£ 15.

PETRARCH'S AFRICA

PETRARCH'S *AFRICA*

Translated and Annotated by
Thomas G. Bergin
and
Alice S. Wilson

New Haven and London, Yale University Press

1977

Published with assistance from the foundation established in memory of
Philip Hamilton McMillan of the Class of 1894, Yale College

Designed by John O. C. McCrillis and set in Baskerville type. Printed in the United
States of America by The Vail-Ballou Press, Inc., Binghamton, New York.

Published in Great Britain, Europe, Africa, and Asia (except Japan) by Yale Univer-
sity Press, Ltd., London. Distributed in Latin America by Kaiman & Polon, Inc.,
New York City; in Australia and New Zealand by Book & Film Services, Artarmon,
N.S.W., Australia; and in Japan by Harper & Row, Publishers, Tokyo Office.

Library of Congress Cataloging in Publication Data

Petrarca, Francesco, 1304-1374.
    Petrarch's Africa.

    Bibliography: p.
    Includes index.
    1. Scipio Africanus Major, Publius Cornelius—Poetry. 2. Punic War, 2d, 218-
201 B. C.—Poetry. I. Bergin, Thomas Goddard, 1904–   II. Wilson, Alice S.
III. Title. IV. Title: Africa.
PQ4496.E29A4   1977   851'.1   77-75380
ISBN O-300-02062-7

To the memory of
Henry Thompson Rowell
Scholar, Humanist, Romanissimo

Contents

Map on pages xx–xxi
The Mediterranean world at the time of the Second Punic War

Introduction

The genesis of the *Africa* is recorded for us by its author. In his *Letter to Posterity*, after a lyric description of the environs of Vaucluse, where he made his home after returning from his grand tour of 1333, Petrarch goes on to say: "While I was wandering in those mountains upon a Friday in Holy Week, the strong desire seized me to write an epic in an heroic strain, taking as my theme Scipio Africanus the Great, who had, strange to say, been dear to me from childhood. But although I began the execution of this project with enthusiasm, I straightway abandoned it, owing to a variety of distractions."[1]

To this simple statement scholars have added a few glosses. That the inspiration came to Petrarch during Holy Week we may not doubt, and the opening lines of the epic seem to contain an allusion to Good Friday, a significant day in the poet's life for it was on that same solemn anniversary that he had first looked upon Laura. The Good Friday of the birth of the *Canzoniere*, as Petrarch tells us himself, was that of 1327; the birth year of the *Africa* is more difficult to establish. Wilkins, with characteristic caution, says "either in 1338 or in 1339."[2] Festa opts for the earlier of the two years; he points out that in the anniversary sonnet written that year (*Rhymes* 62) the poet prays for divine assistance to liberate him from the "pitiless yoke" of his obsession with Laura and to guide him "to a higher life and fairer enterprises."[3] And certainly the composition of an epic such as the *Africa* would be a "fairer enterprise." One is tempted to agree with Festa in assigning the beginning of the poem to 1338, not entirely on the ambiguous evidence of the sonnet but also for another reason. In 1337 Petrarch had had his first view of Rome; it left him so benumbed with wonder that, for once, he was unable to write a word about his impressions (*Fam.* 2.14). It seems very likely that the inspirational vision of the Eternal City must have been the immediate spur to the design of the *Africa* and probably the *De viris illustribus* as well. And it is reasonable to assume that the response to such an inspiration must have been prompt.

That the name and image of Scipio had fascinated Petrarch
from his earliest years is hardly a matter for wonder. The Roman
conqueror had long enjoyed preeminence in the gallery of medi-
eval heroes; let it suffice to mention here Dante's frequent and
laudatory comments, not only in the *Commedia* but also in the
Convivio, the *De monarchia*, and the *Epistole*. Indeed, if Petrarch
needed a Roman hero he had only the choice between Caesar
and Scipio. And for Petrarch Caesar was unsuitable. He was a
dictator and so a tyrant, and no matter what accommodations
Petrarch made in his choice of patrons he was always in principle
a staunch republican and a champion of liberty. Furthermore,
Caesar's private life hardly provided a pattern for Christian virtue,
while Scipio, equally glorious on the field of battle, had also the
reputation of a chaste and temperate man, even a lover of soli-
tude. For "quel fiore antico di vertuti e d'arme," as he defines
Hannibal's conqueror (*Rhymes* 186), Petrarch could feel not
only admiration but kinship. In fact, in addition to making
Scipio the hero of his epic, Petrarch also gave him extensive
treatment in the *De viris illustribus*; it would seem, as Aldo Bernarc
suspects, that the victor of Zama was destined to hold the central
and climactic position in that catalogue of worthies.[4] Bernardo
documents, too, Scipio's recurrent appearances, one might al-
most say invasions, in numerous other works of his admirer,
from the *Rhymes* and the *Triumphs* to the *De otio religiosorum*.[5]

That such a hero's renown still "lacked a song," as the poet
avers in his *Bucolicum carmen* (1.120), was a matter to be de-
plored; at the same time it offered a rare opportunity to an
aspiring bard in search of a subject. (The manuscript of the
Punica of Silius Italicus did not come to light until the early
fifteenth century; Petrarch believed that his only predecessor
was Ennius, of whose "unpolished" *Annales* only fragments sur-
vive.)

The choice of Scipio, too, made available in eloquent abund-
ance that ingredient of historical truth which for Petrarch was
the essential element of poetry—he had but to follow Livy, the
supreme "rerum gestarum memoriae consultor" (*Fam.* 24.8).
Our notes will provide ample evidence of the scrupulous fidelity
with which the poet transcribed his "truth." For its transmission
the appropriate vehicle could be only the manner and meter of

his revered master Virgil, the Parthenias of his first eclogue who inspired him to emulation. Looking back at least, one can affirm that given the three components—the image of Scipio, the respect for Livy, and the cult of Virgil—the *Africa* was a predictable , fruit of Petrarch's humanistic ardors and ambitions.

Finally, in considering the genesis of the epic, we may suspect that Petrarch's decision, while born of his own irresistible desire to imitate the ancients, may also have been stimulated by the example of Mussato, whose *Ecerinis*, a Latin tragedy modeled on Seneca, had moved his Paduan fellow citizens to award him the laurel crown. Nor is it entirely fanciful to imagine that in his desire to create something more substantial than the "trifles" of his *Rhymes*, Petrarch may have had in mind the example of the *Divine Comedy*, the prestige of which was well known and perhaps challenging to him.

At any rate he had embarked, as he soon found out, on a long and exhausting journey. The *Africa* was to be his "croce e delizia" for the rest of his life. That he abandoned work on it "straightway" ("mox") seems not quite accurate; he was fairly far along with it at the time of his coronation in April 1341; indeed, in another passage of the *Letter to Posterity*, reporting a conversation he had had with King Robert a few months before he was given the laurel, Petrarch states: "I showed him my *Africa* which so delighted him that he asked that it might be dedicated to him."[6] It might easily be inferred from the phraseology that the poem was finished at the time of this flattering colloquy. Yet it must have needed some final touches, for in the *Metrical Letter* describing his coronation the poet writes:

> The little book itself, now growing bold,
> Burns with desire to run and cast itself
> Before those sacred feet, and day and night
> Pleads for release.

This letter (*Ep. Met.* 2.1) was sent to Barbato da Sulmona in January 1342, and on the basis of other evidence we know that Petrarch had worked hard on his poem during the *villeggiatura* in Selvapiana provided for him by his host, Azzo da Correggio, Lord of Parma, and also probably in Parma during the months preceding and following that sojourn. Wilkins states: "In Parma

he finished a draft—but only a draft—of the *Africa*."[7] He must
have been eager to present the finished work to the monarch who
had sponsored his coronation. But Robert died in January 1343,
before the poem had grown bold enough to shake off the clutch
of its tenacious author. Clearly the lines toward the end of Book
9 alluding to that unhappy event cannot have been part of the
"draft" of which Wilkins speaks; Festa believes they were com-
posed shortly before the poet's second visit to Naples, in the
fall of 1343.[8] The dedicatory lines in Book 1, probably inserted
after his coronation and indicative of his intention to "release"
the work, were simply allowed to remain. Thus for Festa (follow-
ing Corradini), the work was *provvisoriamente* finished, more or
less as we now have it, in 1343.[9] Even this hypothesis is a little
hazardous, for in a passage of the *Secretum* Petrarch speaks of a
serious illness suffered in 1343 (probably in the summer of that
year), during which his greatest fear was that he would die, leaving
his poem "semiexplicitam"—an ambiguous word which Festa
glosses as meaning "only half set in order."[10]

If we assume that at least in preliminary draft the poem was
completed by the end of 1343 but was not yet polished to such
a lustre as to satisfy its author, we must also assume that the
polishing went on during the remaining thirty years of the poet's
life. Given his habits of work, this is not particularly surprising;
he says of himself (in the *Letter to Posterity*): "My mind was
like my body, marked more by agility than strength; thus I easily
conceived many projects which I dropped because of the diffi-
culty of execution."[11] And if both the *Triumphs* and the *De
viris illustribus* remained unfinished and two decades were spent
on the *De vita solitaria*, it was predictable that the *Africa*, the
most ambitious of his works, would undergo a long period of
gestation.

As the years passed, Petrarch's uneasiness about his epic grew
and became almost a kind of paranoia. In 1343 he had allowed
Barbato da Sulmona to transcribe the moving lines at the end of
Book 6 containing Mago's dying soliloquy, making Barbato
swear that he would not circulate the passage. Barbato, thinking
the verses too beautiful to remain unpublished, broke his prom-
ise. Petrarch was not pleased by this breach of faith and liked
even less some of the criticisms that were aimed at the passage;

his letter to Boccaccio (*Sen.* 2.1) is eloquent in its indignation. Barbato was never permitted to see any more of the epic nor, it seems likely, was anyone else, save possibly Boccaccio, who claims that he was privileged to read it on the occasion of his visit to Petrarch in Padua in 1351. The poet had apparently returned to his labors of revision for a while in 1349; he writes to his friend Mainardo Accursio (*Fam.* 8.3), speaking of Vaucluse, "It is pleasing for me to recall that it was there that I started my *Africa* with such great energy and effort that now, as I try to apply the file to what I started, I seem to shudder at my boldness and at the great framework I laid."[12] Yet the return in 1352 to the source of inspiration was of no avail; Wilkins records that the poet "seems not to have done any further work on the *Africa* either during this stay in Provence or at any later time."[13]

Meanwhile, as the reluctant author stubbornly refused to release his work, the greater grew the impatient curiosity of the literary world. Boccaccio repeatedly urged his friend to publish the poem. In the summer of 1362 (or thereabouts), the faithful disciple forwarded to his master a letter written by Barbato but speaking as well for Niccolò Acciaiuoli and Napoleone and Niccolò Orsini, imploring Petrarch to allow the world to enjoy his epic. "The letter," says Wilkins, "had no effect upon Petrarch except to renew the displeasure" he had felt in 1343 when Barbato had broken his pledge.[14] Some ten years later Coluccio Salutati addressed to the old poet a missive which he called "Metra incitatoria ad Africe editionem," voicing a like plea. This message Petrarch never saw; it would certainly have met with a negative response. On the death of the poet there was much uneasiness about the fate of the great work and sharp competition for the honor of bringing out a definitive edition. It was not until 1397 in fact that Pier Paolo Vergerio gave to a world no longer quite so impatient the first "published" text of the *Africa*. His report of the numerous marginalia, indicative of frequent alterations and emendations, is evidence of Petrarch's lifelong struggle to endow his hexameters with the perfection worthy of their subject. Perhaps, in view of his doubts and uncertainties, we are lucky to have the *Africa* at all.

The *editio princeps* of the *Africa* was published in Venice in 1501 as a part of the *Opera omnia*. The poem appeared again in

another Venetian edition of 1503 and also in the successive
Basel editions from 1541 to 1558, always as a part of the author's
collected works. Not until 1872 did the great epic receive the
distinction of special treatment—in Paris, at the hands of L. Pin-
gaud, working from six manuscripts. Two years after Pingaud's
came the Paduan edition of Francesco Corradini; but only in
Nicola Festa's full-scale and meticulous edition of 1926 (the
first volume of the *Edizione nazionale* of the poet's work, still
in progress) did the poem finally win the scrupulous editorial
attention which had been so lavishly bestowed over the inter-
vening centuries on the *Canzoniere* and the *Trionfi*. As Festa,
dedicating his work to Victor Emmanuel III, defines the *Africa*
as the "poem of the Mediterranean victory of Rome," we may
suspect that the resurgent nationalism of the time encouraged
and facilitated the editor's undertaking.

The long years of editorial neglect clearly bespeak the indiffer-
ence of the reading public and the reservations of the *literati*.
The fortune of the *Africa* at the hands of critics from the time
of its first appearance down to our own day is ably summarized
for English-speaking readers in the eighth chapter of Aldo
Bernardo's *Petrarch, Scipio and the "Africa."* A perusal of those
pages makes it clear that, however persistent the image of Scipio
may have been over the intervening years, the poem itself came
in for little attention until the mid-nineteenth century. For this
oblivion the *Africa* itself is not entirely to blame. The interest
in Petrarch's vernacular works very soon overshadowed his
accomplishments in Latin; this phenomenon was simply a re-
flection of the new tides of culture which began to flow shortly
after his death. Generally speaking, creative writers increasingly
preferred to use the vernacular; Latinists, fortified by the nourish-
ment of humanism for which Petrarch himself can claim much
credit, turned to classical authors and found medieval Latin
writers unrewarding by comparison. Indeed, by the time the
editio princeps of the *Africa* appeared Petrarch's own Latin had
begun to seem unpolished if not downright crude. Nothing was
less likely to attract the reader or the critic than a medieval
Latin epic. One may speculate on what might have been the
fortune of the *Divine Comedy* had Dante not opted for the
Tuscan.

Still, it must be granted that the *Africa* is not quite the master-
piece that its author hoped to make of it. Vergerio, although he
finds much to admire in the poem, defines it as a "youthful
work," and the phrase has certainly a patronizing if not a dis-
paraging ring. The *Africa* has a fatal flaw: it presents us with a
flawless hero. Its Scipio is an unconvincing amalgam of Roman
conqueror and Christian saint; he is simply too good to be true.
The striving for the best of both worlds with the desperate aim
of linking pagan social virtues with Christian other-worldliness
is admirable but doomed to be aesthetically unconvincing. Fur-
thermore, the *Africa* is wordy and lacking in dramatic action.
Yet the poem has had, in recent years particularly, some en-
thusiastic champions. Burckhardt, after making the somewhat
dubious assertion that "the 'Africa' of Petrarch probably found
as many and as enthusiastic readers and hearers as any epos of
modern times," goes on to pose the challenging question: "How
many modern epics treat of a subject at once so popular, so
historical in its basis, and so striking to the imagination?"
Toffanin, while not greatly concerned with the poetic merits of
the work, is impressed by its Augustinian fervor; "the *Africa*,"
he says, "becomes the real Divine Comedy." Enrico Carrara sees
the poem as an expression of the serene reconciliation of the
author's contradictory impulses, a kind of "resolution" of the
conflict documented in the *Canzoniere*.[15] And even Morris Bis-
hop, who finds many faults in the work, grants it the merit of
making "at least an effort to be realistic in its evocation of his-
tory"[16]—a notable advance, one might say, over both the alle-
gorized epics of the Middle Ages and the long fantastical romances
making use of classical figures. On these grounds it seems to us
that the *Africa* should rightfully be seen as the earliest Renais-
sance epic rather than as a medieval artifact. Petrarch's return
to Roman history for substance and inspiration, his Herculean
efforts to revive the Latin language and style of the classical
period, and his perception of the spirit of *Romanitas*, clouded
only infrequently by pious syncretism, distinguish him sharply
from medieval poets. His diction eschews—with rare lapses—post-
classical usage and terminology, no mean accomplishment in
view of the paucity of guidance available to him in such matters
as orthography, etymology, and even vocabulary. It is an injustice

to him to compare the *Africa* to the *Aeneid*. If his hexameters
are sometimes labored and clotted, they still may claim closer
kinship with Lucretius than with the authors of the Silver Age
or any medieval versifier. Petrarch set for himself the goal of
integrating Livy's history, Cicero's philosophy, and Virgil's
poetry: the *Africa* is his great heroic statement on history and
poetry and all the *studia humanitatis*.

It is not our intention here, however, to undertake a critical
study of the poem and much less to anticipate the reader's ver-
dict by appeals to eminent authorities. In preparing our transla-
tion we have been moved by two considerations which it is per-
haps our duty to share with our readers. We believe that the
Africa, for all its imperfections, is a unique monument to a
certain delicate and significant moment in the history of Western
culture. And we believe it serves to deepen our understanding
of a great poet and a remarkably sensitive human being. T. K.
Seung does not hesitate to call the *Africa* "ultimately an epic
of [the poet's] own soul."[17] Petrarch, never doubting that Heaven
was his destination, was yet passionately attached to the beauties
of this transitory world, its aspirations, its tender associations,
the charm of its very fragility. He responded to, and portrayed
with his own special elegance, its alluring beauty, whether of
womanhood, landscape, or art. The *Africa*, flawed though it be,
is replete with such appealing substance. And if posterity has not
so far been kind to it, well, to quote Morris Bishop again, "pos-
terity has still a long time to go."[18]

The *Africa*, for so many years ignored by critics, was likewise
neglected by translators. Even in Italian the first effort comes
late. In 1570 one M. Fabio Marretti of Siena first tried his hand
at it, turning the hexameters of the Latin into Italian *ottava
rima*; his version was published by Domenico Farri in Venice.
Over three hundred years later, Agostino Palesa published a
translation in Italian blank verse, hastily composed to meet the
centenary of the poet's death. And in 1933 appeared the version
of Agostino Barolo, published in Torino. Also in blank verse, it
is the first to be based on Festa's text and the only Italian trans-
lation that is both literal and readable.

Outside of Italy we may count only two published translations
of the complete work: that of Victor Develay into French prose

(Paris, 1882), and the version of Henrik Westin in sturdy Swedish hexameters (Göteborg, 1889). An unpublished line-for-line English translation of the poem was made by James H. M. Campbell in 1933 in partial fulfillment of the requirements for a degree of Master of Arts in the Yale Graduate School; a copy may be found in the Yale University Library.

Our translation follows Festa's text, with a few exceptions, duly noted. We have chosen to present it in verse because the original is a poem and we believe that there is a color in poetry that prose does not reproduce. And we have turned to iambic pentameter as the rhythmic pattern that has proved to be, for a long poem, the most acceptable to the ear of the English-speaking reader.

We are grateful to Edmund T. Silk for his guidance through several troublesome passages.

T. G. B.
A. S. W.

Chronology of the Second Punic War
219 B.C.-202 B.C.

219 Hannibal takes Saguntum, an ally of Rome.

218 Hannibal crosses the Alps; he defeats the Romans at the Ticinus and the Trebia.

217 Hannibal wins a great victory at Lake Trasimenus and moves south.

216 The Romans are defeated at Cannae. Hannibal takes up quarters at Capua. Fabius is appointed Roman commander.

214 Hannibal moves to the siege of Tarentum.

213 Sicily rises against Rome.

212 Hannibal takes Tarentum. Syracuse falls to Marcellus.

211 Capua is retaken by the Romans; the Roman army in Spain is destroyed.

210 Romans capture Agrigentum.

209 The Romans recover Tarentum. Scipio takes Cartagena.

208 Hasdrubal invades Italy.

207 Hasdrubal is defeated and killed at the Metaurus.

206 Scipio drives the Carthaginians out of Spain.

205 Mago invades Liguria.

204 Scipio begins his campaign in Africa.

203 Battle of the Great Plains (near Utica). The Carthaginians are defeated; Syphax is captured. Hannibal and Mago are recalled to Carthage.

202 Scipio defeats Hannibal at Zama. Carthage sues for peace.

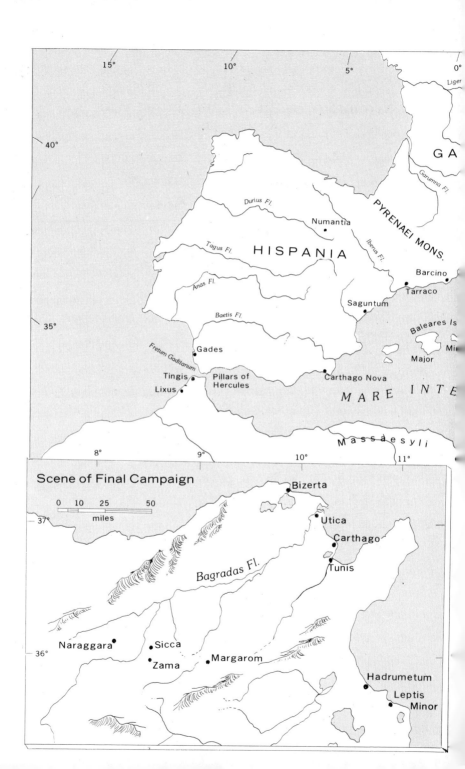

15° 10° 5° 0°

Liger

40°

G A

Garumna Fl.

Durius Fl.

Numantia

Tagus Fl.

HISPANIA

PYRENAEI MONS.

Iberus Fl.

Anas Fl.

Barcino

Tarraco

Saguntum

Baetis Fl.

Baleares Is

35°

Fretum Gaditanum

Gades

Major

Mi

Tingis

Pillars of Hercules

Carthago Nova

Lixus

MARE INTE

Massaesyli

8° 9° 10° 11°

Scene of Final Campaign

Bizerta

0 10 25 50

miles

37°

Utica

Carthago

Bagradas Fl.

Tunis

Naraggara

Sicca

Zama

36°

Margarom

Hadrumetum

Leptis Minor

THE MEDITERRANEAN WORLD

AT THE TIME OF

THE SECOND PUNIC WAR

Book 1

Invocation Muse, you will tell me of the man renowned
for his great deeds, redoubtable in war,
on whom first noble Africa, subdued   *3*
by Roman arms, bestowed a lasting name.
Fair sisters, ye who are my dearest care,
if I propose to sing of wondrous things,
may it be given me to quaff full deep
of the sweet sacred spring of Helicon.   *8*
Now that a favoring Fortune has once more
restored me to clear springs and pleasant meads,   10
the welcome shelter of the sun-bathed hills,
and the soft stillness of the lonely fields,
inspire, I pray, within your bard the song
and give him heart.

           Thou too, Who art the world's
securest hope and glory of the heavens,
Whom our age hails above all gods supreme
and victor over Hell; Whose guiltless flesh   *17*
we see scarred by five gaping wounds, O come,
all-highest Father, bear me succor here.
Full many a reverent verse shall I bring back   20
to Thee—if verses please Thee—from the crest
of high Parnassus. If they please Thee not,   22
then Thine shall be the guerdon of those tears
which long since I might fittingly have shed
save that my wretched blindness checked their flow.

King Robert And you, Trinacria's puissant king and pride   26
of Italy, great glory of our age,
who deemed me worthy to assume a place
among the bards and to receive the name
of poet and the longed-for laurel crown,   30
deign, with a gracious mind, I beg of you,

1

to take the gift I bring; if you read all   *32*
its pages you may find some passages
that offer solace in an idle hour,
and should you find the reading burdensome,
the ending may reward you for your pains.
Your sanction will have launched it on its course
through ages yet to come, for who has dared
to scorn a thing that you are pleased to prize?
One who has known the grace of your good will   *40*
may with the greater confidence affirm
that, merely by inclining of your brow,
you create glory where no glory was.
Mark how the trembling multitudes revere
the gifts disposed upon the sacred altars,
which, once removed, the mob will only spurn.
How greatly then might your effulgent fame
avail me, if within the gracious shade
of your renown my verse might scorn the bane
of odious envy, there where neither years
nor gnawing maggots might erode my name.   *50*

  I pray you, glorious King, accept at last   *52*
this gift; extend a hand in benediction
and give it approbation with your glance.
For with the praise that you have merited
I shall extol your exploits to the stars,
and in a day to come perchance I may
sing of the King of Sicily, his fame
and his miraculous deeds, not yet well known
abroad but which we all have witnessed. Aye,   *60*
if death give respite, not too long a time
I ask. In truth, the poets with such themes
as mine are wont to turn to times remote;
some send their Muse back o'er a thousand years
and others halt not at that ancient mark,
but none as yet has sung of his own age,
and thus the Muse, with no impediment,
wanders through old and unfamiliar years
in freedom. Lo, of fallen Troy one sings,   *69*
a second tells the tale of Thebes and hides   *70*

the young Achilles, while with Roman bones
another fills up the Emathian fields.
I shall not chronicle events still fresh
of recent times; 'tis rather my intent
to utterly destroy the cursèd race
of Africa and curb their power's excess
with the assistance of Ausonian Mars.   77
Keeping you ever in my heart, O king,
and eager to return, I shall set forth
upon this journey ere I make so bold   80
as to portray your mighty deeds. In truth,
they do attract me more; but when I weigh
my skill against your greatness, then I pause
and dare not treat of them. First I would try
my novice hand, and if it fail me not
then shall essay the heights—and with a strength
invincible, for you shall come with me.
Then spacious and renowned Parthenope   88
shall once more welcome me, a bard new crowned
with Roman garland. For the nonce I pluck   90
the tenderest foliage from a lowly bush
and choose famed Scipio to share my course.
One day I'll gather sturdier boughs, and you,
most generous King, will help me with your deeds
and lend more power to my faltering pen.
Another crown of laurel, the most fair
of all our times, will justly then reward
with honor one who holds your person dear.

Origins of The cause of ills so numerous, the source
the Punic of so much devastation I must probe: 100
Wars what gave such passions birth, what folly forced
great nations to fare forth and undergo
so many hardships on much traversed seas?
What stirred up Europe against Libya, why
did Libya turn on Europe, lands both doomed
to be laid waste by all the winds of war?
Nor did I find I had to ponder long
to learn the cause. 'Twas Envy, I perceived,

that root infectious of our every ill,
which, swollen to excess, brings forth the seeds   110
of death and sorrow when with somber eye
it looks upon another's happiness.
Carthage 'Twas jealous Carthage that could not endure   *113*
envies the sight of Rome in flower. The thriving town,
Rome already odious, she hated more
as it became her peer. As she beheld
Rome's waxing strength, she learned she must obey
the rule of a great mistress, heed new laws
and pay her tribute; but within, her heart
was contumacious and unreconciled.   120
Her fatal pride drove her at last to break
her bonds—and double her own misery.
Grief and humiliation racked the hearts
of men who had known lengthy servitude,
and to their bitterness of soul was joined,
with sordid avarice, insatiate greed.
Both cities shared the one ambition, seeking
full sovereignty, for each one deemed herself
apt for the conquest and dominion
of all the world. The Carthaginians too   130
had suffered recently a grievous loss
and a deep wound. Sardinia was theirs
no more, nor Sicily; and reft away
was Spain, a neighbor to both combatants,
exposed to rapine and perfidious thrust
and destined for a long time to endure
anguish unspeakable, even as a lamb
when trapped by wolves that turns now here
now there and seeks to flee their rending fangs
till it is torn to pieces and succumbs,   140
all bloody with the beasts' gore and its own.

   Topography itself must breed mistrust: *142*
Nature has placed the nations on two shores
confronting one another, whence each may
observe his distant foe. The cities differ
in spirit, customs and in gods, abhorred
reciprocally. There is no peace; the winds

and elements stir in opposing surge
the waves to war upon a hostile sea.
There thrice was battle joined in hatred fierce   150
and massive bloodshed. Truth to tell, the first   ›151
clash came about unplanned, the second nearly
ended the strife, the third with three encounters
brought with slight effort warfare to its end.
Of these vicissitudes our song shall sing
the greatest, the vast conflict's middle phase,   156
its glorious captains and its fearsome strife.   157

The Car-   Spain, weary of her losses at the hands   158
thaginians of the star-splendored youth, had shaken off   159
driven out the chains that bound her neck and duly yielded   160
of Spain to Roman arms and the Ausonian yoke.
The Carthaginians, in a panic flight,
had crossed the sea and still were shuddering,
awed by the thundering warrior's crushing power,
his character, his fame, his birth, his new
fashion of waging war, and his campaign
which had wrought bloody havoc. Now at last
perfidious Hasdrubal stood on the shore   168
of Mauritania, casting back a glance
of trepidation, fearful of pursuit.   170
Just so a frightened stag remarks the chase
of dogs and hunters close upon his track
as he looks downward, panting, from a crag.
Scipio in Iberia's conqueror took his stand upon   174
Africa the shore of Ocean where the twin assault
of wind and waves beats on the lofty Pillars
of Hercules, where weary Phoebus sinks   177
into the cleansing deep to purge his scorched
and dusty chariot. And here he stood,
where no resistant hand of man but Nature   180
omnipotent herself has barred the way,
and grieved that from his eager grasp the foe
had slipped, that all too little he had won.
His fretful heart by no indulgent favor   184
of Fortune will be soothed; while Carthage lives

the splendor of his own exploits is dim.
Still could he see, though distant and in flight,
the enemy in arms and with a hand,
though moribund, dispatching tardy darts.
A rumor too of ominous import   190
had reached him from afar: the frantic raids
of furious Hannibal, 'twas said, imperilled
Ausonia's citadels—nay more, to Rome's
own walls the flaming torch of war had come;
it told of many a famous chieftain fallen
and Italy a-burning with great fires
and all the countryside bedewed with blood.
Revenge and filial love moved Scipio
to carry on the task he had begun
and by horrendous slaughter to appease   200
the sacred ashes of ancestors slain
and cleanse of shame the face of Italy.
This was the lasting hope that fed the heart
of noble Scipio; upon his brow
and in his shining youthful glance there gleamed
the glorious flame that burned within his breast.
Nights without rest and days of ceaseless toil
allowed no respite to the general
within whose spirit dwelt such fervent zeal.

Scipio's   Thus troubled—while night slowly freed the earth   210
dream   of its dark embrace, while Tithonus' bride   *211*
still warmed within the circle of her arms
her aged husband, while the nymphs whose charge
is to unfold the hours as yet durst not
fling wide the portals on their crimson hinges
resplendent nor yet venture to unbar
the rosy windows and awake their lord—
the weary Scipio laid down his head
and gentle slumber closed his yielding lids.
Then lo, from the calm welkin high above,   220
clad in a cloud, appeared to him the shade
and visage of his noble sire, who there   *222*
displayed to his beloved son his heart

and breast and flank, transfixed by countless spears.
The valiant youth felt every limb grow chill
and terror caused his locks to stand upright.
Dispelling his son's horror with a voice
Familiar and consoling, the shade spoke:

His father
speaks

"Eternal glory, honor of my sept,
sole hope remaining of our shaken land,   230
put fear aside and with attentive mind
take in my words. For God, who reigns on high,
lord of Olympus, grants to us one hour,
brief but yet promising great joy, if you
but waste it not. For, yielding to my prayers,
he opened wide the starry doors of Heaven
and has permitted you, still in the flesh—
O rarest boon!—to pass the poles and gaze,
with me as guide, upon the stars that whirl
obliquely through their orbits, and upon   240
the trials that vex your fatherland and you.
So shall you see the web the Fates have woven,
still unrevealed on earth but to be spun
by hands inflexible. Look hither now:
southward mark you the walls, the cursed palace
set by a woman's wiles upon yon mount   246
of infamy? See the assembled throng
of madmen and the mob with sluggish gouts

Warning to
Carthage

of blood still dripping. Woe betide that city
whose wide renown is far too greatly grown   250
through our disasters. Woe betide the land,
the source of anguish to Italian mothers.
Would you then brandish your once-shattered arms
again? And would you form anew your lines
of battle for your empty tombs? How then,
O slothful Bágrada, dare you to scorn   256
Tiber invincible? Would you condemn,
insolent Byrsa, our Capitoline?   258
Presume again and learn again to know
your mistress by her lash? The task shall fall   260
to you, my son, and all the honor too

which by the waging of a righteous war
will make you equal to the gods. I swear
by these most justly sacred wounds, through which
I paid the debt I owed the fatherland
and which laid open to my martial soul
the way to Heaven—solemnly I swear
that as the foeman pierced my limbs and while
my soul took flight, no other balm I found
save that I knew that in my house survived   270
a glorious avenger. And this hope
at once allayed the fears that filled my heart
and made more sweet the bitterness of death."

    As thus his father spoke, young Scipio gazed
with mournful eyes upon him, marking all
the dreadful wounds that scarred him head to heel;
his filial heart was stirred and a rich flood
of tears gushed forth. Permitting not his sire
further discourse, he broke in with these words:
"Alas, what see I here? Say, father, who   280
has pierced your bosom with so cruel a thrust?
What impious hand has dared to violate
that brow, by all revered? I pray, disclose
these things to me; for naught else have I ears."
    So with his lamentations and his sobs
he filled the star-resplendent calm of Heaven.
If one might aptly make comparison
between sublime and humble things, I'd say
a fish fled from the briny deep to dwell
in a freshwater brooklet, if it feel   290
once more the unfamiliar bitter salt,
is no more stunned than were the hosts of Heaven.
For here below are grief and tears and doubt
of future fate and fear of death and all
the thousand sorry ills of mortal flesh,
among which, in deep gloom, we quickly spend
our fairest seasons and our sweetest years;
but in high Heaven there is purest day,
shining with lucence inaccessible   299

nor ever troubled by obnoxious grief   *300*
nor mournful sound, nor ever hot with hate.
Most rare in Heaven therefore was this moment
when clamor most unusual was heard
by ears divine, as the son's grieving cries
of piety filled all the soundless spheres
and every recess of unmeasured light.

Then did his father in affectionate
embrace enfold him, comforting his woe
with exhortations and these solemn words:
"I pray you put aside your tears and grief   *310*
untimely and ill suited to this place.
If looking on these wounds of mine so sorely
troubles your heart, if you would care to learn
what ills shall yet befall your fatherland,
then heed me, for I purpose to reveal
in brief discourse much matter you should hear.

The elder   "The war's sixth year had seen our Roman eagles   *317*
Scipio tells in far Hesperian camps victoriously
of his   displayed when, Fortune, you chose to inspire
death   within me, weary as I was at heart   *320*
of all the cares born of the sluggish war,
a grandiose design—for such in truth
the outcome would reveal it. I resolved—
ah, wretched me!—in confidence to share
in equal part the heavy burden with
my brother and accelerate the pace
of laggard war with a twin spur. Therefore
we separated, for the omens all
were most auspicious, and each one of us,
dividing forces, harried far and wide   *330*
the enemy. 'Twas then the weary Fates,
ere yet the spindle of our lives was full,
cut short the threads, and Mars, deserting, fled,   *333*
abandoning our standards. For in fear
of the uneven odds the men of Carthage
in their uncertain hour turned to fraud.

(It is the art in which they most excel
and which we must acknowledge is our bane.)
Suborning with their gold the Celtic troops,   *339*
who hitherto had been auxiliaries   *340*
aiding my brother's force, the enemy
persuaded them to flee. Let this example   *342*
set by our captains warn posterity,
lest by reliance on a stranger's strength
they may end with a want of confidence
in their own soldiery. Vainly my brother
appealed to oaths and justice and the gods;
without farewell our false allies took leave.
Ah, power of gold! To gold alone you bow,
O gods, O honor, O sustaining faith!   *350*
Stripped of its shield, my brother's battle line
turned to its one remaining hope, retreating
through by-paths towards the barren mountainside.
The enemy, relentless and well-skilled
in pressing a retreating force, pursued
until the end. Meanwhile the Punic lines,
with secret reinforcement from the new
perfidious recruits, encircled me,
now widely separated from my friends.
I put my trust in Fate, but all in vain;   *360*
it was not granted me to join my brother.
Three mightier armies blocked my lesser force
where'er I turned, and likewise the terrain
was perilous. We had no hope of flight;
the sole resource remaining was the sword.
In the brief interval the Fates allowed,
with javelins we pierced those savage breasts
and sent in swift descent to Erebus   *368*
those shades of Africa. For pain and wrath
impelled us; no scope was there for refined   *370*
tactics of war nor calculated plans.
Even as the husbandman, relentless, veiled
under a shielding cover, plots his raid
on honey-bearing bees, who in the dark
confusion of the night fly blindly till

they are compelled in sadness to forsake
the combs of sweetness they have built of wax,
and then, in fury buzzing, dart and whirl
in scattered swarms 'round the aggressor's head,
while he, their cunning enemy, remains   380
unmoved, intent upon his task—their stings
are harmless and, victorious, he breaks
and plunders all those holy creatures' hives—
even so we fell upon the hated ranks
with spears and vengeful brands, venting our wrath
in frenzied killing, which affords the doomed
their sole recourse and dearest consolation.
But they remained unshaken where they stood,
as lofty Eryx and star-grazing Atlas   389
stand firm 'gainst Auster's blast. Why say I more?   390
Beneath a weight of arms and fighting men
our reckless charge was buried. Envious Fortune,
as is her custom, spurned the righteous cause.
I felt my blood congeal within my heart;
I recognized that treason had prevailed
and felt death coming on. And fearing then
not so much for myself as for my country,
I swiftly strove, so far as circumstance
permitted, to unite my shattered troops,
and spoke these words: 'Here, men, before us lies   400
the arduous path to death in glory. Now
I bid you follow me whom erstwhile oft
you've followed and with happier lot, I grant,
but never with a greater hope of glory.
Fear not the sharp edge of the sword nor yet
Death's visage. For but little blood Mars grants
great fame; a soldier's death sheds lustre on
his progeny. Be mindful of your stock
and happily embrace this destiny
for your dear land. By nature's self-same law   410
the hero and the coward both must die.
To both is granted a brief span of time,
and were all risks by land and sea removed
still of its own will comes the dreaded day.

But to the brave this privilege is reserved:
to die a happy death. The common herd
succumbs in tears congealed by icy fear.
Wherefore do not regret this sacrifice,
and if the blood of Rome runs in your veins
let death reveal it. Nay, while Fate so willed,   420
we too with arms victorious have slain
full many a foe. Now, since 'tis otherwise,
let our dead bodies break their battle line;
let breasts, fierce staring eyes, and faces grim
provide a dour impediment; let mounds
of piled-up corpses hinder their advance
and form a barricade against their charge.
May these barbarian monsters learn full well
true men have fallen; let them tread upon
brave Roman bodies ever glorious   430
though pale in death. On, valiant soldiers, on!
That death that decent men desire awaits
upon the threshold—win your lasting meed
of incense and fond tears at Roman shrines.'
   "Inspired by my words, they all unite
and like a hailstorm rush into the fray;
and first among them I am borne along—
ah, never to return—into the bright
and shining steel of the encircling foe.
Close after me my gallant comrades come,   440
resigned to death. Struck down, we perish all.
What more could so few do against a host
of many thousands?

He tells   "Now you wish to learn
of his   of my dear brother's final doom. For him
brother's   Hesperia had prepared no happier end   *445*
death   than mine. He likewise vainly strove to cheat   *446*
the final blast of destiny; he too
fell crushed beneath the ponderous weight of ruin.
Nor were it fitting had his fortune been
unlike his brother's. Our life's harmony   *450*
was wondrous, never flawed by disaccord,

however slight. One home, one common fare,
one mind, one death we shared. One site preserves
our graves and ashes. So we came almost
on the same day to Heaven. Here we feel
no longing for our former prison. Nay,
we look down from these lofty heights and scorn
our scattered limbs below, and, shuddering,
we contemplate those chains and snares of old,
which were a burden to our liberty.   *460*
'Tis sweet to us to think we live no more."

   Yet did his son, still tearful, make reply:
"The piety that dwells in you, sweet sire,
touches my heart's deep core; yet the response
of words alone has always ill availed
in weighty matters. But, dear father, say: *466*
would you have me believe that you, your brother,
and all to whom Rome rendered burial rites
long years ago, still live?" The father, smiling
at the son's question, could not but exclaim: 470
"O wretched mortals, by so dense a cloud
obscured! What ignorance of truth enthralls
the race of man! This state and this alone
is the one certain life. What you call life
is naught but death. Behold my brother now:
mark well his state and how he scorns grim death.
Note well the strength of his unconquered soul,
his lively countenance, his shining eyes.
Behind him see his valiant legions stand;
nay, who would tell me that these souls are dead?   480
As is man's lot, they breathed forth their last breath
and left their bodies, which were hers, to earth.

   "Observe, now drawing near, the joyful throng
whose glowing mien reflects the light of dawn."
"I do," the noble Scipio replied,
"nor can I call to mind a fairer sight
my eyes have seen. Fain would I learn their names.
Deny me not, my father; by the gods

I beg you, by great Jove and by the Sun
which sees all things and by the Phrygian   *490*
Penates if they here avail and by
our fatherland if in this heavenly realm
the memory be still sweet. Among this host,
if I err not, meseems I recognize
some visages. The semblances, the gaits,
the very features, though now all aglow
with rare effulgence, are to me familiar.
Nay, I have seen them; and not long ago
we dwelt together in our mother city."
"Aye, you remember truly. Him you see—   *500*

it was but recently—Phoenician guile
stole from earth's store. Marcellus died, alas,   *502*
too unsuspecting for his years, in straits
most adverse. Mindful of his end, he roams   *504*
beside us freely through these spacious skies.
Crispinus follows from afar; him too   *506*
On the same day the treacherous foe struck down,
but he, with festering wounds, was slow to die.
The other, while the enemy's deceit   *509*
was not yet patent, perished as he fell;   *510*
then, soaring hither, his unburdened soul
left his chill members to his murderers.
Now Fabius behold. The majesty   *513*
of his great name and deeds calls him to dwell
in this celestial peace. Mark well this chief,
called the Delayer by his countrymen,
yet justly waxes his unique renown,
born of his wise evasions. Yonder soul   *518*
was reft from Latium neither by the sword
nor yet by fire, but joined us after long   *520*
and tranquil years, while still the Punic war
most fiercely raged below. Now Gracchus see,   *522*
zealous of soul and ardent for the fray;
torn from his fair and unprotected frame
and by betrayal done to unjust death.

"Yet to Aemilius Paulus envious Fate   *526*

was more unkind. Observe the countless wounds
that scar his noble breast. On Cannae's field,
believing he was destined to lament
for the last time the doom of mighty Rome,   530
he chose not to survive the holocaust.
Scorning the charger freely offered him
and the repeated pleas of Lentulus,   533
who urged him to escape, he cried aloud:
'Nay, I have lived too long, but you, dear boy,
beloved for your valor, destined surely
for victories to come and better days,
save your own life and hasten back to Rome;
there bid the Fathers fortify the town,
strengthen the walls, and arm themselves for trials,   540
for Fortune now redoubles her cruel threats
and close at hand the conquering foeman stands,
thirsting for blood. And carry my last words
to Fabius; assure him that I lived
obedient to his orders—and so died,
with you my witness. But the will of Fate
and an imprudent colleague brought about   547
mad tumult and confusion in our ranks
so without order valor could not find
its proper station and was swept aside   550
by the swift onslaught of the enemy.
Begone. Leave me to die. I would not have
my lengthy discourse cause your death as well'
    "Even as he spoke the press of hostile steel
enclosed him, and the youth fled swift away.
Fear made his members light and to his horse
lent wings and sharp spurs to his fleeting heels.
Just as the frightened mother bird whose nest
is menaced by the cunning snake is fain
to flee approaching death but still is loth   560
to leave her darling young, until at last,
unhappy creature, love is overweighed
by fear and yields, so she with beating wings
at the last moment looks to her own weal
and, shuddering from a neighboring bough, beholds

the serpent's frenzy and her fledgling's fate;
then, all atremble, fluttering she fills
the grove with shrill and piercing cries of grief—
so fled the noble youth, with sorrowing eyes
turned often to look back. Upon the field   570
he sees disaster spread, and after scenes
of massive general slaughter he beholds
the barbarous Carthaginians rain fierce blows
upon his cherished leader's corpse, whereat
he raises up to Heaven his bootless cries.
I'll not say more; you'll readily conceive
the number of our gallant youths who fell
for their dear land upon that fatal day.
Truly, while with a superhuman zeal
cruel Hannibal attempts to wreak our ill   580
and strips our helpless city of its brave
defenders, he fills Heaven with our dead."   582

*Scipio
speaks
with his
uncle*
     Oft, as the sire recalled such sad events,
the son sighed deeply. Then he spoke: "I have
been granted satisfaction of the wish
I held most dear, for I have looked upon
the faces of my people. Now unless
you have good reason to refuse my plea,
I fain would hear my second father's voice;
naught would I welcome more." The answer came: 590
"Lo, here he stands before you. Speak forthwith."
So charged, the youth stepped forward; he inclined
his head, embraced his kinsman, and thus spoke:
"Fair uncle, dear to me as my own sire,
since God has granted that my mortal eyes
may look upon you, opening to me,
although unworthy, Heaven's lofty gate
and bright Olympus, one brief hour concede
to our exchange of voices. For the time
allotted me is short and my return   600
to camp awaited. Where from Ocean's shoals
high Calpe towers, looming o'er the waves   602
to touch the heavens with its summit—there

the Roman army waits its general;
thither impetuous war runs to its end."
The noble hero, clasping in embrace
the youth, made answer: "If, as it must be—
no other source could yield such privilege,
vouchsafed to you alone—that you stand here   610
by Heaven's edict, truly I know not
how to express the hopes I have in you.
For to what living person have the gods   613
ever before thrown wide this thoroughfare?
Had not Divinity Itself decreed
your journey, never could capricious Fortune,
dispenser though she be of bounties, e'er
have granted any man so much: to see
celestial mysteries, learn of things to come,
behold the souls in bliss, and stand above   620
the shining sun and the vast universe
stretching from pole to pole. Such rights reserved
for God Almighty Fortune cannot give.
Wherefore if so much favor God bestows
upon you, how shall others glorify
your name with fitting honors? And well earned,
for we have seen full many of the foe
dispersed and slaughtered on the fields of Spain,
and know we are avenged. For centuries
your name for filial piety will live.   630
Ask therefore what you will and you will find
my ear and all my thought at your command.
So fill we this brief hour with ready speech."
"Tell me," the nephew asked, "if life endures   634
beyond the grave, as my dear sire attests,
and never dies, while life we mortals know
resembles death, then why, on earth abandoned,
must I yet linger? Why may not my soul
arise and, leaving earth behind, fly up
to its appointed mansion where you dwell?"   640
His uncle made reply: "You do not grasp
the matter rightly. God and Nature by
eternal laws ordained a man must bide

in mortal flesh until he is recalled
by express edict. Hence it is not just
to hasten on the journey; we must bear
the tribulations of our mortal lot,
though they be many, with humility,
lest we appear to seem recalcitrant
to God's commands. For to this end mankind   650
was made: to populate the lower realm,
and hold in fee the earth and everything
within it and the seas. So in the flesh
must you and every good man serve the spirit
and let it not its proper home forsake
and by some chance break forth, abandoning
the body, flee the senses and betake
itself to Heaven, impelled by lofty cares
and zealous love of contemplation. This
is suited only to the rarest souls;   660
this is the manner of departure used
by holy men who follow paths sublime.
But for the short span while the members still
are vigorous, do you my counsel heed.
Hold sacred rites and faith and justice dear.
Let piety abide within your hearts
a holy guest, aye and a partner too
in all your acts. This is to your sire you owe
and to your country more, but above all
to the all-highest God. A life adorned   670
by practice of this virtue will assure
the way to Heaven; hither will it bear you
when the last day relieves you of the weight
of flesh and bears off your ethereal soul.
And I would have you know that there is naught
more pleasing to the Lord of earth and sky,
our Father and our King, than cities built
on righteous laws and human covenants
on justice founded. And a citizen
who has advanced his country by his art   680
or when it is oppressed has lent his strength
in bearing arms, may rightfully expect

for all eternity a place secure
within this tranquil kingdom and so reap
the merited rewards of a good life.
This is the law of God's own justice which
leaves naught unpunished, naught unrecognized."
He spoke, and his attentive nephew's heart
was stirred within by goads and flames of love.

The
ancient
kings of
Rome

Came now advancing yet another throng   690
of faces unfamiliar; all were clad
in like attire, wearing mantles light
that glittered with a sparkle like the stars.
A few stepped forth, of august brow and graced
with majesty and venerable age.
"These are the kings—their mien reveals their state—
who in the early years ruled over Rome.
The first is Romulus, the origin
of our great name and father of our folk;
mark you the fire that still so fiercely burns   700
within his soul; our future realm required
a leader such as he. And on his heels
with slower pace one comes who with new rites   703
tempered a savage people. Greatly prized
in Sabine Cures, his first fatherland,
for virtuous ways, he was translated thence
and came to reign in our high citadel.
See how his brow shows his solicitude
to institute—well counseled by his spouse—   709
wise and just laws and rightly to divide   710
the cycle of the year. By Nature born
already agéd, from his early days
he had the face you see, the sunken cheeks
and the gray temples. Close on him the third   714
and bravest of our kings appears: he shaped
all arts of warfare that you practice now.   716
Thunderous in aspect, he could be struck down
only by Jove's own bolt. The fourth in line   718
with ploughshare closed the city in its walls
and founded Ostia at Tibermouth,   720

with prophecy that thither would yet flow
the wealth of all the world. He also yoked
the city's quarters with an ancient bridge.
The visage of the fifth is less well known   *724*
to my perception. He is one, I think,
who long ago from noble Corinth came
to be our ruler. Aye, 'tis he; I mark   *727*
the tunic, toga, fasces, stately robe,
the curule chair, the breastplate all agleam,
the chariot, the steeds, the panoply   *730*
of martial triumph. Sixth in line one comes   *731*
who from a lowly birth was high upraised
to regal throne, and kingly is his heart
though humble be his name, that yet endures.
His deeds and virtues far outweigh the shame
of vulgar origin. He was the first
to institute the census, that great Rome
might know her strength and in that knowledge fear   *738*
no other power." He ceased. His nephew then:
"If rightly I recall the chronicles,   *740*
seven were the chiefs that wore the royal crown
of Romulus and I remember all
the names they bore. The seventh—where is he?"   *743*
"Dear child," replied his uncle, "idle lust
and cruel pride to Heaven never come.
His crimes unspeakable, his wickedness,
his fame for violence have thrust him down
to deepest Hell. But since you ask of him
who for the last time bore the sceptre, know
he was a king most cruel, whose cruelty   *750*
yet served us well, for it inspired our city,
which had so long endured his tyranny,
with the first love of liberty. But now
I pray you contemplate the happy host,
friends of true virtue all, and citizens
of this, the better world."

Roman   Then, arm in arm
heroes   from out the festive throng three souls came forth,   *757*

and all the shades in the encircling ranks
acclaimed them joyously. The nephew stood
in wonder. "Why is such great homage paid 760
these three, and say, what loving union binds
their shades together as they go their way?"
"Begotten of one sire, fruit of one womb:
hence springs their love. And once our liberty
was to their hands entrusted; hence their grace.
Mark the harsh wounds that two of them display,
with dreadful scars still showing on their breasts.
The fate of a great people long ago
was in the prowess of six brothers placed,
three from each nation, that an end might come 770
with least bloodshed to the great sum of slain.
While from opposing camps the hosts looked on
a final duel was fought between the six.
Then was our freedom, trembling as one
that falls beneath a vacillating Mars,
by one stout hand preserved. Two brothers fell,
and Fortune seemed to smile on Alba's cause
until the third, unhurt, at last avenged
his siblings and assured his country's fate.
For he, still sound, turned to engage the three 780
opponents, weakened by their wounds and far
apart, and slew the slayers, one by one.
So still exultant in the memory
he goes; his brothers too rejoice that they
arose to heaven avenged, and all to whom
his valor gave the Empire close around
the hero, hailing him. But to what end
should I call every name? As you perceive,
thousands inhabit our far-ranging realm.
Before all others stands Publicola, 790
for patriotism and public service famed."

Eager to see yet more, the nephew cast
a glance around and near at hand discerned
a vast array of spirits where, with stars
innumerable aglow, the galaxy

turns toward the fixed North Star. Amazed,
he asked the names and exploits of them all.
"Dear nephew, if I spoke of every act
worthy to be remembered, I should need
another night and more. Behold the stars   800
now fall into the sea, sky changes hue
and, eager to arise, Aurora's face,
dispelling sleep, lights up the Orient wave.
Already pointing to the stars, your sire
gives warning and forbids delay. Let it
suffice that you know this: all of these souls
are Romans whose one thought was the defense
of their dear country. Many by their blood
poured freely forth have won to this abode
and through the bitter sacrifice of death   810
have gained the prize of everlasting life."

Book 2

The youth stood wrapped in revery, from which
his father's gentle voice recalled him: "Now
Time bids you leave these heavens. To but few
has such grace e'er been granted. Go in peace."
"Nay, father let me tarry. Leave me not
unsure of what the future holds." "My son,
you ask the solace of a transient hour,
for soon these dubious visions of the night
and all the things you've seen while wrapped in sleep
will fade and vanish from your waking eyes,   10
and, if some shreds of memory remain
you'll deem them fancies of a wandering mind.
Yet would I not refuse you. Freely ask
what frets you most to hear; steal, if you will,
some moments from the night ere Phoebus come."

Scipio   "My father, if the everlasting Will
inquires of be known to you and if your eyes can read
the future the future's scroll, then would I yearn to hear
what destiny prepares. Now all we see
is cruel war that with its clash and clamor   20
shatters our Latin land, while at the gates
perfidious Hannibal stands poised, and all
our effort falls to ruin. With Roman blood
the fields are sodden; our great chiefs are slain,
ye twain, twin glories of our country's pride,
felled at one stroke. The sun no longer shines
on Italy, and lofty Rome, twice shaken,
reels to her ruin. Say, what now remains?
What doom awaits our city, the world's queen?
Must she submit? May she yet stand erect?   30
For if it is in vain we wield these arms,
why then, declare an end to all our cares
and all our travails and let welcome slumber

23

bring peace to wearied eyes and grant repose
to flesh and bones. Nay, if it is God's will
that I must fall and fall our fatherland,
what shall it serve to rally human strength
against a grim fixed fate? Best die in peace
while savage Hannibal lives on, the lord
of the wide world!"

                              Intolerant of such   40
Prophecy   embittered speech, the worthy sire replied:
of the   " 'Tis not so written. Rather, with your arms
elder   you'll drive the one-eyed brigand from the shores   43
Scipio   of Italy. Reluctant he will go,
uneasy in his mind, with unslaked thirst
for blood and booty and afraid to leave
the alien land but summoned back to home
by his affrighted countrymen hard pressed
by stress of war within their own domain.
And then, in Africa, fearing to face   50
A fatal clash, he will approach your host
and seek to parley. Now prepare yourself
against the wily tactics he will plan.
Let our twin ruin, savagely contrived
by that barbarian city, give you warning.
Go then and look upon his wicked face
And hear him speak—but, ever vigilant,
mark you the sly beguiler's cunning words,
and if you waver or recede one step
the world will call you cowardly or vain.   60
With wiles and new-found schemes he will attempt   61
to circumvent your will and guilefully
cry "peace" and ever mouthing "peace" will clothe
his treachery—the only bane of peace—
in garb of peace. But you, tenaciously,
must hold your ground and keep your purpose firm.
Your majesty, your fatherland's prestige
must not be cheapened. Seeing his dire fate,
he'll rage within but with a humble tongue
will feign submission, cautioning a youth   70

accustomed to success to ponder well
Fortune's caprice, painting in wily words
the hazards and the trials of leadership.
But when he sees no arguments can shake
your steadfast spirit, then in rancorous wrath,
with threats of war he'll hasten to his camp.
Then will ensue a conflict, viewed by Fate
with changing visage, and the whole wide world
will fear its outcome: ours a noble chief
and theirs an impious general; on our side   80
see Virtue, foe of Evil, modest Honor,
Decorum, suasive Faith and Piety
and Justice with her sisters all in arms;
on their side mark you Fury, Frenzy, Fraud,
hearts deaf to truth, Contempt of God, and Lust
unbridled, Wrath that grows and swells with strife
incessant and dire semblances and Crime
in all its forms. Yet, when all's done, you shall
prevail in battle, nor will victory
rouse overweening pride within your heart.   90

Hannibal's From him will Fortune turn and cast him down,
destiny and he shall flee, a vanquished fugitive,
to seek an alien shore where the wide flood
of Hellespont divides the Asian lands
from Greece. There, desperate, he'll embrace the knees
and feet of worthless kings and, suppliant,
beg for command of foreign soldiery,
eager to try again the Ausonian coast,
in hope of Fortune's smile. But she, at last
with evil surfeited and well-disposed   100
to us, will thwart his wicked schemes. And then,
a wretched exile, he will wander far,
spewing his venom throughout many lands,
dreaming of slaying Romans. Aye, as on
a thoroughfare we see a hissing snake,
under a rain of stones, spit out defiance
with venom, and from head to tail in coils
unending writhe and twist its scaly shape,
a fearsome sight; then finally upraise

its glazing eyes and with a dying gasp,   110
blood-choked, essay in vain to strike its foes—
even in such fashion will that frenzied man,
though moribund, yet try a thousand schemes.

"It shall fall out in that time yet to come
that on your country's service, you, secure,
will meet him in his abject state, and look   *116*
once more upon that face that terrified
the world, and happy Ephesus may witness
the encounter and the courteous colloquy
of men of such regard. For Fame, 'tis true,   120
ever mendacious, with false eulogies,
is wont to pair the wicked with the good.
In truth, she celebrates throughout the world
the most atrocious and most dreadful acts,
indifferent to their ends. For one is praised
who was the mainstay of his tottering land,
and equally another is esteemed
and lauded for the carnage he has wrought   *128*
to sack a realm and rest on stolen gold.
So shall both Scipio and Hannibal   130
win equal praise from blind posterity
although a pair most disparate and born
under opposing stars upon our earth.
The vulgar multitude cannot discern
the gap that yawns between magnificence
and deeds of foul enormity. He then
at once will set about with fulsome words
of flattery to win you to his side,
either because such is the wonted way
of Punic tongues or because valor craves   140
a foeman's praise, a tribute truly rare.   *141*
Such chatter doubtless with a placid smile
you will ignore. And Hannibal, as death
draws near, will sadly call again to mind
his fond illusions, nourished by false hopes,
whose promises could never be fulfilled.
Drawing his last breath in Bithynia,   *147*

still dauntless, the ferocious chief at last
will free from fear our city and the world.
And now you know the fortune of that foe   150
who brought such anguish to Ausonia.

    "If yet more of Rome's destiny you'd hear,
give heed: attend to what the Fates yet hold

The
coming
triumph
of Rome

in store. This victory will clear the path
for easier conquests. No folk need feel shame   155
henceforth to shelter in the port that holds
once-mighty Carthage; she'll teach other lands
to bear the Roman yoke and willingly
to pay their tribute. Let the frivolous
Aetolians arise and take up arms,   160
Antiochus rush in—you will prevail
under your younger brother's auspices.   162
Thus, famous in the west and rain-drenched south,
your name will win renown through all the east.
Wars will breed wars, but Rome shall e'er prevail
against all challengers and rule the world
subservient, as vanquished kingdoms yield.
Galatia, aye, and fiery Macedonia   168
will both submit, nor shall a royal name
avail them, nor the glory of their past.   170
Let mighty Alexander, oft invoked,
rise from his grave again, yet (well you know
what I would tell you here) all Greece shall fall
and in brief time lie prostrate at our feet
to expiate the slaying of our sires.   175
Here Glabrio shall win his meed of fame   176
and modest Mummius, and with great deeds   177
high-souled Flaminius shall achieve renown   178
to rival yours. In many years of trials
much will be done. A generation comes   180
rich in skilled soldiers: see the Scauri rise,   181
the Drusi and the great Metellus clan
of glorious surname and the Neros, long
to merit praise, though from this very trunk
in later days a poisonous branch will spring,
baneful to all beneath its noxious shade.

Rigid with virtue, one by one come forth   *187*
the Catos—I could wish their stock might show
less envy of our own. The Aemilian clan
comes to the fore; from them you'll choose your heir.   *190*
He'll bear a name like yours, by valor won,
and will with fire and sword conclude the work
begun by you, and harsher will he be
than you towards those who merit his just hate.
But to resume: next come into my ken
ferocious Sulla and the Pompeys, grave   *196*
of mien, and high-souled Brutus—and, amazed,   *197*
I see where he would aim his dagger thrust.
Next we attain the loftiest peak of all,
for, lo, the great Caesarian tribe comes forth   *200*
to rule the earth. To what end further words?
For never will our city be more rich
in noble minds and meritorious chiefs.
Nay, who would credit what I now reveal?
Leaving his rustic plough, a mighty leader   *205*
will bear our ensigns south in victory,
enslaving Libya again, and force
the heads of haughty sovereigns to bow
beneath his arch of triumph. Latium, twice
Prostrate in abject terror, he will save,   *210*
twice breaking parlous sieges. Then, returning
at Rome's command from scorching shores, he'll cross
the snow-capped Alps and in the vale called Aix   *213*
will turn aside the mad Teutonic surge
with fearful carnage and thereafter deal
likewise with the ebullient Cimbrian hordes.
Then, in the hidden corners of the earth
where once, O youth whose rare unrivalled deeds
shall live on through the years, you pitched your camp,
I see another come—and none more worthy   *220*
than he to win the title of "the Great."
Tagus and Baetis he will force to yield   *222*
and Ebro: all shall feel the Tiber's yoke.
Beyond due measure he will castigate
a rebel. Nay, let not your honest soul   *225*

feel envy; suffer others, like yourself,
to tread high roads of honor. For no man
who was or shall be can claim all of glory.
Capacious, she is ever readying
new places, for one lifetime's span is short   230
in the progression of the universe,
and mortal effort would but little serve
if each age of itself did not bring forth
champions to battle fate's on-rushing tide.
Could one but have sufficed for endless time,
then might the state have bided well-content
under your leadership. But with me here
as wars rage on, you shall abide in bliss
and praise from Heaven that most gifted youth.
From many things to tell I'll choose a few   240
and leave to loftier muses yet to sing
the story of his other mighty deeds.
He, moving as it were from setting sun
in headlong brilliance to the break of dawn—
for so his conquering course may be described—
will raise the name of Italy aloft
up to the stars. Before him all will bow,
and Fortune, generous in triumphs, will
reward the victor. He, with modesty
sincere and asking little, will depart.   250
It will suffice him that three times his brow
will have been girt with laurel and that thrice
Rome saw him on his awesome chariot pass.
More, he will sweep the pirates from the sea   *254*
and vanquish stubborn Judah and therewith
the twin Armenias, all of Araby,
and Cappadocia and Ganges, broad of girth,
and Parthia and Persia. Rome, in brief,
will conquer every land from the Red Sea
to the far regions of the frozen North,   260
the ice-bound plains, the Don, Maeotis, and   *261*
the Riphean peaks that pierce far-distant skies.   *262*
Vanquished in lengthy strife, the kings will flee,
weary of life and kingship and of war.

The Caspian strand the conquerors will tread   *265*
and penetrate to Saba, force the homes   *266*
of incense-burning peoples, enter temples   *267*
and peer into the holiest of shrines.
Nor will they lust for purple, gold, or gems,
for with bared sword into the treasure store   *270*
comes the austerity of Rome, unmoved
by such allures. No isle in all the seas
nor any land under the steadfast stars
by ocean girt will keep its liberty.
Great Cyprus and its princely palaces
shall fall to us and Crete, the home and school   *276*
of superstitions; the Euboean gulf
and Rhodes with its far-famed and sunny port;
the wide Aegean, where the Cyclades
glitter like stars in a clear sky; the shield   *280*
of mighty Sicily; Sardinia, dark
with clouds and Corsica with sun-drenched hills
and fields infertile—all the three seas span:
Tuscan, Iberian, or Adriatic—
all must succumb. But who will lead his fleet
into tumultuous Ocean? One will come,   *286*
bravest of all Rome's sons, whose name henceforth
shall be forever sung throughout the earth.
He will bring terror to the land of Gaul
and foul its rivers with dark streams of blood   *290*
and overcome the tribesmen, golden-haired,
of Britain's isle, a land remote and veiled
under strange skies, beyond a distant sea.
The hostile Rhine, unvanquished hitherto,
with bridges he will span, o'er which his hosts
will march into the foeman's land and bring
the waste of war to blue-eyed German stock.
Ah, happy conqueror could he but learn
to set due limits on his flashing blade.
For this the wretched man lacks wit and will;   *300*
he lays in madness his victorious hands
upon the state, and laurels won abroad
with blood of fellow Romans he defiles,

in strife unseemly sullying deserved
triumphs. Ah, shame to mar such high renown
with folly infamous! How brazenly
the lust for office sweeps all else aside
so that the power may lie with one alone!
He for the first, and giving sad example,
will loot the Treasury with rapacious hands   310
and bind the hapless Senate with new laws!
Nay, of such deeds I'll say no more, nor speak
of the Corinthian war nor of the deaths   313
Pharsalus witnessed, nor of Thapsus nor   314
of Munda, nor the Capitol outraged   315
by bloody desecration.

               After him
a nephew comes, born of the illustrious stock   317
his sister made her own. And he shall bring
beneath our rule the far-off lands of Ind
and feral Egypt, and he shall subdue   320
that consort of the Latin lord who shakes   321
barbarian rattles. Everywhere his blade
coruscant strikes; he tramples down proud kings
and teaches Ister and the plains that lie   324
under the Bears to heed the Roman rod.
Thrice crowned in triumph he will sit enthroned
and give the world new laws, and at his feet
monarchs will lay their sceptres, generals
will come to pledge their faith, and throngs of folk
will bring him gifts, all studious to please him.   330
Last of his labors it will be to crush
the obstinate Iberians, which achieved,
he will then close the somber portals, hung   333
on copper hinges, of the two-faced Janus,
and thus ensure calm centuries of peace.
Old and revered he goes down to his tomb,
leaving the arms of his most cherished spouse.   337
When he has gone, I see the fates of Rome
reversed and all our ancient practices
once fair degenerate. Alas, that you   340

must die! The stock that bears our name is doomed
to die with you. And you shall surely find
a merited abode in Heaven's vault.
But of the herd that follows, what's to say?
the shame of their forebears and to the world
a laughingstock. For them the Stygian caves
and Tartarus stand ready—nay, too soon   *347*
I speak, for I can see a sire and son,   *348*
a noble pair, that crown the Capitol
with double triumph and a double wreath,   350
two purple mantles; but I seem to see
one chariot alone whereon, content,
rides Piety, a portent notable
and rare. Before these chiefs Jerusalem
will fall and force of arms shall overthrow
an ancient faith; and rightly shall the sword
invade the holy places and the folk
suffer the punishment their sins deserve.
It pains me to continue; hear but this:
Decline   the rule and glory, fruit of all our toil   360
of the   to build an empire, alien hands will hold,
Empire   Spaniards and Africans—ah, who can bear   *362*
to think that mankind's dregs, the base and vile
survivors of our sword, shall come to reign?"

The other, helpless to repress the grief
upswelling in his heart, mixed words and tears
and spoke: "O sire, what weight of misery
you prophesy! Say, can the Fates permit
such dire events? Nay, let the shattered stars
fall to the Stygian swamp ere such things be,   370
and let the Lord of Orcus rise to claim
the throne celestial, thundering from Heaven,
ere Africa, victorious, steal Rome's power
and her eternal name!" His father's words
left him not long unsolaced in his grief.
"Banish your fear," he said, "and weep no more:
our Latin honor stands; the might of Rome
shall through the ages have unique renown,

albeit not always shall a Roman grasp
the reins. Soft Syria will try her hand,   *380*
and callous Gaul and ever-prating Greece,
Illyricum and finally the cold clutch
of Boreas' clan. So fate whirls human things.
In years far off perchance, in the world's ruin
Fortune may yet return to her old dwelling.
Yet deeper cast your glance and scrutinize
our city's destiny in years to come.
This is but one of countless future things
that God Who reigns above enshrouds in mist,
but insofar as it is granted me   *390*
to prophesy, know this: though fallen, Rome
shall ne'er be vanquished. To her and to her stock
alone of all the nations of mankind
this grace is granted. Age will sap her strength;
she will grow weary and in crumbling dust   *395*
decay. No generation, nay, no span
of years shall pass exempt from furious wars
and civil discord. There will come a time
when scarce a single Roman shall be found
within the city's wall, but rather all   *400*
the dregs of every land; and if no chief
above all others strong, of ancient virtue,
comes forth with forceful will to intervene,
then shall the old and sober seed of Rome
destroy itself with sanguinary brand,
in internecine carnage pouring forth
what little of the true blood yet remains
in breasts degenerate. But this comfort keep:
our Rome that under favoring stars arose,
though rent by strife and treason, shall endure   *410*
and in her time of wretchedness to come
shall still be the world's queen, if but in name
alone. This title shall she never lose.
Even so an aging lion, long bereft
of strength and courage, may well still possess
his venerable mien and fearsome roar,
and though, a shadow of his former self,

he totters as he goes, yet all the jungle
obeys its feeble lord. And who would dare
predict the certain ending of this tale?   420
Shall I add more? Your ravaged Rome shall live
until the end of time and she shall see
the last of centuries, dying on the day
the world dies." And he sighed and said no more.

　　Then, with his listener's hand in his, he moved
along the shining path. With easy step
they left the high place, following the curve
of the celestial vault. Behind them shone
great Lucifer, and where two figures walked
cast but one shadow. From the crest of Atlas   430
Cynthia descending shone against the face   431
of her resplendent brother. Yet again
the father, in austere and sacred speech,
unloosed his tongue, while motionless the world
stood in delighted trance and the bright stars
stayed their eternal course. "My dearest son,"
he said, "my life's delight and fairest part,
who bring this joyous Heaven yet more joy
in causing me, as I look on a soul
still in the flesh, to feel a greater bliss   440
though I already dwell in blessedness—
a thing I would have thought impossible—
hear me with piety and so take back
a heart replete with truth. My stay is brief:
night's jealous shadow wanes, and in its depth

The
fragility
of earthly
things

the sea now hides the stars. All that is born   446
must die and after ripeness comes decay;
no thing of earth endures, wherefore what man
or race of men can hope for what's denied
even to cherished Rome? In hasty flight   450
the ages pass; all time is swept away,
and ye who rush towards death, ye are but shades
and only shades, light dust or wisps of smoke
tossed by the wind. This blood-stained glory, then,
what boots it? And what purpose, say, is served

by arduous effort on a transient earth?
Though fain you'd tarry there, a breathless flight
bears you to Heaven. See what little room
within its bounds our sorry empire fills,
though with great toil enlarged. And now by you—   460
with what great danger! —it must be preserved.
Ponder what can and must be if but Fate
repent not of the good begun. Let Rome
reign the sole queen of all the subject lands.
Is that so great a thing? And do you find
it worthy to be reckoned a true glory?

The
world is
small and
narrow

Lo, the whole world, in straitened space confined,   *467*
is one small island, by the curving crests
of ocean girt. Observe, how small it is
though great in name! Nor is this whole expanse   470
for habitation apt. For much of it
is swamp or jungle or a rock-strewn waste.
One part is ice-capped and another seared
by scorching heat; there under fiery blasts
lie burning deserts, habitat of snakes.
Look thither if you would see all. Remark
how at the orb's extremities, beneath
the poles that mark their summits, all the land
lies covered by the everlasting ice.
That sector far remote is closed to man,   480
for there grows naught that would yield nourishment.
Look yonder, there where through the wandering stars
the slanting sun pursues a wider path:
there the fields glow with heat and in their midst
the waters of an ever-boiling sea
serve not to moderate the blazing fire
rained down from Heaven. There once the gods
          convened   *487*
(so feign the Argolian bards) and took their rest
refreshed with meat and drink, and passed a night
of tranquil ease beneath the shade of Atlas   490
in converse with an Ethiopian king.
So might they fable because they believed
the stars were great divinities who first

rose from their dwelling in the waves that beat
on Ethiopia's shores and then, grown weary,
seemed to turn westward where great Atlas strains
bearing aloft the last of lands. He waits
to take them as they come and shelter them
in his vast cave. However, to return: *499*
there is no access to the central zone,   500
for on this side the all-pervasive cold
repels you, while the fringes of the ice
melt in fierce flames. Thus mortals might enjoy
two habitable zones, but one of them
yields no approach, for fire and ocean form
its boundaries. One site alone remains,
but fragmented by vast unpeopled deserts.
So it falls out that different usages
and varied and discordant tongues prevail
to check the course of fame. World-wide renown   510
is given to none. A name on all men's lips
throughout the farthest North will be unknown
where rise the hidden sources of the Nile;
what glory clamorous in Taprobane   *514*
shall find an echo in Hibernia?
Say, truly, to what end do men direct
ambition? They would seek far-reaching fame
but narrow walls constrain them. Thus enclosed
in prison cells, their solace is their dreams.
But when the light eternal dissipates   520
all shadows and all dreams, the wretches then
perceive the truth too late. With vain regret
for wasted years and all that they have lost,
in bitter lamentation they depart.

"Such folly, though ridiculous, ever fills   *525*
your minds. You burn to have your name endure
through all of Time. Oncoming ages claim
your every thought; in your mind's eye you see
distant posterity and long to live
on lips of learned men when you are dust   530
and, though within your sepulchres confined,

to journey far o'er fame's free thoroughfares
to the world's ends. And sweet it is, I grant,
to flourish after death and so deride
devouring destiny—and yet 'tis naught
to live on as a name. A better life

True im- you have, and surer. Heaven's arduous slope
mortality you may ascend with joy and leave behind
our miserable earth. For here above
a life awaits you which the centuries   540
shall never alter. Winter's piercing cold
shall here do you no hurt, nor summer's heat.
Here is a life unburdened by the cares
uneasy wealth occasions or the blight
of poverty, a life that fears not death,
free of all ills of spirit or of flesh
the baneful stars may bring. Live beyond time,
for Time devours both you and your renown,
fruit of such arduous toil. For true it is:
what seems most lasting does most swiftly fade.   550
Virtue alone, that heeds not death, endures.
Virtue alone prepares the way to Heaven.
So hither, heroes, come! Let this last burden
be not too great for weary backs to bear.

    "But if your wayward heart still would find joy   *555*
in empty glory, know what prize you seek:

Scipio's the years will pass, your mortal form decay;
future your limbs will lie in an unworthy tomb
which in its turn will crumble, while your name
fades from the sculptured marble. Thus you'll know   560
a second death. Though honors registered
on worthy scrolls have long and lustrous life,
yet they too in the end are likewise doomed
to fade away. Your children's age, mayhap,
will venerate your name and your renown,
but later generations will bring forth
forgetful progeny. Much have you done
and will do more. You will yet wage great wars
on far-flung fields and by your prowess win

a glory worthy to endure. Your feats,   570
by many praised, yet many more shall praise.
Far down the centuries to come I see

An Etru-   a youth, Etrurian born, who will narrate   573
rian youth your splendid story; he shall be, my son,
will cele- for our renown, a second Ennius.   575
brate him
I hold both dear, for both of them possess
a memorable ardor. One of them
brought rustic Muses, in rough fashion clad,
to Latium, and the other with his notes
detains them as they flee. And each will sing   580
in manner of his own of our exploits,
thus striving to prolong our lives' brief course.
Dearer I count him who in distant years
will backward cast his glance upon our age,
for no compulsion shall inspire his zeal
nor fee nor fear nor hatred nor yet hope
of our reward, but only reverence
for high-souled deeds, and simple love of truth.
Yet still, what serves it all? Books too soon die,   589

All   for what with futile art a mortal makes   590
human   is also mortal. Should posterity
things   strive to preserve such works and so oppose
must   voracious age, eager to check time's march,
perish   it were impossible, so numerous
are the impediments. Destructive floods,
fierce fires that burn whole cities to the ground,
assaults of tempests from both sea and sky,
wars that rage madly through the world and leave
nothing unharmed—nay, more: the earth itself
must die and take with it its dying scrolls;   600
so yet a third death you must undergo.
How many from the distant East or South
have won renown, whose names they could not save
for you to know? How many, in time's dawn,
hoped for a name enduring and have passed,
forgotten all? Ye mortals, O my son,
are held in narrow bonds of space and time,
and one who understands this truth were wise

to hither, Heavenward, lift up his thoughts.
The vulgar herd on earth may prate of you   *610*
as they esteem you. If you'd heed my word,
ignore them one and all. Have but contempt
for earthly approbation; place not there
the best hopes founded on your highest deeds.
Let fairest Virtue draw you by her own
allurements. If for fame you yearn you may
attain it, but all fame must fade and pass.
But if your goal be Heaven, then, my son,
what you achieve is yours beyond all end
or measure in eternity of bliss.   620
However, if the sweetness glory brings
yet moves you, and you feel her pricking spur,
then I can promise that your deeds will bring
fair glory and you shall have the reward
you seek, my son. In truth, though you might strive
to flee it, yet your fame will follow you.   *626*
As under the bright sun a shadow follows
each movement of a man and turns or rests
according as he moves, even so fame clings,
whether we will or no. And would you not   630
count him a fool who walks in scorching dust
that he may watch the shadow at his heels?
No wiser surely is the man who wastes
his strength in empty effort through the years,
with care-encumbered spirit, to obtain
in recompense naught but the vain applause
of vulgar gossip. My intent you ask?
Let one man, with attendant shadow, rush
to reach his goal, another strive for Heaven,
impelled by love of virtue, not of fame,   640
which, though well merited, his heart ignores.

Paternal   "Take then the path I show you, arduous
counsel   though it may prove; or, better, I should say,
cleave to the way you've chosen for yourself.
May the state thrive as you direct its course
and by its victories rise to eminence

on Fortune's highest rung. And from the stars
the Lord Serene, of vast Olympus King,
will mark your deeds, rejoicing in your fame,
and pleased the more to see you stand in truth   650
a pillar of your stricken country, thus   *651*
well meriting the name of Scipio
joined to the other title your exploits
will consecrate. One further thing I urge
upon you—and heed well my counsel here:
after the love of justice and that due
the fatherland, let your most tender care
be for your cherished friends. Aye, treasure well
the friendships that true virtue offers you.
There is naught sweeter in the lot of man   660
than intimate exchange of trust and faith
with a true-hearted friend. And happily
one such stands with you now, the firmest, he,
of all your company. May Laelius share   *664*
and counsel your most secret thoughts and guide
your habits and be free to scrutinize
your deepest mind, from other men concealed.
Another Laelius after many years
shall by another scion of our house
be cherished and deserve a special love.   670
And men may err and blend the twain in one
and speak of Laelius and Scipio
as but one case of friendship and unique
since time's beginning, though between the pairs
like-named a lengthy space will intervene.
Do you first claim your Laelius, nor allow
your noble blood to shrink from one base-born,
for many a worthy hero, made the peer
of senators by active virtue and
a spirit loftier than his state, has come   680
from a plebeian stock." He said no more.

His son spoke then: "I've followed hitherto   *682*
upon your traces, ever mindful of
my father's honor; henceforth even more

attentive I shall follow where you lead.
Yet somewhat I must wonder, dearest sire,
how is it, that among the things disclosed,
you have as yet said nothing of my fate?"

Scipio's
end Sadly the father answered: "My dear son, 690
your virtue must instruct you to accept
great hardship. What your destiny reserves
as end to all your toils choose not to learn.
With anguish and in shame I tell you this:
your country will show you no gratitude,
but see you take your leave of her content
with temperate vengeance; you are not to turn
to wars nor take up arms, although for you
occasion be not lacking. Best submit 698
and suffer what your fortune brings. Do not
seek to destroy the land that once you saved 700
and darken thus the light of your fair deeds.
She drives you forth? Depart. She will not call 702
you home? Endure. In splendid exile die
and with a word avenge the unjust disgrace 704
that she imposed on you in life: deny
your thankless fatherland your last remains
and leave inscribed upon your tomb the tale
of cold ingratitude. So much is right;
no more shall you express. And now must I
no longer tarry. Dearest son, farewell! 710
Remembering your father, tend with care
your brother's youthful years. It may well be
that he will follow in your footsteps." So
he spoke and turned to leave, with pace to match
the swiftly falling stars. The dawn meanwhile
shone on the tents and sent its rosy sheen
to the rude cot whereon the general slept.
The trumpets' awesome blast aroused the camp,
and in affright fled sleep and spectral sire.

Book 3

Lashing his chargers on, the tireless sun
rose through the sky, and all the trembling stars
vanished from the horizon, one by one,

Scipio
ponders
his
dream

as if in fear. The mighty hero then
uprose, and long he pondered on the dream
vouchsafed him in the dark and quiet night.
"Ah, why did I not claim my sire's sweet kiss?
Why, as he turned aside, did I not seize
and hold his hand? Why was I not allowed
with tranquil discourse to prolong the night?   10
Why fled it fast away? For there was much
I would have sought to learn: in what domain
must the last battles rage, or in what zone
of the deep sea? Can an ally be trusted?
What room for loyalty is found within
the hearts of barbarous kings? And where shall be
my grave? What style of death has ruthless Fate
allotted to my brother and to me?
My cherished cousin of well-proven worth,   19
how shall he end? Must I alone bear all   20
the wicked wrongs my fatherland endures?
Haply such things are better unrevealed,
lest with foreknowledge of finality
Virtue might furl her canvas 'gainst the gales
that rise to thwart her. Nay, what is begun,
let it proceed. Forgive your maddened land   26
that knows not what it does."

                        And so he pondered;
then summoned his friend Laelius, who straightway
obeyed and stood before him, wordlessly

He
speaks
with
Laelius

regarding his lord's mien. "Dear Laelius,"   30
the leader said, "my soul is much perturbed
by heavy thoughts. What we have so far done

42

would be enough for others to have wrought,
yet weighed against the carnage and the woe
of Italy, it is but a slight thing
to have destroyed the power of Spain; that host   *36*
is scarcely dangerous. Nor, even so,
is that task yet completed. It might seem
we fear to look upon the awesome chief,
but rather have sought out a foreign field   *40*
nor dared approach our native shores to lend
our aid in guarding the invested walls
of precious Rome. Will citizens and foes
see in our presence here the evidence
of exile or of flight? I cannot tell
what purpose or what strength of heart is yours,
yet I do deem them great. Let others rest
content with great beginnings; as for me,
naught is achieved if aught is left undone.
I must yet see fierce Hannibal spew forth   *50*
his wicked soul to satisfy our leaders,
and treacherous Carthage sink into the pit
before the exalted ire that fills my heart
subsides. And if my death may serve to match
the Punic hurt with ours, I'll die content.
Will not a just God draw his sword for us
in judgment of such crimes; shall thunderbolts
not rain from Heaven? Affronted by such sins,
shall not great Atlas, shield and guardian
of an abominable world, uproot itself   *60*
from out the depths of earth and so make way
for swarming vipers, hills of burning sand,
and yield free passage to the scorching blasts
borne from the south? Shall Bágrada not turn
its sluggish course and, swollen like the cold
and raging Ister, swamp those impious walls
and drown the caitiffs in its vengeful flow?
We yet prevail; let weakened muscles bear
weapons for yet a while and God, grown tired
of so much perfidy, will end the strife.   *70*
This burden, I foresee, falls on our backs.

"Delay is vexing, but still many things
must be well weighed and future risks foreseen.
All Africa is now aflame with hate;
no shore, no port, no hearth will welcome us
nor give us sustenance. Where'er your gaze
may fall it meets with harsh hostility.
What harbor shall our fleet first choose; what strand
receive our host? Where shall our chiefs encamp?
Who, say, will guide us to a road secure,   80
who tell us of the countryside and towns
and all the alien customs? Who will show
our cohorts, fearful of deep running streams,
where fords lie hidden? Matters such as these
must be considered with sagacious care.
First would I learn: can any trust be placed
in barbarous hearts? It may be you have heard
of Syphax. Rumor says he stands supreme   *88*
above all kings by right of birth and wealth
and subject tribes and scope of fertile land.   90
Him shall we try. If word of Latin glory
has penetrated Libya's hidden land,
he may be moved perchance by courteous pleas,
for not uncommonly even barbarous hearts
and rustic spirits may be moved and won
by dreams of glory. And should we invade
that hostile land—as is now my intent—
his province would provide our best approach.
Be this your charge, O best of men, for you
have a persuasive tongue and the sure skill   100
a tranquil soul provides. Try then with words
to mollify his savage heart." He ceased.
And Laelius, tarrying not, cast off the coil
that bound his ship to shore and made his way
across the waters of the narrow strait
between Iberia and the Libyan strand;
landing that day in Mauritania's port,
he hastened to the king.   *108*

    On snowy pillars raised the palace stood,

and through the stately halls, agleam with gold,   110
bright clusters of rare gems diffused their glow.   *111*
Here might you see the sparkling topaz shine,
and from the lofty ceiling emeralds
glanced down like stars. The curving Zodiac,
traced all in gold, pursued its oblique path
under the vaulted roof. And there with craft,
ere he was turned to stone, had Atlas set   *117*
seven gems to ape the seven spinning stars.   *118*
There one, more sluggish, shone with hue to please   *119*
an old man's frigid heart; another glowed   *120*
with threatening red; but yonder gentler hues
shed kinder rays, and with a light serene   *122*
the vault was cheered. A great carbuncle, placed   *123*
in the mid-point, with splendor like the sun's
effulgence, banished every shadow. Well
you might have deemed its lustre could avail
to generate the day and banish night—
true image of our Phoebus. Further shone,   *128*
with matching clarity, another pair,   *129*
of which the one of russet hue had power   130
to rouse swift passion in a watcher's breast.
The moon, with tawny horns of iron down-curving,
unwearied followed her descending course,
dark, yet aglow and swathed in heavenly beams.

Dispersed above were sundry creatures seen,
awesome in visage, carved in divers shapes.
First stood the Ram with twisted horns, his head   *137*
turned back in sadness as if he could still
behold the body of the lovely maid
upon the waves. Next came the fearsome Bull,   140
bearing Agenor's daughter as he swam.
Followed two glittering youths, the high-born Twins,
fair Leda's progeny. The fourth in line,
ugly to look upon, the deep-sea Crab,
was followed by the Lion, swift of foot
and awe-inspiring for his mighty head.
And close on him the rosy Maiden trod,

and then the Scales with ponderous arms outspread
on either side to weigh with just assay
the fleeting hours; next, with waving claws,   150
the Scorpion, threatening the vault with tail
high-reaching; after him the dual shape
of beast and man combined, from Thessaly.
Visage and arms like to an aged man's,
yet well skilled in the taut-stringed bow and fierce
to look upon, he bore an ivory quiver;
horse-like his nether parts. And after him
the agile Goat with his twin horns of gold
boldly uprose, firm on his cloven feet.
Came then a naked man of massive bulk,   160
head veiled in storm clouds even as when he bends
to pour down Heaven's rain. And last the Fish
swam through the waves with flickering fins and tails.

While the observer's eyes, through shifting light
moved swiftly, following the Pole's twelve signs,
enraptured by the beauties of the work,
lo, all about them in bright gold appeared
the gods and heroes of the days of old,
The   depicted in their actions. First of all
pagan   sits Jupiter in pride on his high throne   170
gods   with bolt and sceptre, and the bird of Jove
to high Olympus bearing in his claws
the lad from Ida. Next, with faltering stride,   *173*
in glaucous mantle, reverend with years,
comes rustic Saturn, holding in his clutch   *175*
mattock and pruning fork and there portrayed
devouring his own progeny. Comes then
a dragon belching fire from its mouth   *178*
wherein its tail is grasped, and all convolved
in giant coils. And after him Neptune   180
swims through deep Ocean's dark unfathomed depths,
armed with his trident that can quell the waves   *182*
however stirred to anger; choirs of nymphs
surround him, and the Tritons from afar
show veneration for the sea's great lord.

He strikes the rock but once, and at the sound
his swift-paced steed bounds to the sandy shore.

   Next comes Apollo with his flowing locks,   *188*
a beardless boy, a youth, and all at once
with temples shining white. Before him stands   190
his sacred courser, quivering, swift of foot,
pawing the earth and champing at the bit.
Beside him sits a monstrous beast, three-mawed;   *193*
mark how he fawns, placated when the god
rewards him. Triple heads he has; the right
a dog's, the dusky left a raging wolf's,
and in the midst a lion's. These are joined
by twining snakes that show the shrinking skull.
And from the sacred lyre there portrayed
one seems to hear the plucked chords yield sweet
     notes.   200
There too are seen the quiver and the bow
with sharp swift arrows on the shoulder slung;
and lo, within the Delphic cave in death
the monstrous Python lies. And there appears   *204*
the sacred laurel, green and gold, the plant
beloved by the bards of Italy
and Hellas. Far it casts its fragrant shade,
cooling the bowers where the Muses nine
seem with alternate song and sweet refrain
to charm the stars and halt them in their course.   210
Close on his heels his younger brother treads;   *211*
his brow bespeaks his cunning, and he bears
a wand which fuscous serpents twine around.
A brilliant helm adorns his head; his feet
are shod with pinioned sandals all agleam.
See how the cock stands viligant—mark there
how Argus falls upon the curving blade;
see on the left his youthful bride, well pleased
with her exotic dower, proudly preen,
parading her rare charms.

                And close to her   220

the far-famed Gorgon sisters stand. Perseus   *221*
with blade fraternal cleaves the snake-bound neck
while he averts his eyes to look into
his glass. Mark too the ancient turned to stone,   *224*
the beast from blood upsprung, the wingèd horse,   *225*
the fountain sacred to the gracious Muses.   *226*
Mars the destroyer, on his bloodstained car
raging comes next, and see with him the wolf,
and the mad train of Furies crying ruin;
he wears a shining helmet on his head   230
and in his hands he bears a flail. See next
Vulcan, aware that he has been betrayed   *232*
and in his shame preparing to depart
but hindered by his lameness, while the gods
throng the high heavens to mock the clumsy spouse.
Then with horns stretched aloft and ruddy cheeks
behold great Pan, his breast adorned with stars;   *237*
his shaggy legs are stiff as on goat hoofs
he prowls the caves, in shepherd-fashion holding
a crooked staff, and as he goes he plays   240
upon a huge pipe shaped from seven reeds.
Yonder with sceptre in her grasp the Queen   *242*
of all the gods is seen, dear sister she
and august spouse of Jove. Her lofty head
is somewhat veiled by an adorning cloud
which many-colored Iris furnishes: *246*
mark how the peacocks flock about her feet.
Next comes the dread Minerva, whom men style   *248*
"the Virgin," in full panoply attired;
an awesome spear she carries and she wears   250
a lofty plume; a brightly glittering shield
graven with semblance of the Gorgon's face;
above her in the dark the birds of night
hover, and where the keen-eyed goddess goes
they follow. And the fields of Cecrops, rich   *255*
with fresh young olive trees, are likewise seen.
Mark how the daughter of Jove's brain derides   *257*
the shameless issue of her sister, Venus,
and her unseemly source. And it is she

we next observe, as, new-born, she comes forth   260
out of the sea, her lowly origin,
as legend tells. See how, lascivious,
she rides within the cradling conch, adorned
with crimson roses while swift-flying doves
provide her escort; mark her company,
three naked girls: the first averts her face,   266
the others outward look with smiling eyes,
and all have snowy arms entwined in sweet
reciprocal embrace. Nor absent is
the Boy, his quiver charged with pointed darts,   270
slung from his wingèd shoulder. Once he shot
with his death-dealing bow and made his mark
Apollo. Then the clamor of the gods
disturbed the stars above; the naughty lad
took refuge in his mother's loving lap.
Comes next Diana, and her sequent train   276
of Dryads throng the grove, and Oreads,
and nimble fauns and satyrs follow them
and in a circle all dispose themselves,
applauding while the shepherd cherished by   280
the goddess, sleeping on the grassy bank,
snores on. There hapless Actaeon caught sight   282
of lovely limbs bathed in the crystal fount
and was dismembered by his fierce-toothed hounds.
In memory of him the sacred stag
is on the Scythian altars sacrificed
in vain to win the favor of the goddess.
Last comes great mother Cybele, to whom   288
no land is fairer than Mount Ida's slope.
In ease disposing her vast body's bulk,   290
in garb of many hues the ancient dame,
revered for her great sceptre and the key
she holds, is seated. Rich in progeny,
she wears upon her head a lofty crown
of Phrygian towers. The old legend tells
that she brought forth the family of the gods,
aye, and the Thunderer himself. 'Tis true
her fickle womb likewise the Giants bore,

a scourge to all the world in ages past.
Yoked lions draw her chariot.

                                        Afar,   *300*
The   the violent ruler of the lower realm
nether   from his sulphuric throne calls forth the shades
world   of Tartarus; beside him, all forlorn   *303*
               his bride sits, ravished—so the story runs—   *304*
               from Enna's vale in Sicily. Here groans
               and lamentations issue from the shades
               who suffer punishment and expiate
               their sins on earth. And here are seen as well
               the nine dark provinces, each walled from each   *309*
               by barricades. Mark the black Stygian marsh;   *310*
               these pools are flooded by the murky flow
               of somber Acheron that chokes the tarn
               with clots of mire. See how Cocytus' flood
               of bitter tears here in its doleful course
               surrounds Avernus and, meandering, laves
               the caves and choirs of the damned. Here too
               yawns Phlegethon's abyss, a scorching mere,
               and silent Lethe whose dark night benumbs.
               Behold the ferryman of this bleak stream   *319*
               plying the oar of his funereal bark.   *320*
               The lord of Styx with his sad spouse surveys
               the spectacle and probes the distant dark,
               feasting his lurid glance upon the sight
               of varied torments, urging on his slaves
               with harsh commands; his servants are grim Death
               and Misery, the Furies and the Fates
               who spin the twisted thread. Before him sprawls
               the dismal realm's three-headed guardian.   *328*

                   In varied style and wondrously designed
               such scenes of Heaven and Hell were here portrayed.   *330*
Laelius   Nothing less dear than gold met Laelius' eye:
received   he trod on what is counted rich and rare,
by   as, having traversed all the spacious hall,
Syphax   he found the king. The latter rose at once

up from his lofty throne, in eagerness
to give the embrace of welcome. And then both
were seated. Laelius quietly began:
"Great King, whom Fortune has deemed worthy of
so great a friend, the like of whom the sun
through his discerning path from Indian shores   340
to his Hesperian resting place sees not,
has never seen before, nor—if my mind
play me not false—shall ever see again,
attend me and let not my utterance fall
on empty air. Most puissant Scipio,
renowned in every corner of the earth,
greets you. If aught exists to be revered,
if stainless faith, if care for fame endure,
all these are met in fullness in one folk,
and one man only does that folk obey.   350
Rome is the head of all things and her chief
is Scipio; nor do I feign these truths.
He now, O King, requests your friendship. You
have seen the Punic nature, marked how frail
its faith. If Fortune should—believe me—grant
them victory in war (and may the God
of gods forbid it) then your kingdom's state
would be unhappy and your life beset
by many perils. Now they are restrained
not by the bonds of friendship but by fear.   360
But Romans know no debt that's more compelling
nor duty dearer than to keep their word.
Allies we value, counting them our wealth,
as Italy and near-by Spain attest.
Now Africa will learn how firm the oath
sworn by the men who wear the toga stands.
Nor is there aught that shall avail you more
than our alliance. As we dwell afar,
not neighbors, we'll not chafe each other. Yet
if summoned we shall cross, however slight   370
the favoring winds, with ready fleet to aid
if need should press you, and your foes will quake,
surprised to see our armor in your camp.

And truly, unless Fate should interpose
obstruction, we have come here but to further
a labor now in hand. Our people seeks
to sweep away the crowd of petty kings
and from unworthy despots wrest the rule,
so that but few may hold the power supreme;
for the condition of a state best thrives   380
under a monarch, as it wastes away
in hands of many lawless herds. At last
all Africa may yet accept the rule
of one prince only. I need scarce say more,
for who between the Red Sea and the shores
of the Atlantic seems more fit than you?

*Laelius
presents
Rome's
gifts*   "Scorn not the gifts sent by your mighty friend: 387
from the Apulian plains a charger swift
and skilled in battle, rivalling in its course
the blasts of Auster and the Thunderer's bolt;   390
further, he adds a breastplate for the steed,
and a gold collar for his snowy neck,
reft from a Samnite tyrant, and thereto
arms for the rider, durable and hewn
from solid ore of sundry metals mined
in fertile Elba. Mark the dusky helm,
the flashing sword; see how the sturdy plate
protects the breast, how supple are the greaves,
how glows the purple of the belt, concealing
the sword's dark metal, how the pointed goad   400
glitters with tawny gold. The javelin
see here, apt for far-reaching thrust. Observe
how with protective curve the studded shield
deflects the stroke. Henceforth, in frays to come,
put on these Roman tokens. Arm yourself
in happy auspices as Scipio's friend.
This he and friendly Rome would ask of you:
give us your faith and pledge, so may this day
forever be propitious for us both
and honored long in song on either shore   410
of Africa or Europe." Having spoken,

he let his voice fall and cast down his gaze.

Syphax
replies
    The king gave gracious answer: "I embrace
your offer gladly, Roman, nor would I
disdain the gifts of such a friend nor yet
the alliance you propose. Yet I do fear
to make a pact and choose a side, incurring
new and alarming risks, unless I first
may meet your great-souled leader face to face.
My highest wish it is to grasp the hand   420
of the great conqueror and in loyal pledge
to seal the bond, a gage of peace for years
to come. His merit well we know, how famed
throughout the world his honor stands, for none
among all Romans held such high renown
nor could by noble discourse so well bend
reluctant spirits, charming every heart
by his aspect alone. His mighty name
and glory move us and it is our hope
to meet him, so may hand clasp hand and eye   430
meet eye and word respond to word; thus may
his presence verify his wide renown.
Not so untutored are our minds, our hearts
beat not so barbarously within our breasts
that with blind eye we look on beauty, nor
does Virtue, once perceived, leave us unmoved.
I am constrained in an uncertain realm
by anxious care. I dare not move beyond
the boundaries of my ancestral land,
surrounded as it is by hostile tyrants.   440
Else had I gone to meet him; such a voyage
to seek a great friend over the wide sea
I would have deemed a glorious enterprise.
But he is not impeded by the check
of craven fear, and his more youthful years
more readily accept the trials of travel.
Let him then, if his love for us be true
and you have faith in me, seek out the hall
where dwells a friend prepared for words of peace.

The sea will offer him a path secure.   450
But now the dying day and thickening shade
bid us to hasten to the waiting feast.''

The   So speaking, he uprose and grasped the hand
feast   of Laelius and sat him in a place,
outspread with purple, high above the rest.
The tuba, heard through all the darkened hall,
gave the awaited signal. Servants then
with lively clatter hurried back and forth.
It was no simple banquet that they served,
nor were the settings primitive and crude.   460
Vessels of gold some bore and others plates
of sparkling unflawed crystal; goblets carved
from massive gems brimmed with the honeyed draught
that nurturing Meroë, by Phoebus fired,   *464*
had erstwhile proffered, while the household shone
in splendor, ringing with the festive hum.
Even such, unless you credit not the word
of Homer, was Alcinous's feast—   *468*
there sat Ulysses, wily and astute,
and here did Laelius play the part of guest,   *470*
like him most affable and honey-tongued.

The   Scarce was the feast concluded when a lad
minstrel's arrayed in purple rose before the throng
song   to pluck his tuneful lyre in native style.
Rapt by the music, all there held their peace
to hear the words accompanying the notes:
"The mighty Hercules, who through the world   *477*
subdued wild beasts and thus hewed for himself
a living path to Heaven, taking leave
of Nemean woods and Lernian marshes, cleft   480
the passes of Haemonia which of yore   *481*
had awed the shadowed Erymanthian hills,   *482*
vanquished two famous cities, laid in dust
the prideful centaurs, and slew Geryon.   *484*
Thence did the warrior deign to turn his steps
to where we dwell and, slaying Antaeus   *486*

on his own forebears' soil, brought to an end
our long dismay. So was our freedom born.
The hand of Hercules that overthrew
that dire oppression made our realm secure,   490
enticing to the fields the husbandmen
long absent. He then, knowing all was done,
leaving the world at peace, went boldly forth
to seek the vestibule of Orcus, daring,   *494*
eye close to eye, to meet the fearsome gaze
of dire Megaera, and not far remote   *496*
from our confines, raised high—a wondrous feat—
twin pillars o'er the turmoil of the deep,
and thus decreed that here was fixed the end
of human journeys. So it long remained.   500
But newly, from the east, a savage youth   *501*
has dared to spurn such limits, yet has failed
to change the name they bear since Hercules
defined the frontier, he to whom old Atlas,
lord of all Libya's kingdoms, wearying
of his great burden, gave in trust the stars
and lofty heavens while he took his ease.
Nor did the wretch repose for long; bewitched,
he burned to look upon Medusa's face   *509*
and so was turned to stone. Behold him now: 510
darkening the world with his vast shade he stands,
far reaching into space and with his head
touching the highest stars. Eternal snow
enshrouds him and he towers for all time,
harassed by thunder, wind and cloud and storm.
But not for long remained he unavenged:
out of Arcadia an avenging youth,   *517*
armed with the arts of Pallas, came and bore
away the dreadful monster's severed head.
The dripping blood gouts staining Libya's sands   520
spread poisonous infection. So in death
as in her life the dread Medusa brought
woe and calamity to all the world.

"Later a queen came hither, fugitive   *524*

from Tyre and closed within its lofty walls
great Carthage, named after its origins.   *526*
Then, having spurned the hands of neighboring kings,
flouting her people's wish to see her wed,
forever mindful of the cherished face
of her dead spouse, by her own death she chose   *530*
to assure her virtue. In this fashion then
the fierce queen, founder of the city, died.
What cruel injustice will be done to her—
but who will believe it?—if it yet should be
that some detractor, trusting in his art,   *535*
will, in his verses, tarnish her fair name
with taint of shameless passion! In brief time
the city grew to greatness, flourishing;
but always in the web that Fortune spun
was envy interwoven, stirring up   *540*
great states to enmity. In early days
lived violent men, and Carthage still reveres
for patriotic zeal the far-renowned
Philaenian brothers, holding they have risen   *544*
to swell the immortals' ranks and worshipping
at their twin shrines. And had the ardent pair
denied the fatherland the sacrifice
of their own lives, then on Cyrenian fields
had perished thousands of their countrymen.

*The   "The present age is rent with bitter strife,   *550*
present   nor can the raging Middle Sea nor strength
state of   of ravenous Scylla with Charybdis joined
Africa*   protect Ausonia from the Punic hordes.
Worthy of fame, immortal Hannibal
has stormed Italian hills and made a way
with acid for his troops through pathless crags,   *556*
where even mountain goats would find hard footing.
More he has done. Lo, now streams run with blood
and fields are sodden, while the unmown hay
stands high in Italy. But now a youth,   *560*
to be remembered long, comes, sent by Heaven
to aid with his strong arm his stricken land.

Spain has observed his glorious deeds and now
all Africa has heard of them. So Fate
stands poised unsure between two chiefs; the end
will be Fate's choosing. Great things are at hand."
So far the song; the singer then fell still
with fingers fondling the silent strings,
while lords and humbler folk, alike well pleased,
applauded. Then the king spoke: "Honored guest,   570
the ancient Libyan legends you have heard,
and our beginnings. If it seems that thanks
are called for, may it please you to describe
your nation's origins and ancient chiefs."

*Laelius
tells the
story of
Rome*   And Laelius, gently smiling, made reply:
"Ah, what a mighty tally of great deeds
you ask for, best of kings! You think perchance
to hear the story of our triumphs told
in a brief span of time? Nay, the account
might easily require a year or more.   580
You'd have the tale told in one meagre night
more than half spent and at a time when tongue
must fail the teller, who for need of sleep
grows weak and weary. The remaining hours
are far too few for all I might narrate.
Who in brief words could tell of Italy
so long embattled in the ages past,
of Tuscan ranks and Samnite wars and Gauls
so often routed? Or our deeds upon
this continent, or in mid-ocean where   590
chance brought the fleets together, each on each
rushing headlong, plying destructive oars?
Or of the bitter warfare waged in Spain
where rivers choked with corpses could not flow,
where fields reeked ever with blood newly shed?

"All this our chiefs have done. The ancient annals
hold but the thousandth part, which Scipio
will have transcribed from the Tarpeian rock,   598
where in the temple guardians preserve

our chronicles. From them can much be learned,   600
yet still the merest portion of the truth.
However, facts provide such evidence
as to require no word of witnesses.
Rome, unlike Greece, where such are found in number, *604*
produced few chroniclers. For us, to act
is better than to write, and eulogies
we leave to others. Should you see set forth
our glorious deeds in books, note that such books
were written by the hands of foreigners.
Nor can Greek genius, though its subject be   610
Roman achievement, find the fitting words
to do full justice to our chronicles:
this I must ask you to bear well in mind.
However, for such time the tardy hour
permits me I am willing to discourse.

"Our early fathers came from distant Troy
whose walls, men say, in ten long years of war
the Grecian conquerors befouled with blood;
and now perhaps in Italy is born
one to avenge that ghastly crime. But I   *620*
would not digress. In that calamity
thousands were brought to ruin and scarce one
escaped unharmed. There, on the Phrygian shore,
where ashes from the pyre of Mother Troy
rained down to cover the defenseless dead,
Anchises' son, the illustrious chief renowned
afar for feats of arms, when he could find
among his folk nor yet in friendly towns
no hope of safety, was constrained to flee
in tears, abandoning his fatherland   630
and the long-cherished partner of his bed.
After long wanderings, many trials by land
and all the thousand perils of the sea,
he came at length, impoverished, to land
on the Ausonian shore. There, when the clans
of Latium, vanquished by this son of Troy,
had yielded and when from Lavinia's lips   *637*

he had obtained the kiss of peace—at last,
entrusting to the venerated stream
his sacred mortal part, the hero died.   640

"Iulus, the boy, his son, came after him,
and others followed; so for long endured
the kingly line that reigned in Alba's halls.
Then a great-hearted chieftain, his forebears'   *644*
avenger and a punisher of crimes,
came to raise high new walls on Tiberside.
Him does our race call father and in death
has deified him, calling him Quirinus
and offering incense to him. Now you know
of Rome's foundation and its early times.   650
What names, what leaders shall I mention next?

The line   I see their number swell past reckoning,
of Roman for Freedom planted a most fruitful seed
heroes   for dwellers in that tranquil town, and gave
an awesome valor to their sturdy hearts.
I could more easily enumerate
the scintillating stars, the grains of sand
that line the shore, the ripples on the sea,
than all the shining names of mighty chiefs
my Rome may vaunt: the clan of Curius,   *660*
Camillus and the Pauli, great in war;   *661*
and of the Fabian name three hundred sons   *662*
all in one day together sacrificed
on the occasion of their country's need;
the fierce Torquati and the Lepidi,   *665*
the virtuous Catos, the Fabricii,   *666*
content with little, and the hero called   *667*
by appellation that his winning race
bestowed upon him, and the one who took   *669*
his surname from the bird sent from above;   670
the brave and noble line of the Marcelli,   *671*
the stubborn Gracchi and the Reguli   *672*
of loyal faith, whose name, I think, reports
of war have brought already to your ears;
and finally, above all other clans,

the Scipios, whom the Cornelian line
brought down from Heaven so that men might vie
in progeny with the gods. And from this stock
our chief of chiefs is sprung. Nay, to relate
merely the names of families such as these   680
is no small task, but should I undertake
to count their exploits there would be no end.
My tongue is mortal, not of iron wrought,
nor are your ears. However, lest it seem
we lack examples of the faith displayed
by the Philenian pair your song has praised,
I'll match them with a few accounts I'll choose
from an abundant store to tell you here

The   "Once on a time a sudden chasm yawned   689
sacrifice   deep in the Forum, opened by the blast   690
of Marcus   of some mysterious wind or other cause
Curtius   unknown. The Fathers gathered in amaze
and terror seized the city. From all sides
assembling in fright the townsmen came:
some cast great boulders into the deep pit;
some strove to shore the gaping void with beams
and baskets filled with earth. But since such vast
accumulations naught availed, 'twas clear
the anger of the gods had been aroused
and in their hands must lie the remedy.   700
The priests, besought by timid postulants,
after deliberation made reply:
'O noble folk, by this strange case disturbed,
in a far different way from what you deem
this cavern must be filled. Vain is the hope
to move the gods with piles of worthless stone
or useless clods. Were the Tarpeian rock
with six attendant hills all cast within
the void and o'er them massive Apennine
with Aetna added, it would not suffice   710
to fill this pit, for what it truly seeks
is to devour what you hold most dear,
whereof but little part will seal it up.'

At these words faces paled and hearts stood still.
And many brought their jewels and their gold,
things deemed most precious by gross intellects
unskilled to recognize the truly good,
for man is ever moved by his blind greed,
in his dark fleshly prison seeing naught.
Then one addressed the crowd, a valiant youth,   720
raising his voice: 'Ye dullards, whence comes this
stupidity? Besought for what is dear,
you bring but worthless things; for what is great,
mere trifles. Here there is no need of gold
which earth disgorges from her foul entrails,
nor yet of pebbles culled from sandy plains.
I tell you that the gods have given us
naught better than our might and arms, and these
true Roman virtues are Rome's best of things.
And since the best is asked, lo, here I bring   730
arms and the man.' And speaking so, he lifted
his eyes aloft and eyed Jove's fane that crowned
the citadel, in supplication raising
his arms to all the gods that dwell on high
and to those spirits whom he strained to meet,
then spurred his stalwart courser on and plunged
into the pit. And bright his armor shone
with resonance like thunder as he rode.
A crash was heard and the opposing sides
of the abyss were joined even as the tip   740
of the bold horseman's spear was lost to sight.
Just so a mighty flash of lightning splits
the welkin and reveals the sacred realms
of the eternal world—and then, scarce glimpsed,
the bright flame, driven by the wind, departs
and the sky's calm serenity returns.
How great this hero whom you here behold
yielding his life up to his fatherland
and offering his living corpse to earth!
He rides in armor toward the Stygian shore!   750
Most notable this Curtius and his act
in all the lengthy chronicles of Rome.

"Shall I recall the Decii? The first   753
of that line, when he saw our men in flight
before the Latins, stood his ground and gave
a mighty groan, then called upon the gods
and as a self-devoted sacrifice,
head filleted in the Gabinian mode,   758
rushed 'midst the foemen. They from every side
thrust weapons to undo him. But his death   760
gave us the victory, as his brave charge
brought with it sudden fear and anxious doubt
into the hearts of all the Latin foe.
For he, high seated on a dusky steed,
in manner more than human, with a mien
to strike stark terror, had been seen to ride.
As if by right of birth, sometime thereafter
his son revived his glory in a fray
with the embattled Gauls. His father's name
and righteous actions were renewed in him;   770
for, with raised voice invoking his great sire,
through sword and javelin and Gallic arms,
through file on file all eager for the thrust,
he rushed to certain death and with him bore
into the victor's camp the seed of fear
and panic flight and death. The third in line
of this great tribe, like sire and grandsire called
though fame allowed less lustre to his name,
with dedication similar to theirs
and a like forcing of the Stygian shades,   780
broke the Lucanian strength. So on three fields
three Romans gladly died and each in turn
found his reward in death. O glorious clan,
well meriting the praises the long years
have justly sung! nor may oblivion
with step insidious prevail to dim
the splendor of your memory 'mongst our folk
which to this day holds you in reverence.

"The rest I leave. It is a tale far told
and known to you. You have remarked—for scarce   790

so many years have passed—with what a price
of anguish patient Regulus preserved   792
his oath and loyalty, with what great love
of fatherland this hero was imbued.
Nay, noble sire, your fame will never fade
though you may die; it lives and grows forever.
Why linger more on mighty men or clans?
Have we not often seen the legions charge
to meet sure death and heard their leader cry:
'Onward forever; there is no retreat,'   800
and as he urged them neither step nor glance
is backward turned, as all with measured pace
march on to meet their doom. As you must know,
it is the way of Romans to despise   804
the tricks of chance and calmly to accept
death when it comes and to despise such things
as other breeds admire and esteem,
to welcome what men fear and to ignore
affliction, tread down pain and choose to die
rather than drag out an ignoble life."   810

    With this he ceased. The king said: "You break off
a tale half told, omitting much. Say why
you tell us nothing of your last of kings?"
His guest replied: "'Tis right a king, I own,
should ask the fate of kings. For brevity
alone I spoke not of them. My omission
perchance has troubled you. Now, lest you think
if we have dared to speak ill of our kings
it was because, aroused by simple lust
for plunder we have sought with a fair name   820
to cloak the work of villains, hear me now
and learn the true cause of our change of state.

The   The light of liberty, unrealized
tale of but long held dear, shone in our hearts the while
Lucretia a haughty sceptre held us all in thrall.
Though from the palace harsh dictation came,
and overweening tyranny with threats
to hapless subjects had aroused our ire,

yet torpor held each citizen inert,
unmindful of his rights. I blush to tell   830
how much we granted to that wicked house,
how many wars on foreign fields to serve
an impious ruler we endured, and how   *833*
we bowed our necks in shameful servitude.
He thought it no disgrace to style himself
"the Proud"—a title earned by heinous crimes—
nor yet to flaunt that name in wrongful acts
intolerable to his country and the world.
Ah, monstrous and disgraceful spectacle,
where thousands to whom Virtue had disclosed   840
a path of honor—a folk foreordained,
so Destiny already had decreed,
to subjugate so many kings and realms—
stood terrorized by one unworthy man,
obeying as they might a sacred law
the merest hint of his depraved desires.
Not otherwise the honey-making bees
revere their king and offer bold defense
against subversive drones and swarming gnats—
nay, often to the owner of the hive,   850
quaking with fear, they will deny approach
and scatter dogs and flocks and grazing herds,
and all for reverence of an impotent
and petty king, whom every citizen
and soldier counts a creature marvelous—
and ever through the regal halls they swarm
and bear him to his nuptials on their backs.
So with like awe did we revere our king
until his pride with self-indulgence swelled
and evil lust was joined to arrogance.   860
Then men could stand no more; the knife alone
could cure the monstrous cancer; healing hands
were needed for the city's grievous ill.
One shamefully immodest act at last
drove past all toleration those who still
remained submissive to his stringent rule.
The royal youth, with foul desire inflamed   867

and vilely pandering to his naked lust,
in dark of night forced wide the chamber door
of a chaste matron. She, suspecting naught,   *870*
received him courteously; and there by force
he overcame her. Silently he left
the scene of his excess, content to win
the spoils of victory, a woman's shame,
and all the dark night's pleasure, well aware
of his deceit and pleased. But she in grief,
disdainful of her body and her life,
berated her own flesh: 'Woman,' she cried,
'will you live on, vile vessel of foul lust,
bearing the dark stain of adultery   880
for all your days within you? Can you dare
to look again upon the bed whereon
you were despoiled of all that you hold dear,
husband and honor, virtue and fair name?
Nay, rather die, unhappy soul, and quench
a light bedimmed and break these hostile bonds.'
So did she chide herself, then straightway bade
her husband and her sire be summoned home,
having but one desire in her heart:
that in their presence she might put aside   890
the burden of the flesh she now despised.

    "Her father was in Rome, her spouse at camp
some distance from the town; a messenger
found first the father, then, as chance fell out,
came on the spouse as he was hastening home;
and as his mistress bade him so he spoke:
a dreadful thing had happened in their house—
he knew not what it was—and both at once,
the husband and the father, should make haste
and homeward turn forthwith. The former, stunned   900
by such a message, in his troubled breast
pondered uneasily and asked himself
what stroke of Fortune had befallen him
and what his destiny might now require.
Meeting his wife's sire at the gates, he found

him likewise shaken; so with shared concern
they reached their doorsill. Their arrival moved
the wife to sudden tears. The puzzled husband
inquired the reason; was she not unharmed?
'By no means,' she replied, 'for all that's dear   910
at one blow we have lost; naught fair remains.
For all fair things must be accounted dead
when chastity is ravished. Dearest lord,
the loathsome traces of another man
defile your bed. My body is besmirched,
my spirit clean. Death be my witness here.
Put forth your hand and swear that evil one
shall not bear with him to the Stygian shore
this crime, nor an adulterer unscathed
survive to mock my tomb.' And mingling then   920
such prayers and lamentations with her story,
she told them of the ill that night had wrought.
Her husband strove to soothe her and affirmed
that where the mind was pure no blame could be.
But she replied: 'If I absolve myself
of crime, I'd not evade the punishment,
and no adulterous wife shall live in Rome
by my example cloaked.' And as she spoke
she drew the sword concealed beneath her robe
and plunged it deep into her snowy breast,   930
sinking upon the blade as if to raise
by such a wound her prostrate modesty.

     "And as the mother bird, in the old tale,
raised high aloft the nestlings she found dead,
stung by a loathsome snake, and then remained
to spend her life in mourning, even so,
seeing the gaping wound, they all made moan
and their loud lamentations shook the house.
Brutus alone refrained from tears nor spoke
an idle word of bootless grief; for he   940
was a strong man, within whose noble heart
a lofty spirit dwelt. He grasped the brand
and drew the steel all bloody from the wound,

still fresh and foaming. 'All ye gods,' he cried,
'and mighty wielder of the thunderbolt,
and blood once chaste and pure, I swear to you
I shall pursue with fire and sword the race,
the odious house and all its progeny,
the king's own head and his proud diadem
today, tomorrow, and while I yet live,   950
with hate undying. Nay, he shall not hold
this realm while my right hand may wield a sword.'
A like oath too he made the others swear,
while they could only wonder from what source
had come such boldness into Brutus' heart.
The folk he summoned next, and as they watched
he dragged out to the light the piteous corpse;
to some he showed the brand from which still dripped
the tepid blood, to others pointed out
the breast transfixed and the deep gaping wound.   960
To one he mentioned a dear daughter's name,
spoke of another's sister, to a third
mentioned a wife whose tenderness was known
to bring a special sweetness to their hearth,
thus indicating whither led the path
of kingly rule, where lust and pride were joined.
His anger lent him fire and eloquence
befitting the occasion. And the blood
still flowing from the purple wound, the pale
and frigid corpse, the dreadful sight of spouse   970
and father sore distressed, the fearsome oath
of Brutus stirred them all. Where'er he turned
his steps were followed by a mighty crowd
of men all girding on their swords, and flocks
of women weeping for the sad mischance
of fair Lucretia, held in high esteem.
But why prolong the tale? The weightiest part
I've told you. It was under this great chief
the kings were banished; aged Tarquin died
in exile far from Rome; his cruel wife   980
and all his sons suffered due punishment
and died unhappy deaths. To ashes fell

the mighty royal household of the Proud.
"Such was the end of kings. Then better times   *984*
ensued; our age of liberty began.
An oath, repeated annually, has banned
despotic rule; a just authority
shatters the rigid sceptre. Two rule now
in place of one. More modest magistrates
with double emblems of their vested power   *990*
you now behold. And that high office first   *991*
was held by him who was the primal author
of our new liberty. With wonted zeal
he propped it, for in tranquil freedom's cause
he sentenced his own sons to painful death,   *995*
scourged by the lash and mangled by the axe,
for seeking to restore the rule of kings,
both upright citizen and hapless sire,
both consul stern and Freedom's loyal son;
for after, when the warfare was renewed,   *1000*
in battle he encountered and dispatched
to Orcus, by a mortal thrust transfixed,
the son of Tarquin, fighting to regain,
as 'twere by right, his father's lost estate—
a boastful youngster, voicing haughty threats—
but Brutus, charging, fired by hate and rage,
marked not the other's blade. So in fierce fight
they fell together, but the mightier Brutus,
already dying, covered the supine
frame of his foeman—victor at the last.   *1010*
For, reckoning naught the peril to himself,
he slew that wicked prince, and as he dealt
the mortal stroke, he cried: 'Perfidious one,
I, your avenger, follow after you
with biting sword to the Tartarean shades.'
So nobly perished Brutus. Romans all,
of every age and sex, lamented him,
and sounds of mourning never heard before
echoed throughout the land. Above all grieved
the mindful matrons, counting him their lord   *1020*
and chastity's avenger. So they mourned
and for a year they sang his funeral dirge;
nor shall the fame of Brutus ever die."

Book 4

When Laelius had done, the king began
serenely: "Of great things, in truth, you speak.
What gulf lies 'twixt the great and the sublime
I now perceive, and how Rome's destiny
differs from other races. I can see
likewise what your chaste matron sought of death:
that our fair Dido might not claim alone
such honor; and the youth by heartless earth
engulfed, the valiant line from sire through son
to grandson, you praise here lest lasting fame   10
to our entombed twin champions be reserved.   11
The greatest wonder that your words arouse
is how such lofty valor could descend
and penetrate the folk. The final hour
more than all else dismays the heart of man,
breeding a fear that fortitude alone
can mitigate. Few men of any breed
possess such virtue, yet it would appear
all Romans are endowed with this rare strength.
Such resolution dwells among your host,   20
ever prepared to die with face to foe,
that precious freedom never shall be lost.

Syphax
inquires
about
Scipio
                "But what above all else I yearn to know—
the life and exploits of your present chief—
you say naught of. I pray you, this disclose:
his mien, his manner, and what heart abides
within his breast, the majesty bestowed
on one so young—such matters we would hear,
for hither wandering rumor brings his name
and nothing further. Chiefly we would learn   30
of his late actions in Iberia,
if I may ask of things well known to you
since you have been a witness to them all

69

and you alone have shared his secret thoughts,
for ardent friendship hides naught from a friend.
Nay, speeding night, I pray you, linger yet
a little time while Laelius relates
the glorious tale, and may Aurora lie
content beside her aged spouse (and he,
with rare unwonted ardor, clasp her close   40
in fettering embrace) and so forbear
to lead forth on their course her snow-white team
and grant us leisure for our colloquy."

Scipio's   Perceiving that the ears and minds of all
gifts and   in deepest silence waited on his words,
virtues   Laelius began: "Ah, what a mighty task
is set my tongue if such a high behest
I would obey. For not to me is given
the smoothly flowing stream of eloquence
of the Cecropian tongue, nor yet its grace   50
abundant. As once peerless Homer spent
long vigils following a youth of wrath,   52
so with like zeal now rustic Ennius   53
devotes his hours to one of excellence.   54
The latter were more worthy of the Greek,
the former rather of the Latin bard.
Achilles' fame required a herald's voice;
the man I speak of has no need of such.
His fame, with no embellishment of art,
grows daily greater and his praises swell.   60
Nor does my love for him deceive me: I
foresee a time to come when simple glory
shall raise this hero to the skies. Ere now,
were it not for the malice envy spawns—   64
nay, rather turn we to our pleasant task.
Never, 'tis said, to any man before
has nature shown such bounty. From him flows
a rare ethereal aura, and his brow,
whence two yoked flashes hurl a single bolt
that no man may sustain, makes manifest   70
in tranquil majesty the worthy chief.

Over his shoulders his luxuriant locks
expose their gold to sun and wind—disheveled: *73*
for burden of the helm and sweat of toil
assiduous and constant, and a mind
content with simple things, make him eschew
refinements unbecoming to a man.
Tall above other men he stands, and when
the armies join in battle, from afar
his towering frame brings terror to the foe   80
and courage to his legions. Thus his mien
bears with it truly hope and fear alike.
His chest is broad and deep, a dwelling apt
to house a lofty soul; all else concurs.
His arms and shoulders show a lord of war.
Among a thousand thousand him you'd mark
and know him for a chief. His presence moves
many to quake before him as in awe,
or holds them, in a rare enchantment rapt,
in silence, long forgetful of themselves.   90
It can likewise arrest the flow of speech
and scatter words or turn aside their course
into another channel. More than man
he is, more wondrous; splendid Jove himself
or quiver-bearing Phoebus in the heavens
could scarce compare with him.

                       "No more of such
details; a righteous mind correctly scorns
the petty fleshly attributes of form.
His tranquil mien you may yourself behold
perhaps, and, seeing it, you'll say that I   100
have told you less than truth; to him alone
is granted this rare glory: that for him
presence takes naught from prestige, as 'tis wont,   *103*
but rather adds to it. As to his age,
I must confess he has not yet attained
three decades' span—and with each passing day   *106*
his virtue waxes. Men of riper years
could find example in his gravity,

while tender youth might seek to imitate
his pleasing grace. Naught to a foe more harsh   110
than is his way, nor sweeter to a friend.
You'd see him as he hurled the javelin,
or, arms put down, with open countenance,
and could not say which style became him more.
Elated by no favoring boon of Fate
nor yet cast down by Fortune's hostile dart,
unchanged he stands, whatever be his lot,
with spirit of serene tranquillity
in happy times or seasons of mischance.
Riches he scorns and all the empty praise   120
the fickle mob bestows; he venerates
true glory and he seeks for loyal friends:
these are his treasures; these he ever holds
by the same faith that wins them. Now through Spain   *124*
run wide reports of this youth newly come
like an immortal from above, 'gainst whom
no strength of any mortal may avail
and who with friendly grace can win to him
the foeman he has bested in the fray.
And as the radiance of the skies outshines   130
earth's darkness, even so the flowering soil
of Italy outstrips all other lands,
and as one sector of the heavens glows
more brightly than the rest, so mighty Rome
surpasses Italy itself, and as
the sun dims with its rays the lesser stars,
so Scipio excels.

                   "Nay, let the truth

Scipio's be granted: you would swear this youth was not
birth   made in our fashion. Nor is rumor here
entirely false, thus raising a mere man   140
to heights divine. For truly, many hold
this man comes down to us from lofty realms.
All that is told I need not here repeat:
it were too burdensome; let it suffice
to cite the rumor widely spread abroad.   *145*

'Tis said a glittering serpent oft was seen
upon his mother's bed, that terrified
all who beheld it. Hence came the belief,
now held in many corners of the land,
in origin celestial. And for sure   150
the child thereafter born, as he grew up,
in semblance seemed no mortal man. Moreover,
His piety his piety, his great-souled rectitude
strengthened such credence; for it is his wont,
at earliest sunrise, all alone, to seek   *155*
the shrine of Jove, whose holiest citadel
crowns the Tarpeian hill where the god's priests
in reverence perform their sacred rites
and offer praises. There, with portals closed
and locked behind him, drawing near the altar,   160
long he will stand as in communion rapt;
thence swiftly come away, and you might mark
his mien display his loftiness of soul,
his glance infused with a celestial power.
So, when the times urged action, he would come   *165*
with confidence aglow and bringing faith
of happy issue from great wars, as though
he had the promise of the god himself.

His   "'Tis thus on many fields his presence brings
leader- zeal for the fray, inspiring every heart   170
ship and making possible what had not seemed
to be so ere he came. For confidence
breeds strength; without it mortal flesh and bone
are helpless. Oft I've seen the battle line
turning to flight with vulnerable backs
exposed, and standards waver in the hands
of trembling bearers—then the general
would seize the staff and plunge into the fray
crying the while: 'See how the god leads on!
Shall we go where he leads or flee? Myself,   180
I follow. I am promised victory;
should Fate deny it, then alone I fall.
Flee then and live ignobly after me,

degenerates—not so will heroes die.'
Then I have seen the serried ranks surge back
and turn their breasts toward death and, often spurred
onward in this way, win the victory.
So great the love they bear their chief, so strong
their sense of honor, calling them to arms!
For when the troops observe his constancy,   190
his faith in powers above, and how great Jove
protects him, then they rally to the charge,
believing they obey a god's command.
Wherefore, since arduous and weighty things
have been accomplished under his command,
he'll be remembered as a mighty chief
who in long warfare never lost a field.

His   "Now you would know what further are his plans
plans   and what success he dares anticipate
for the   as issue of his present toils. Already   200
war   within his mind he shakes the lofty walls
of Carthage to their ruin, now he sees
the storming of the citadel and Byrsa
collapsing in the waves. And even as
a lion, moved by avid hunger, spies
a well-fleshed heifer as she crops the grass,
and, furious and harassed by darts, marks well
his distant enemy and holds in check
his rage as he draws near, and all the while
in mind foreseeing, not yet with his claws,   210
he tears and rends his prey and ravishes
the hidden entrails with vain savagery,
mauling the hated corpse, just so in truth
our lion rages, and no force he fears
so greatly as he fears the foe may flee;
with eye alert to close off any path
of flight, he stalks his prey. And he believes
that what he purposes can be achieved
and what he wills is possible, for he
has never failed to win what he desired.   220
But his desire is only for the best;

his goal but to accomplish worthy deeds.
Need I speak of his piety, far famed
alike for sire and country well displayed
in many moments of dire peril? Here
let two examples serve. The enemy
had wasted savagely the fields of Gaul,
dismaying the Cisalpine husbandmen,
and from the Po the fiery smoke was borne
to the Capitoline. The valiant sire   230
of our great general was then dispatched
northward—in sorry auspices, for when
the armies met upon the open plain,
to the Phoenician fell the victory.

How   The Roman leader would have fallen there
Scipio   had not his son, a lad whose tender years   236
saved   numbered a scant eighteen, with fierce assault
his   snatched from the hand of death his stricken sire
father   who lay upon the ground with wounded flank.
A boy's work, thus to cleave with thirsty brand   240
a way through ranks of foemen to his father?

His   "Again, when Fate extreme stood poised to strike,   242
firmness   when Hannibal with threat of fire and sword
after   was subjugating once great Italy,
Cannae   when Cannae's ravaged town, notorious
for blood we shed there, had rent Latin flesh
with savage wounds, then terror cast all hope
from out our hearts. It was as when a bark
founders beneath the waves, a helpless prey
to blasts of heaven and the pounding sea,   250
and sailors quake and every face grows pale,
and each man thinks how best to save himself:
one plans to leap into the sea and swim
to shore, another hopes to find perchance
a friendly footing on some reef outthrust
from a sheer rocky cliff that looms near by,
another plans to grasp a mast or spar
reft by the gale and somehow keep afloat,
yielding his arms to the devouring sea—

even such was then our city's plight and such   260
our remedies. The tottering pinnacle
of empire threatened to collapse; the fall
of such a massive peak must surely bring
a train of dire calamities. Nay, why
should I prolong the tale, though all be true?
In this dire strait the young men came together,
Metellus at their head, and all agreed   267
that it was best to flee, abandoning
a country marked for such catastrophe,
and leave Hesperia to the conquering might   270
of Africa. This rumor, spread abroad,
cast down all spirits, filling every heart
with chill forebodings. But the Tribune, then
by chance a youth with down still on his cheeks,
alone remained unmoved—'twas Scipio.
When every man proposed his vain advice
in this emergency, thus wasting hours
in rambling words, our Scipio spoke out:
'Why stand we idly here? We have not time
immeasurable for counsel. We must act.   280
Shall we not draw our swords? Come, follow me,
ye nobles in whose hands the final fate
of state and city lies. I'll show the way.
The cause we all defend is not yet lost.'
So with his speech he roused new courage, born
of shame. And all of us rose up as one
to follow where our general led. With stride
no firmer did Amphitryon's son advance   288
when long ago he moved with dart and sword
to face the rebel Centaurs in grim war.   290
And when at length we reached the house where lay
the diffident Metellus, he went in
before the rest. The panic-stricken crowd
was still assembled, planning shameful things
in voices hushed, so hardly could be heard
the murmurings of men whose trembling tongues
could scarcely shape their words. Such hue was theirs
and such despairing aspect as appear

on brows of conquered men condemned to die
by savage ordinance a painful death;   300
they quake with fear and as the end draws nigh
are all undone, yet gazing all about
they seek for means of flight when only one
sure issue of their suffering is clear.
He broke in with drawn sword and fearsome mien—
'I swear,' he cried, 'by the high power supreme
of Heaven's Thunderer, that never I,
while I am still possessed of life and limb,
shall turn away from sore-tried Italy
nor Rome. Nor shall I tolerate the flight   310
of others. Now do you, Metellus, swear
as I have. If you will not, by this sword
you die. And all like-minded here must know
the last day of their lives is now at hand.'
He raised his blade and all were seized with fear.
Metellus too, the author of the plot,
grew rigid. The audacious act had dazed
their startled hearts; it was as if Jove's wrath
had hurled his three-pronged missile on the roof
of an imperiled home. Or say they shook   320
before his irate glance as if they'd seen   321
the standards of all-conquering Hannibal
loom over them, portending cruel death
or captive's fetters. So as they were bid
they swore the oath, each man, and first of all
their leader. Thus did he with valor rare
foreclose a shameless flight. And but six years
had passed since he had saved his father's life   328
on that first field.

           "Then, when the two great lights   329
of cherished Rome were quenched, for ruinous Fate   330
almost at one same time erased the name
of the great Scipios, and all the realm
of Spain, astray on dubious paths, had changed
its ancient fealty and none came forth
out of so many thousand knights, not one

His
Spanish
campaign

dared lend a hand to rectify the wrong
of that vast slaughter till the son arose,
avenger of his uncle and his sire.   *338*
With ardor greater than his army's strength
he crossed the Pyrenees and once more brought   340
under the rule of Rome the Twilight Land
in all its scope from where it swells most wide
to thrust between and part two distant oceans
to where, upon its longest-ranging flank,
it looks upon your sea and the great peaks
called after Hercules and, turning thence,
uprises towards the massive mountain chain
that takes its name from its perpetual fires,   *348*
wherefrom the plains of Gaul may be surveyed.   350
All men, all goods within those wide frontiers
won from the foe, are ours by Fortune's will.

The
siege of
Cartagena

   "From many glorious deeds I'll choose a few.
There is a town upon the Spanish coast   *353*
founded by Hasdrubal; it bears a name
derived from mighty Carthage. Massive walls
on one side gird it, while the raging tides
of ocean shield the other. Hither came
the power of Phoenicia in its pomp,
with standards, arms and men and generals.
They reckoned that if battle should be joined   360
either by sea or on the spreading plain
this spot would be most apt and rightly placed,
with passage opened to the motherland.
Thither the neighboring peoples made their way
in search of safety, just as when a fire
puts forth its flickering flames and whirling smoke
blackens the air, the folk will flee, dispersed
by the approaching plague, and leave their homes,
bearing with them such treasures as they have,
and from all sides converge upon and fill   370
a sheltering refuge. Hither, following
the spoor of rumor, Scipio made his way.
Heedless of other fields he sought this spot

with all his forces and encircled it
within a Roman camp. He dug a moat,
not deep but guarded by a palisade.
I tell you things both marvelous and true:
those thick and turret-studded walls, so well
constructed and so stoutly garrisoned,
and soldiers well directed to their goal,   380
and ranks of guards, devices of defense
past counting and great catapults that strike
from far an unprotected camp—not all
of these availed a whit against our chief,
who scaled the walls and pierced through armored ranks
and fought his way into the city's heart.
All history reports no shorter siege;
one day saw its beginning and its end.
No quicker do the peaceful doves forsake
their nests as Jove's arms-bearing bird swoops down,   390
and no more swiftly flees the frightened hare
that hears the lion treading near his warren
than the defenders fled—a few in fear
conceal themselves in the walled citadel;
the rest disperse and scatter through the town.
The air resounds with shouts and clamorous noise
of clashing steel and groans of dying men—
even as when upon our northern shore
a tempest rushes, stirred up by the gales
of Ethiopia, fearsome from afar,   400
and swollen storm-clouds break and torrents flow
and bear great stones away, now rivers rise
and even the brooklet that a while ago
so gently flowed now roars and rushes on,
rivalling the churning rapids in its rage,
and in a panic all the husbandmen
take to their heels, while terror from the skies
pursues them; in the furious waters' swirl
the cattle perish and where'er you turn
your frightened gaze you see through fissured clouds   410
sharp-pointed fiery forks that blind the eye.
Death stands before you whether you stand firm

or turn to right or left; here misery
and horror join and through the misty gloom
comes sound of lamentation far remote.

"Our new chief's action at this time displayed
his character, in hour of battle great,
great when it's ended. For with no more force
than his against the adverse ranks of arms
did Mars urge on his dreadful car of war   420
against the Thracians, nor more fiercely thrust
when madly he plunged into Hebrus' stream   422
his foaming steeds. But when the citadel
was forced and, downing arms, the enemy
knelt to beg mercy, fury fled away;
the wrath of battle vanished from his heart
as swiftly as the sword fell from his hand.
Thus Jupiter will thrust his visage clear
and peaceful through a heavy cloud, and all
the winds are stilled, the storm abates, the sun   430
shines forth, or stars, if it be night, emerge
and earth resumes its mien. And so in peace
the conqueror approached the citadel,
gave orders that its towers should bear the seals
of Roman victory, and bade the fee
of sacrifice be paid and to the gods
due thanks be rendered. Mantled in his robe
of office, the attendant priest stood by
and pierced the rough breast of the stalwart beast
offered for sacrifice, and to the rite   440
he summoned the Almighty Jupiter,
the Phrygian Penates and the souls
of Romulus and all the guardians
divine of Latium through whose viligance
Rome keeps her sacred trust to rule the world.

*The
soldiers
rewarded*
"This done, the due rewards and honors earned
he gives his soldiers, being well aware
that valor thrives on praise. An ancient use
Rome's chiefs have practiced since the earliest days:

Whene'er a city, strong, and by steep walls   450
protected, fell by storm, on him who first,
whether by chance or valor favored, scaled
the rampart, was bestowed the Mural Crown,
the name deriving from the deed. Such prizes
are held most dear since only honor moves
the minds of men and makes them heed not risk.
Discerning this, our chief exalted courage
and with such spurs aroused it. But the crowd
cried out, asserting that at one same time
two men had reached the summit, whereupon   *460*
a factional uproar swept through the camp
and some cried up one favorite, some the other.
Likewise, when dogs in rivalry have forced
out of his den in the thick underbrush
a snarling, thrusting boar and laid him low,
and with their murderous fangs have torn away
his limbs so that his massive bulk upon
the earth lies mangled, then there will arise
among the young spectators of the sport
hot-tempered wrangling, as they dispute   470
which dog first dared to fix his teeth into
the hirsute haunch, which was the first to spring
upon the shaggy back, which first drew blood;
and as the hunters angrily debate
the merits of their hounds, the latter raise
their loud exultant baying to the skies.

Scipio's
wise
judgment

"When Scipio saw his turbulent soldiery
brandishing arms, and marked the sprouting seeds
of new dissensions, he at once commanded
both factions to attend him in his tent   480
and calmed with eloquence their mounting wrath.
'When it falls out,' he said, 'that two men's fame
so brightly glitters as to far surpass
all others' merit and may only cloud
itself alone, then is the glory due
to neither or to both. Since he is first
whom no one has preceded, we adjudge

the latter verdict best.' With these calm words
spoken he circled with a verdant crown
the brows of both the rivals. Whereupon   490
all wrath and turbulence were stilled; so ended
the unbecoming brawl. Yea, even as
when sturdy bulls are stirred to violence
by jealous rivalry for some fair mate,
and horns at bodies slash and bellows fill
the air and all the ample herd takes sides,
choosing a champion, then the vigilant
cowherd, if he but hears them, hurries up
well knowing what has caused their restlessness
and quiets their unease with soothing words,   500
then crowns both combatants with grassy wreaths
of victory and leads them both away,
each to his pasture, pacified and mild.
Meanwhile a sound of sobs and lamentation
betrayed within the city's walls a throng
of frightened, tearful women. Hearing which,
that righteous and compassionate youth assumed
the role of Virtue's guardian and straightway
gave his commands: all who because of sex
or age might fear assault, and likewise all   510
in need of aid were in the citadel
securely sheltered and a guard was set
of sober men; the women were denied
access to gates and windows, since bold eyes
mock shame and the fair bloom of a chaste face
is plucked by brazen glances. Fearing this,
our captain set these prisoners apart.
Now mark, Olympians, what majesty
dwells in a mortal's breast! In youthful prime
behold maturity! For it is hard,   520
in truth, at one time to resist the spur
of youth and lure of beauty's fragrant flower."   522

Book 5

Massinissa enters the Numidian capital
The great-souled conqueror through the shattered walls *1*
of Cirta passed, surveying joyfully *2*
the effigies of his ancestral gods
and the old dwellings, cradle of his clan;
then, posting sentinels around the gates,
he made his way towards the high citadel
with eager step, even as the prowling wolf
by hunger driven that spies a well-stocked fold
of fattened sheep will straightway enter in,
leaving behind the sharer in his toil 10
and booty to stand watch so, undisturbed,
he may from out the now well-guarded store
safely bring forth the stolen carcasses
to be devoured. In like way he approached
the splendid palace of the luckless tyrant,
where after his downfall his queen abode *16*
Sophonisba meets him
uneasy in her heart. And she, still numbed
by Fate's swift stroke, at once came to the portal
to meet the victor, hoping some fair chance
might yet alleviate her wretched state. 20

All the great palace shone with gold and gems
of star-like lustre; than its lord no king
had e'er been richer while yet Fortune smiled
upon him; now—ah, false felicity! —
none was there poorer. Yet his queenly wife
outshone the splendor of the royal hall,
Sopho-nisba's beauty
more dazzling she than light itself. That face
unrivalled by the very stars of heaven
need fear not—if the arbiter were just—
comparison with Phoebus. And that brow, 30
as white as snow, might stir almighty Jove
to wonder and his jealous sister find it
more dangerous than any concubine

her errant spouse might cherish for her charm.
With brighter gleam than gold of any land,   *35*
putting the sun's own rays to shame, her locks,
encircled by a fillet of light gold
and softly stirring in the gentle breeze,
formed first a frame for her slim, graceful neck—
a peerless, milk-white column, sweetly rising—   *40*
then spreading wide, in pleasing fashion twined,
encased her slender shoulders as they fell.
So purity of white and glamorous
allure of gold were joined; the flaxen strands
commingled with the white of milk and cream
and virgin snow shone 'neath a golden sun.
How shall I tell you of her eyes? So clear
their radiance gleamed beneath her beauteous brows
that gods might covet them; her glance divine
cast all around her a compelling charm,   *50*
and where she wished to turn it she could rouse
desire or bend a will however firm
or to Medusan marble change the heart
of an admirer—nay, it is to wonder
that Africa has no second monstrous breed.   *55*
Those eyes, now filled with freshly flowing tears,
shone with yet greater sweetness than their wont,
like to twin stars in rival splendor gleaming
in evening skies, dew-drenched, when showers have fled
and all the welkin is serene again;   *60*
above their glow two winsome arches curved.
The pure hue of the lily in her cheeks
blended with red of roses, and beyond
her lips of ruby dazzling ivory gleamed.
Her bosom's curve, exposed and softly swelling
in tender palpitation, brought forth sighs
which, with enticing blandishments conjoined,
had often driven her unsettled spouse
beyond where she could bid him to return.
See too those arms that Jove would choose to wear   *70*
clasped as a wreath forever round his neck;
those hands so long and slender and the fingers

tapering and tipped by shapely, lucent nails.
Mark her soft yielding flank and other parts
all charged with grace down to the dainty feet
on which she moves not as mere mortals do;
but so discreetly do they touch the ground
they seem to tread on air and leave no trace.
Such semblance did the timid Venus bear
when, cloud-veiled, on Olympus she addressed   *80*
the high-souled Thunderer, beseeching him
to aid her shipwrecked son, or when she prayed   *82*
for her dear grandson, lying nigh to death,
while Ilion stood to founder on the wave,
or when the earth shook, threatening sacred Rome.

   In beauty that no goddess might surpass
the woman meets the youth, as well prepared
in art as charm; a purple bodice graced
with divers jewels swathes her heaving breast,
and grief itself is her adornment. Aye,   *90*
distress enhanced her beauty, lending her
a charm more irresistible than that
of happier moments. Massinissa felt
a flame consume his marrows, even as ice
melts in the heat of summer or as wax
dissolves in the proximity of fire,
so as he looked he melted, captive prey
of captive foe, a haughty conqueror
subdued by conquered victim. What can stand
against Love's might, what thunderbolt could match   100
the force hurled at him? Drawing nearer now
with timid step, she knelt before the one
whose arms and visage and the deference
of all his followers proclaimed as chief,
embraced his knees and made to seize his hand
while in submissive accents thus she spoke:

*She ad-
dresses
Massinissa*   "If I, a captive and a widow, may
touch your victorious hand, let me implore
by all the gods your pity and your grace.

Little it is I ask. Enjoy your rights,   110
do with your captive as you will, mete out
a bitter death or dark imprisonment.
It is but just and, truly, as for me,
since envious Fortune has so changed my state
life differs not from death. Wherefore command
as you desire; I only beg you, choose
a worthy death for me and, above all,
I ask I be not sadly borne away
to live in slavery. My lord, perhaps
sisters you have, whom sight of my distress   120
may conjure to your eyes; as is their lot
so once was mine. But often times of grief
follow on happier days. Yet I would not
foresee you any ill. I pray you rather
use well this happy land until your end
and leave it to your heirs; and may no man
foment intrigue among their progeny.
May they be spared the evils I have known:
a kingdom's tragic fall and the cruel turn
of Fortune, made more bitter to endure   130
as following happy times. Her power spent
by injuries dealt to me, she may now rest
in peace, more docile towards another's rule.
Towards me, as you well know, the Romans bear
deep hatred; me alone they deem the cause
of armed invasion, the sole source of war.
Nor is the accusation false. I pray
you, put me safely past the reach of those
who now would mock me, and beyond the grasp
of those who look for arrogant revenge.   140
And by the manner of my death, great king,
whom Fate has favored and who yet aspire
to greater things, you shall be known and judged."
Her tears bedewed the earth while her lips pressed
repeated kisses on his gold-shod feet.

Massinissa   Oblivious of arms, the youth, from whom
is moved   all martial zeal had fled, with heart o'erwhelmed

by her   by new and unexpected images
words   of sweetness, and within him all ablaze
with flame unwonted, sighed and made reply: 150
"O queen, I do implore you, grieve no more,
and from your thoughts dismiss your trembling fears.
you ask but little; you shall have much more:
your birth, your beauty, and your regal mind
proclaim you worthy of far greater things
if such be your desire. You shall remain
a queen and be the sharer of my couch,
and through the centuries your fame will live.
Say me not nay, I beg you, nor permit
past ardors to infringe upon our love."   160
Then, while as yet, incontinent, she clung
clutching her liberator's feet in all
humility, with suppliant lips, the king,
in tears himself, bent down and raised her up.
How could a fragile arrow have such strength
as to subdue a conquering prince, long tried
in fiercest wars; how came it that his heart,
pierced by so slight a wound, could yield and bend
to serve a woman?

                She, now more at ease,
They   made answer: "Glorious King, the comfort once,   *170*
reach   when it was worthy, of my fatherland
accord   and now its greatest terror, if it be
that after such dark days my fortunes rise
again and hope survive so many blows,
what greater joy could life, though many years
it span, reserve for me than to be bidden
to turn to such a spouse and so arise
auspiciously from ruin? Yet since Fate
moves on and nearer draws the end appointed
to my life's course, my dearest, strive no more   180
to raise my broken spirits. On such seas
fares not a shaken bark. I know full well
the faith that Fortune keeps. It will suffice
that you bestow on one who seeks but death

this greatest gift: that she, with freedom lost,
may by the straightest path convey her soul
to shelter 'mongst the shades. All I would ask
is to escape the yoke of Rome. No more.
And for your many merits may the King
of Kings Supreme bestow his best rewards   190
on you, who with such rare benevolence,
strive to exceed the compass of my pleas."
She spoke and once more hid her countenance
and so once more moved him to tears. "Nay, spare,"
he said, "your mourning and my eyes, which, ere
the need be, you would charge with idle tears.
The mind, exhausted, has no strength for hope
and looks to earth and can see naught above.
Think now on better things. Ill Fortune may
turn to afflict another and, appeased,
leave scope for great events. Should this not be   200
(the heart rejects the omen), then at last
as I have vowed you shall be granted death.
I swear it by the lofty stars and on
the faith of kings, the Manes, and the gods."   205

With trembling voice he ended and with heart
disturbed entered the empty citadel.

The tides   Ah, who can comprehend the ebb and flow
of Love   of tides lashed by the tempest blasts of Love?
Nay, turbulent Euripus may not vie   210
with such great storms, nor roaring Scylla nor
savage Charybdis. The disordered mind   212
of an impetuous lover knows no peace,
nor any light of day nor polar star,
nor placid mirror of a tranquil night;
his ship sails helmless by a shore that owns
no sheltering port and all that meets his eye
are skies vexed by unending tempests, reefs
that menace him on either side, and seas
ever at war with boisterous gales, by which,   220
poor wretches, you are swiftly borne away
into uncharted channels, perilous deeps.

Entering alone the high hall's inner chamber
beyond the secret threshold, the king sits
in silence pondering his course. He knows
for one who loves, fulfillment of his pledge
will be a hard thing; for the captive state
of the forsaken queen affrightens him,
and knowing well the purity of heart
and lofty spirit of the Roman chief,   230
he cannot doubt that Scipio will oppose
his passion. But although he clearly sees
what destiny must bring him in the end,
yet Love's imperious rule holds him fast bound
in rigid chains. And, as a pilot, lost
on the deep main, may see before his prow,
up-looming, great gaunt rocks or shallow sands,
and yet, for all his skill, be powerless
to veer away, so falls into despair
and, yielding to capricious chance his ship,   240
the oars, the rain-soaked canvases and all,
sits helplessly lamenting in the stern,
the prey of wind and wave, just so the king,
with mind at sea, clings to his certain ruin
nor finds the strength or courage to change course.
So for some time with lamentation long
and varied he continues; now he sees
before him the bright visage of the queen,
now he calls back to mind her honeyed words,
feels once again her humble kisses pressed   250
upon his feet, the soft touch of her hand,
recalls the teardrops falling on her breast,
her dewy eyes yet glowing with sweet fire.
But when into such thoughts the Roman chief
with brow austere intrudes, then craven hope
takes flight and ardor in his heart is chilled.
As when into a red-hot kettle pours
a stream of ice-cold water, for a while
the heat will lose its fury, cooling off,
until the fire intensified augments   260
its former strength, thus, when his cares were calmed,

the self-same goads would stir him up once more
to hot rebellion against reason's rein.
So when injurious love routs reverence
and present beauty's charm and baneful bliss
banish the distant leader from his mind,   *266*
the hard-pressed and tormented prince takes thought
and finds a foolish way to his desire.

He will make Sopho- nisba his queen
"Why tarry now?" he chides himself, "Behold:
Hymen and Jove, indulgent, offer you   270
a splendid marriage and long years of joy.
I glory in the trials I recall:
an exiled, helpless fugitive, despoiled
of my ancestral realm, a suppliant
'mid countless dangers wandering on land
and sea through alien realms and palaces
over long years—but now: enough. Henceforth
it may be, you will know a time of peace.
For if all ills in one short life were counted
no man on earth could match your years of care.   280
See how your kingdom, sweeter to enjoy,
Fortune returns to you at last, restoring
all that was lost. You hold the foe in thrall—
most precious of delights—and you stand now
the arbiter of life and death, the judge
who may claim all things for himself alone.
So all comes back to you. At one same stroke
the foul usurper, groaning, is cast down
and a fair woman, like the shining nymphs
in beauty, widowed of her spouse (for so   290
the laws of war decree) before you stands
and seems disposed to love you if it be
permitted, though yet fearful, mindful yet
of Fate. Truly in modesty she seeks
what she seems fearful to express in words.
What loveliness in lamentation! How
her tears do lend her grace! What majesty!
What joys are yet to come! How fair a queen
she will be, surely, seated on a throne

if such great glory in her suppliant state
she shows, such dignity in captive bonds! 300
O sweet the life of lovers with accord
never disturbed by alternate complaints;
two with one visage always, one sole mind,
all effort shared and likewise all repose.
The world would never see a fairer pair
unless I err in judgment of myself.
In race and birth and quality of mind *307*
and in all else we are well-matched. The gap
in years between us, pleasing both, I think, *309*
will serve to lighten life's oppressive cares. 310
And, as I well observed, our hearts concur
in what alone suffices to unite *312*
the mighty and the lowly: love. So haste
and have no fear lest Scipio condemn
your plan of marriage, for he too is young
and will take pity on another's youth.
Seeing your tears, assuredly he'll grant
full pardon to your passion. He may well
deem it no stolen sweet but sacred troth.
And, gentlest of leaders, he'll respect 320
the queen, once she is sharer of your couch."

The   After such inner council, all his friends
marriage he summoned and revealed his plan to them.
Forthwith he ordered preparations made:
a modest wedding feast, no Tuscan clang 325
of brass, no compliments of friends, the hall
but sparsely filled. No frequent torches flared;
one torch alone, soon destined to be quenched
by their own tears, inflamed the loving pair.
Hesperus, hastening to plunge beneath 330
the Atlantic wave, brought on the longed-for night—
the selfsame star that in his morning role,
hostile to lovers, brings on tedious days
and bears the hated name of Lucifer.
How with its opaque mist the dawn of day
beguiles us! In his fancy, it may be,

while joyously he passed the festive night
in nuptial bliss, the king embraced his sons
and grandsons yet to be. Ah, but for her,
not her new husband's countlessly renewed   340
caresses nor the ancient kingdom's power
promised by all the gods could cast out fear
still dwelling in her heart. Before her eyes
all trembling she called up death and tombs.
No respite came in dreaming; there she saw
herself reft from her second spouse, the first
voicing reproachful taunts. And in her dream   348
enthroned she seemed upon a windy summit
and gazed below and looked upon her lands   350
and migrant folk—when suddenly a mountain
of bulk more massive rose and crashed against
the one on which she sat—O monstrous sight! —
and all the ridge quaked with the shock, while down
from either peak an icy torrent poured
and all the mountain melted soon away
and downward she was whirled through empty space
to dismal Tartarus and the Stygian marsh.

The
rumor
spreads
abroad

Soon through the neighboring towns the rumors ran:
the vanquished had subdued the conqueror;   360
a hero undefeated on the field
was servant of a girl. The common herd,
judging their love fanned by unworthy flames,
amid war's tumult cried "adultery! "
Did not the other king, her lawful spouse,
yet live? What more? A captive beauty seen
by a victorious chief, at once desired
and by intemperate ceremony seized—
not by the rites of the ancestral gods,
and with calm judgment—rather, all was done   370
for lust, delaying not for decency.   371
So everything the wordy gossipers
twisted to its worst sense. And to the ear
of Scipio repeated rumors brought
varying reports. For his part the great chief

Scipio's distress was grieved and pitied his good friend's mischance.
He pondered how to end the sad affair;
and inwardly, as he deplored the act
of lust, inopportune and rash, he planned
to chide the absent one. So might a vexed   380
and anxious father, pouring from his pen
torrents of wrath, berate a wandering son—
and then, relenting, with a calmer mien
resign himself and moderate his words.

Came then a second tale upon the first
Syphax a prisoner to please the wagging tongues. Syphax, 'twas said,
in chains had reached the camp. And all the host
put down their arms and thronged about to see
the spectacle. For in their gatherings
oft had they spoke of him, admiring one   390
who held dominion over many realms,
mighty in war, who once had entertained
the Roman and the Carthaginian chiefs,
both suing peace and seeking his good will,
and scorning not, these two great arbiters
of all the world, to flatter him—to whom
at one time vows were made as to a god,
and who had driven Massinissa forth,
that mightiest of kings, to roam in fear,
an outcast from his realm—now this same man   400
Fate had cast down with mighty overthrow,
withdrawing bounties she had erst bestowed.
Stunned by the crash of such a towering mass
the mind could ill conceive the fall. It was
as if a man might see Olympus quake
or lofty Athos with its shattered peaks
collapse submerged beneath the Aegean wave,
or yet the crest of Eryx or our own
great Apennine give way and sink below,
deep in Tyrrhenian waters—nay, such sights   410
would not be credited but would be deemed
rather the figments of some monstrous vision.

So in a thronging press the king was borne
whither our general waited in his tent.
Ah Fortune, what devices dost thou use
to bring to ruin mortal enterprise!
How envious art thou of mighty realms!
Behold the downfall destined for the great;
mark here the measure of prosperity!
Lo, this great king of kings, erstwhile supreme,   420
lies like a purchased slave in chains, undone
and dragged before a hostile company.
The Roman's heart is moved as he recalls
the ancient ties of hospitality,
now broken, that once bound him to this man   425
and sees once more the winning countenance
of one whom he had thought of as a friend,
whose hand had clasped his own, whose very board
he once had shared, whose wretchedness contrasts
so sharply with his former regal state.   430
Such were the thoughts within him. Then he spoke:

Scipio
reproaches
Syphax   "Vain Syphax, what was it you sought to gain?
Whence your perverse decision? Were you not
content to have withheld the aid you pledged?
Needs must you turn against us as a foe?"
The other, hitherto unmoved in thought
and countenance, now broke his somber silence
and humbly spoke: "O soul magnanimous
and greatest leader of our age, naught worse
has Fortune dealt me than to let me not   440
leave this flesh rigid on the battlefield
among the many mounds of slaughtered men.
What grieves me most is that I have survived
to look upon your visage and there read
the just reproof of my perfidious fault.
But if a wretch's words may be believed
and truth find harborage among these chains,
I'll speak the truth. I own I well deserve
full punishment. Misled by passion vile
and shameful, I scorned every solemn rite   450

of law and justice and of piety.
I broke my pledges to a noble guest
and to the gods who were my witnesses—
nor do the gods forget the sins of men.
And yet my ruin's true cause and sorry root
you may not know; now briefly I'll disclose
the final truth. It will not palliate
the blackness of my crime but rather spur
the pricking of my shame.

The evil done by Sopho-nisba

                                  "When in my house
an alien woman first set foot, she brought   460
omens of ill and augury of doom;
then did I perish and my majesty,
then from my hands the sceptre fell and from
my brow the diadem. My palace in the grip
of hidden flame already was afire.
She bore funereal torches. By her wiles
she bent my purpose; with her artful plaints
she made me heedless of my sacred friend,
my name, myself, and the great gods above.
But why delay you? To her wretched spouse   470
with her own hands she brought the arms of war,
arrayed him for the field, placed on his head
the helmet, thrust the sword in his right hand,
bound to his left the shield. The trumpet called
and him, a-tremble, hating thoughts of war
she sent to dubious battle and compelled
him to attack you, though the gods denied
their favor. When the battle lines were formed,
then did my course of error reach its goal!
Such were the causes of my ruin: I joyed   480
excessively in impious blandishments
and loved a savage wife. A queen indeed—
a queen disposed to wed a train of kings
past counting, all in fickle faith espoused.
With fire such as this may you consume
my foe's Penates! Aye, and so you will   *486*
if my prevision does not play me false;

I'll bear this solace with me to the grave."
Then, troubled, he was still and said no more
but downward turned his glance. And Scipio   490
could see his rancor; in the speaker's glance
and in his visage clearly showing hurt,
he saw love wounded to the death. And more
and more he grieved and shuddered at the thought
of his friend's crime: "For the king's love had been
lawful and right, and if your plaint was just,
yet, Massinissa, it might not excuse
rapine and rage and lust so rashly roused. . . ."
The king was led back to his prison cell.

Massinissa
returns to
the Roman
camp

    Then came fresh tidings to the Roman camp: 500
the troops and chieftains of the royal host,
and with them Laelius, were drawing near.
And when they came, with aspect most serene
Scipio received them, publicly rewarding
the captains with rich gifts; and then he drew
the king apart to sit beside him. When
no other ear could hear him, he began:
"Unless I am deceived by the high hopes
that, Massinissa, I have long maintained   509
of your great qualities, it was no slight   510
and trivial reason that made you seek out
your Scipio, entrusting to his hands
your destiny and scorning former friends.
For as vast seas divide your Africa
from Latium, so are we held separate
by different customs. Weighty reasons then   516
impelled you to traverse so great a gulf
amid the tumult of a world at war.

    "For my part I avow—if my words seem   519
not too ignoble, coming from my lips—   520
no other virtue that I may possess
makes me as proud as this: that in my hands
I firmly hold the reins of pleasure's lures.
No foe in arms against me on the field

The
dangers
of passion
nor Aetna's summit loud with roaring flame
nor all the flood from dark Euboean depths
rising in angry force deserves such fear
as this same throng of pleasures which surround
and strangle us. Youth in its early bloom
is subject to this evil, quick to spread   530
its nets to trap our unsuspecting years.
For Aetna's wrath may pass, the mighty flood
recede, the foe be beaten off or checked
by walls; but ruinous pleasure rages on
through night and day; no rampart may avail
to ward it off, past sentinels it sweeps,
past faithful watchdogs to the inner chambers
and through the armed gates of the mightiest.
If by your virtue only you were moved
to leave your hearth and home and realm and
          shrines,   540
relinquishing your princely name to serve
in my command, prepared to follow me
o'er land and sea and look to me alone
for safety—then, how great will you appear
before the world if this one honor more
be added to the many you possess.
To vanquish Syphax is a glorious thing,
but doubt not it is greater to put down
the strong emotions raging in the heart
and hold tight rein on the intemperate soul.   550
You'll have in me a herald of your virtues
and gladly I'll report your words and deeds.

          "Ponder such matters in your heart and let
Massinissa
reminded
of his
duty
your conscience, before any utterance,
cause you to blush. In truth this war has shown
the valor of your arms. However (pray
forgive me here), our vast, far-flung campaign
has been conducted under my command
and all that we have won belongs to Rome.
Forget not that the captured king himself,   560
his kingdom and all that it may contain

are ours. And so to Rome the king must go
with his fierce consort. She it was who prayed
for war; moreover she is daughter to   *564*
a famous foe. Her presence will adorn
our triumph. Now be master of your heart
and of yourself; let not one lawless act
besmirch your glory. Mark well how the fruit
of waywardness, the wrath and woe it brings,
should give you rightful cause to be afraid   *570*
of an unwholesome love. Bethink you too
of what becomes a king and bear in mind
how vile a thing is passion in itself."

*Massanissa
shamed*   As Scipio spoke the other's copious tears
covered his face, as when the gleaming snow
melts 'neath the breath of the soft southern wind
and soon the drops fall headlong. Then he spoke:
"The greatest care I have is to obey
your will. My fate and my security
are in your hands. You quench an ardent breast   *580*
and temper a despairing lover's mood.
Naught shall you ask in vain. But give a thought
to my fair name. I ask of you but this:
allow me, if I must lose my dear wife,
to keep my pledge to her." Then, breaking off
his speech with raucous sobs and murmurs, he
retired into his tent, there to remain
with somber mien, while with self-hurtful hands
he beat his breast. As when a sentence read
has marked a criminal for death, the blast   *590*
borne from the tuba's mouth sounds the decree,
and the poor quivering wretch, his face o'ercast
with a funereal pallor as he looks
on death and at the lictor's word lays down
his head to meet the ax, and then, in truth,
anticipating what is soon to be
he sees his lifeless body, gushing blood
and feels the anguish of the severance
of head from trunk; so to that hapless youth

the mistress he was fated soon to lose   600
seemed in his wretchedness already lost.
His state, past all restraint of quiet grief,
compelled the venting of his woe in words:

His   "Alas," he cried, "for such sad threads of life   *604*
dilemma   protracted through such anguish and by Fate
drawn to the cruel pass! Now shall we choose
a death with honor. So my chief commands—
unless he deems that I can bear to live
bereft of heart. Ah Scipio, if yours be
a heart of senseless flint within a breast   610
of firmest adamant, what portion then
of Roman harshness think you apt for me?
Would you destroy a friend who well deserves
a better fate? My life offends you? Ah,
what wounds have I not taken on my breast,
wretch that I am, to die at last of love,
releasing my spent soul in sighs and tears.
There is no death that less becomes a man,
yet more I may not hope for." So he raved
and to the circling stars above uprose   620
his poignant grief; his lamentations reached
the ears of troops in distant stations where
the cohorts broke their stride to hear his moans.

Night   Phoebus, meanwhile, had led his breathless steeds
comes on   to their Hesperian bed, remembering
perhaps the ardent flame the comely maid   *626*
of Thessaly had kindled in his heart,
and to his vision came once more the frond
of sacred laurel marvelously reft
from his hot hand, the life so sadly lost,   630
the weight of sorrow, and the kisses pressed
upon the tender boughs as breath of life
grew ever colder while it ebbed away.
Wherefore with pity for the king whose love
was like to his, he bathed his tear-stained face
beneath the ocean wave and, as he sank,
yielded to waiting Night the chariot reins.

But Scipio—for Fortune gives no rest
to any save to those whom she ignores,
since her hostility brings pain and woe,   640
her favor but new cares—through the long night
lay sleepless, pondering his battle plans.
Should he assault the bastions and the walls
of Carthage behind which the terrified
Phoenicians cowered, or move to devastate
the outlying Libyan fields, or should he first
give his exhausted cavalry some rest,
granting to all his troops a short surcease?
Then to the cautious general recurred
another care: how best to send across   650
the mighty deep the captive Punic host
to the exultant Romans. Most of all
the king and consort troubled him. How strong
a guard should be provided and to whom
the office be entrusted? Even thus
a merchant whose propitious enterprise
has yielded wealth and profit may with care
ponder which galleons he should charge with gold
and precious stones and treasured merchandise
and to which captain he should give command.   660
The leader, cherishing above all others
his Laelius, would, when weary with his cares,
to him alone entrust affairs of weight.
So in the dark of night he sent for him
and, ordering that a hundred ships be staffed
with crews and armed, he bade him be prepared
to travel with the fleet to Italy.

Massinissa's   But for the hapless lover those dark hours
torments   were drawn out in another, sadder style;
what arts should he employ, what gods evoke,   670
what prayers would serve to loosen Fate's black threads
and so redeem his cherished lady's life?
Now he considers in a sudden flight
with her beside him sailing far beyond
the barrier set by Hercules to seek

the Blessed Isles; and then the notion comes 676
to hasten with all speed and make his way
past the high walls of Carthage, there to sue
humbly for pardon and compassionate grace
for him and for his spouse from friends of old; 680
next his thought turns to the deliverance
offered by sword and noose, the tools of death;
he thinks of fashioning the fatal knot
with his own hand and by the ready cure
of self-destruction ending all his woes.
Often he grasped the sword, nor was it fear
nor wish to linger in a widowed life
that held his hand, but sense of shame alone:
he would not stain his honor with a crime
irreparable. So moved, he would restrain 690
his impulse and once more into the sheath
his hand would thrust the sword, half drawn to strike.

Thus on his sleepless couch he turned and writhed
through the long night, and passion racked his breast
and fierce desire gnawed at his heart, and grief
and wrath and madness gave him no repose.
Repeatedly he would embrace the bed
as if it were his absent love he held,
murmuring endearments; when his raging grief
could brook control no longer, he broke forth: 700
"O Sophonisba, all too dear to me,
sweeter than life itself, farewell! No more
hereafter shall I look on you, my love,
as with a smile on your angelic face,
all sweetness, you confine your flowing locks
within their wonted band of gold; no more
I'll hear the soft notes from your fragrant mouth
shape words to charm all Heaven and its gods.
Alone I'll lie, my lifeless limbs disposed
on a cold couch. Ah, dear one, would that I 710
might share with you a common sepulchre
wherein, together, we might spend in joy
the years denied us here—oh, that one pyre

might to one glowing ash reduce us both
and death unite forever our twin souls.
Then Scipio could not divide our love!
Nay, would that even now in darkest Hell
we were one shade, through meads of myrtle granted
to roam together. Scipio might not then
divide our love. Then shall we go in tears   720
with matching steps, in harmony conjoined
eternally. And Scipio, whose soul
is forged of iron, will not divide our love.
I shall depart, a shade that all the gods
of Erebus will envy and the king
and all the dwellers of that silent realm,
the happiest of shades, and Scipio
shall do our tender love no injury.
Let him, a pious leader, rise aloft
to Heaven's starry heights, so high above   730
the ways of mortal men, nor be concerned
to follow us to the drear plains of Dis
and the infernal realm and vex no more
two ardent lovers. Would he ne'er had come
into the Libyan land, would he had stayed
forever on the Latin shores! Alas
for my mad outcries; if he had not come,
my dearest, then your loveliness, your face
radiant as sunshine would have been unknown
to me, and therefore in that case likewise   740
life would have held no joy to warm my heart.
What paradox is here: he brought me life
and took it from me! Noble Scipio,
you should have swiftly carried off to Rome
your prize of standards and your captive king,
leaving the queen behind, unknown to you.
Alas, the gods I call upon are deaf;
the victor, august master of the hosts
demands his prisoner. Shall I give her up?
He urges—ah, how cruel is the prayer   750
that only hurt fulfills! He but requests—
yet with a wordless glance he threatens too;

he sues, but I can sense a stern command
beneath the gentle plea. Shall I obey?
Rather let angry Jove upon my head
hurl all his bolts and earth devour this flesh,
or let a treacherous king's accursed bowels
be cast in fragments over the wide sea!
Shall I, to please a Roman, violate
the sacred marriage bond? I might have reigned,   760
'tis true, without a wife—and better so,
perhaps, as Scipio by example proves,
for he remains a celibate—and yet
it would be wrongful to forswear a pledge
made to a wife. But his command is clear,
inexorable his veto. What remains?

His
resolution   Dear Sophonisba, you must die—and die
by your own husband's gift; a cruel Jove
finds satisfaction in such gifts as these.
You shall not be borne off to Italy   770
in chains, doomed to a life of servitude
to Latin women. My decision thus
cannot appear to you as treachery
nor will you blame my broken faith. So die;
and in grim death and death alone must end
our love. Nay, pity, all ye gods, for faith
I must betray. Let us through Libya's sands
flee to the last frontiers of earth and find,
where serpents reign, a dwelling more secure
than we own here. So far will Scipio   780
not follow. Be assured no venomous fangs
shall sting your dainty feet with noxious force;
nay, seeing you, perhaps the very beasts
will spare me too. Dear wife, I am resolved
on flight. I shall protect you from the death
that waits us here. I'll readily endure
exile and poverty and every ill
with you beside me. Nay, I know the heart
of womankind: you will not follow me,
queen as you are and wont to sit enthroned   790
in majesty. And even if you would

I've naught prepared for flight, and Roman power
precludes escape; the name of Scipio
is feared throughout the world. There comes to me
a dream recurrent in the night's dark hours,
troubling my rest and heretofore unclear.
Were you that graceful doe, by violence
snatched from a wounded stag, and finally,
by order of an unjust shepherd, reft
from her new guardian? Even so disguised,   800
you pleased me. But what meant the sequent dream
wherein you died? Ah, to oblivion cast
this omen, mighty gods. And yet I fear,
noting the ordered sequence of the acts,
that vision showed the truth. What then to do?
Nay, you must die; there is no other choice,
my hapless wife, and of your death 'tis I
must be the cause. What of my life to come?
You, Venus, and great Jupiter who look
from Heaven downward, you well know the trials   810
and toils of life on earth. Who then, tell me,
will with soft words give comfort through calm nights
or banish cares when spirits lie oppressed?
Who will provide me solace of sweet kisses
or warm embraces? Life without you holds
no sweetness. Palaces that throng with slaves,
a bed adorned with Tyrian purple drapes,
or mansions glittering with countless gems—
what do all such avail? What serves a crown
or all the splendor of a spacious realm?   820
Remorseless flame consumes my burning heart:
your dear face, to be cherished after death,
say, whither does it go? Dear love, farewell,
since I must mourn for you while you yet live.

He bids   "O Sophonisba, loveliest of all
his queen   fair creatures whether of the race of gods
farewell   or mortal born in any age or time,
mirror and model of all excellence,
who have in human form exemplified

what beauty dwells beyond the stars, what grace   830
clothes the immortals—hear, I pray, my plaint
with gracious ears! Ah, even in wretchedness
how sweet are memories to me! Those eyes
that with celestial fire enchant the heavens
must suffer their rare splendor to be hidden
in a confining tomb, those precious eyes
made to enrapture the immortal gods
and calm the wrath of cruel men, those eyes
that drew me from myself and all my cares;
that brow, a shining glory framed in gold,   840
nobler than mortal mold, must lie unseen
under cold stone; that smile, so quick to pierce
a breast of iron or shatter clouds that blot
the skies, is doomed alas to sink for aye
beneath the Stygean depths. Ye happy souls
to whom that quickening light will come to break
the gloom of centuries! Oh, blessed, born
in time to see so fair a sight that death,
my foe, withdraws from me! That milk-white foot
with god-like step will board the dreary bark   850
and soon be carried over Lethe's wave.
Ah, happy Charon, would it were my task
to steer your skiff; I'd linger between shores
and leave to you the ruling of my realm.
O enviable ancient, have you seen   855
a paragon like this, and can you hope
hereafter ever to look on its peer?
'Tis true you saw the bride reluctantly   858
ravished and borne off to her sombre bed
from Aetna's slopes, nor were your eyes denied   860
the sight of our Elissa. You have seen   861
the dreadful Gorgon, awesome to behold,   862
and Laodamia following on the steps   863
of her ill-fated husband, noose in hand,
and winsome Procris, and the bane of Troy   865
and one of Minos' daughters (for the other   866
with starry crown now dwells in Heaven above).   867
But who bears glory such as this in such

a lovesome form? Doubt not my word, old man:
no age to come will look upon her like,   *870*
nor did the first age, though it vaunt its worth,
behold such rare perfection. Aye, that sight
will stir your passion, old man; have a care.
Soon it may be that you'll receive me too,
close following on the footsteps I adore
of my unhappy wife. Nay, not for long
shall I lie captive here. If joining her   *877*
is not allowed me and I must again
put on this mortal flesh, then I am lost.
Old man, take pity; as an honest judge,   *880*
and burning with a flame akin to mine,
be not unmindful of my ardent youth.
Ah, Cerberus, if the Thracian singer's lyre   *883*
had power with its notes to banish wrath,
what must my spouse's beauty not effect
when you and the great lord of Tartarus
behold her? He, I truly fear, will be
so smitten as at once to make assault
upon my love, and you, Proserpina,
to your old mother may once more return.   *890*

      "With such feigned visions you delude yourself,
mad Massinissa! Happy were your lot
if faithless Fortune had but ratified
her pledges. Now, unhappiest of kings,
put down your lamentations, stay your tears.
O my sweet beauty, O my soul's true half,   *896*
O rapture brief, O sorrow long to bear,
O peerless spouse, doomed by the shortest path
to reach the Elysian fields, forsaking me
and my deep grief! But soon I'll follow you;   *900*
I find my solace in this thought alone."
He ceased. And sleep drew near and for a while
his weary limbs were comforted in rest.
But in his dreams complaints and charges vied
and accusations hurled against cruel Fate
and chaos and mankind and all the gods.

Soon, to conclude the course of this sad love,
Phoebus comes radiant from the eastern wave
and trumpets sound the dawn. The prince awakes;
his passion mounts again, again his thoughts   910
turn to the same laments. He sees the camp
in busy preparation, and he fears
his general's command and well suspects
that force will be employed if he resists.
Wherefore he carries out a base design,
dreadful to tell of, born of love's despair.
He gives a golden goblet to the slave
entrusted with the poison. When he sees
the vessel brimming with bright lethal foam
the prince commands: "Go to my luckless queen   920
and bear her this sad gift and so discharge
my vow the gods have witnessed. She will know
that I remember both my promises;
the second I fulfill. The other way,
God knows, would please me more, but all in vain
I've sought for a solution whereby she
might have remained to share with me my throne.
There is no way but this. The Roman chief
forbids it. And the gods above have willed
and Fortune granted that his power and strength,   930
far mightier than mine, should overcome me.
Let her reflect upon her past estate,
her present ruin, and what her fate must be
shorn of my name's protection. And therewith
she must consider the respect she owes
to her first husband and her sire. Then, surely,
this option, suited to her birth and rank,
she will elect. We offer her the key
to flight and freedom. We can do no more."
He spoke and turned away his swollen eyes,   940
and straightaway to the chamber of the queen,
bearing the fatal gift, the servant went.

     A crone, as rich in years as rags, came forth,
remarked his aspect and the cup he bore,

and told the queen. She stood a moment, dazed
and terror-chilled, then, putting fear aside,
she bade him enter. He with eyes downcast
and quaking told his mission. But the queen
Sopho-   broke off his words and, "Willingly," she said,
nisba's   "I take the regal gift you offer me   950
last   if my dear lover has no fairer thing
words   to send me now. If I may speak the truth,
I should have better died than madly wed
upon the grave's edge; not—hear me, ye gods!—
that aught my cherished spouse might send to me
could be unwelcome, but that sooner I
might, rising to the stars, have cast aside
these fetters of the flesh. When you have been
a witness to my death, return and bear
this last word with you. Now, immortal gods   960
of Heaven and the vast seas and ye too
of earth's dark core and all the shades of Styx
whom I approach before my rightful time,
if what I ask is just, lend favoring ear;
let me be heard by sky and sea and earth.
Now I must die, and sadder far to me
than death is what occasions it. Wherefore
has our rare pleasure irked the Latin chiefs?
What a presumptuous tribe! 'Tis not enough
to drive a foe from his ancestral realm;   970
nay, they must rob the soul of liberty
and dare assail love's sacred bond and force
the spouses and assault the marriage bed—
aye, and the Roman leader is assured
of victory; no human power can change
what from eternity Jove has decreed.

She   "So be it; but as for the conqueror,   977
curses   may his last days of life be dark, may Rome
Scipio   be thankless for the trophies he has won,
may he grow old far from his native land,   980
a lonely exile on a barren shore
and far from every trusted friend. Ye gods,

let him who has all sweetness reft from us
find no sweet for himself; may he be racked
by anguish of a brother wronged and grieve
for cruel injustice shown his house, and may
a worthless son rob his last years of joy.
Ah, death will come upon you, Scipio,
far from your native country, left by you
in bitterness. And on your sepulchre,   990
mean and unworthy, you will carve in stone
your querulous reproach to shame your land.   992

    "And you, dear spouse, if you hold fast to him   993
as his ally, will endlessly be vexed
by turmoil of your neighbors; you shall see
your children die untimely and their sons
dishonored in the brawls of civil strife.
And from that very stock a bloody churl
shall rise to harry and revile your heirs   1000
with insolence and drag them through the walls
in bonds before cruel chariots; aye, that Rome
you love will crown her triumphs with your kin."

    Great lamentation followed on her words
and all were shaken at her hapless end.
She grasped the goblet, raised her eyes to Heaven
and cried: "Sweet sun, farewell; farewell, ye gods;
farewell, my Massinissa; think of me!"
And then, as one who quenches avid thirst,
she quaffed, with tranquil mien, the envenomed
    draught   1010
and her fierce spirit fled to Tartarus.

Book 6

*Sopho-
nisba in
Hades*

Not since the whole vast cosmos was disposed   1
in three unequal shares had e'er a shade
drawn near the Stygian lake with such a train
of wonder-struck attendants. On all sides   4
stood Punic ranks in awed amaze; thereto
the Furies with their wordless jaws agape
and unkempt hair up-raised and pallid cheeks
looked on and marveled. But the queen maintained
a regal virtue in her glance; her brow,
though pale, yet bore the majesty of old.   10
Resentful of the gods and death itself,
with gently downcast eyes she made her way,
and when she stood before the infernal judge,
great Minos moved his hoary beard in speech   14
and uttered his decree: "Madly she turned
upon herself; hers be the second cell,   16
allotted to the guilty souls that scorn
life's final cares." The verdict was confirmed
by harsh assent of Rhadamanthus, whence   19
the monstrous lictor made as if to seize   20
the wretched soul. And then, while all the wide
vexed plain of Tartarus was still, the voice
of Aeacus, the arbiter supreme,   23
rang loud and clear across the Stygian marsh:
"She died for love; she was cast forth from light
by force; the third precinct of my domain
claims her by right. And thither let her go
and suffer at our hands no further hurt
that she has not deserved. Her lot in life
and manner of her death were harsh enough."   30
Thereat, the people of the shadow realm
and all the bloodless Senate of the dead
in ghostly concord clamored their assent.
And even as when a convict first condemned

110

to shameful noose or cross or burning stake
feels his heart shaken not by thought of pain
but of disgrace, then, if a nobler style
of death be granted him, his aspect alters
and tears spring to his eyes as in his breast
some consolation rises, so the queen,   40
more joyously and, rancor now assuaged,
more fair, moved on with stately step to view
her longed-for dwelling, while on either hand,
as if renewing dreams of her old life,
thronged youthful bands.

                    Not distant from the shore
of Lethe's stream which first receives the tread
of those who quit the bark and make their way
to gloomy caves beyond, a dusky plain
extends, girt 'round by dark, oppressive hills.
Here 'midst the ample acres stands a wood   50
of ancient myrtle, in its bosky depths
holding the silence of eternity.
Here is no clang of arms nor charger's snort   53
nor care of flocks nor dogs nor husbandry
of cattle—only grief and tears and sighs   55
drawn in recurrent anguish, bootless yearning,
self-hatred and the pallor of disgrace,
misguided passion, folly, crime, deceit,
and thieving plots by adulation cloaked
or seeming jest, and woe, offensive mirth,   60
and perjury pronounced with placid mien,
and a few scattered truths among the host
of treacherous falsehoods. There, as she stepped through
the narrow portal, on its very sill
the queen marked Iphis, humbling his neck   65
in the constricting noose, and Byblis, crushed   66
by burning sorrow. And beyond she saw
Myrrha, with visage buried among leaves,   68
seeking to hide her dreadful shame. There too
stood Orpheus, the ravager of Hell,   70
still bent on his vain purpose to retrieve

Eurydice, and in the deeper grove,
treading the pale green moss, Achilles strode
with pace still war-like. On a facing path
as if still fearful of his foe's pursuit
Paris in silence trod, and on his heels,
imploring him, Oenone came in tears,   77
but he turned from her. There the royal maid   78
and matron, bane of earth and source of woes
past count, and Turnus, for his spouse's rape   80
resentful, roamed the plain. You might have seen
two others in the valley, wandering
together side by side, each with an arm
cast lovingly about the other's neck.
Observing them, the queen could not but sigh
and murmur: "Happy Thisbe," for that love
unbroken in Avernus touched her heart
and moved her, as no other of the shades,
to envy. The forsaken wife was stirred,
as ne'er before, to yearning for her spouse,   90
so warmly cherished. All in vain, alas;
far from her side, his destiny decrees,
and weary, after many years of care,
he will arrive at life's last hour and pass   94
thereafter to his own eternal home,
encloistered with the heroes of renown.

    When Rumor, in its wonted circuit, brought
report of her undoing, every heart
was moved to pity; all the cohorts wept.
Some grieved for the doomed queen and some were
        stirred   100
to anger at the wrong done by the king,
who, piling crime on wicked crime, had sought
by one foul deed to expiate the rest;
and others, marveling, could only praise
the courage, worthy of a hero's heart,
shown by a woman facing dreadful death.
But Scipio, fearful lest the fiery youth,   107
now fully conscious of his double crime,

might plan more grievous injury to himself,
with words of consolation sought to soothe   110
the anguish of the chastened prince, and raise
his downcast spirits. So a doctor speaks
who sees a dubious illness reach its crest
and offers reassurance in the hope
the patient may not learn his perilous state.
And thus another sleepless night of care
oppressed him till dawn came. But when the stars
scattered before the light of Lucifer
and shining day moved from the Indic sea,
while myriad birds began their sweet complaint   120
and Procne broke the stillness of the night,   *121*
then he rose up and bade the herald call
the troops together. Taking his high place

He ad- above them, he began: "O noble Romans,
dresses victorious veterans of great campaigns,
his ye whom the western lands, for long oppressed,
troops have nurtured and whom Africa has known
through numerous defeats and will yet know
the better in her ultimate collapse:
your leader asks of you attentive ears   130
and open hearts. And that I speak the truth
be Jupiter my witness from on high.
In this long labor never has vain glory
moved me nor yet pernicious lust for power,
but mighty love of country led us all
to cross the unquiet sea and pitch our camp
beyond the Syrtes. With such comrades I   *137*
would never fear to cross the Riphean Alps,
though lightly clad, in winter's gelid season,
nor yet to traverse, under Leo's sign   140
and fully armored, Ethiopia's bare
and barren desert with its scorching sands.
Whether in dubious fight it be my fate
to conquer or to die a happy death,
not to myself but to my fatherland
my life and my security belong.
The payment of that debt of piety

I shall account no loss. What this portends
I'll now disclose. All ye who have followed me
in toil, turn now your minds to this supreme   150
effort; the end draws nigh and with it comes
our highest glory. It is my design
to encircle savage Carthage and her walls.
Then must the man to whom that treacherous race,
hostile to us alone, has given the power
to harm itself, return, and then the peace
of old shall once more dwell in Latin lands
and we shall win such lasting fame as falls
to victors in a final fray—or else,
should he choose to remain far from the field,   160
he will confess himself a beaten man.
O undefended land of wickedness,
now at my hands shall you receive in full
your rightful punishment and pay in blood
for all our countrymen so cruelly slain!
Shall barbarous footsteps stain Italian fields
and just revenge be not permitted us?
If Hannibal—the very thought alone
is spark and tinder to our righteous wrath—
stands threatening beneath our walls and looks,   170
albeit with one eye, in arrogance
on the Capitoline, why then should we
not in like fashion eye his city's walls?
Aye, if that second Carthaginian Mars   *174*
should come full-armed across the Stygian wave
to encounter me and guarded on both flanks
by those four savage lions bred by him
for warfare, yet I would not turn aside
but rather challenge him. O sons of Rome,
so much your martial virtue tried and true   180
has taught me. With the bloodless shades below
lies that notorious sire; his count of sons
has dwindled down to one, so keen has flashed
the sword of Latium on those stubborn necks.
And the survivor has been spared that he
may prove the crowning glory of our arms.

Let his long life so meet an honored end!
Aye, boast of battles won and Romans slain
by your spear thrust; your hour too will come.
By this hand shall you fall, but ere you die   190
the honor will be granted you to learn
the name of him who slays you: Scipio,
and on the marble of your sepulchre
that name shall be inscribed. But now to deeds:
avengers of your country, turn your thoughts
to mighty triumphs.

             "Massinissa, you,
most puissant pride of kings, whom neither waves
in raging storm nor Jupiter descending
in one great flame nor warlike Mars himself
with lethal force onrushing could perturb,   200
come, open up your heart and hear my words.

His gifts   I know your worth in war and how the gods
to   have favored you; I offer you these gifts
Massinissa   as from our city, meager, I confess
against your merits. Count them but a pledge
of greater gifts to come. This mettled steed   *206*
remark, full-armed and glittering with gold,
impatient of repose. Behold this car,
likewise agleam, and therewith trophies such
as generals in Rome would choose to bear,   210
marching in triumphs. How it scintillates,
this jasper-studded crown; how in the hand
lies heavy this stout bowl of tawny gold!
See this rich robe? In all of sacred Rome
you would find none more precious. You have learned
already how high Roman virtue stands
among mankind, but treasures such as these
you could not know; 'tis not our use to give
such honors to an alien—but to you
we freely offer titles, vestments, arms   220
and dignities and honor. Our ally,
in every triumph Fortune shall decree
for us you'll have a share. For you a place

within our Senate shall be made and kept,
and every token of the privileges
the sons of Romulus claim, you too shall wear;
and so we hail you: king, ally, and friend.

*His gift
to
Laelius*
And you, most worthy Laelius, pray accept
and cherish this bejewelled chaplet, rich
with gold. And now speed on your way and take   230
with you the captive Syphax and his train.
The fleet awaits you on the open sea,
with placid waves beneath the south wind's breath.
And as for you, my comrades in long trials,
you shall have fitting honors and rewards.
With us you shall ascend the Capitol,
exultant in the car, with laurel decked,
while thousands all around applaud the victors
and among carefree throngs almighty Rome
from all her seven hills will honor us.   240
That day the Fates, whose promise never fails,
have promised me draws near." He said no more.

And now from every side arose a great
and joyous murmuring to high Olympus
as Laelius and the king sought to express
the thanks they owed their chief. As for the king,

*Massinissa
consoled*
great hopes cast out his former cares and filled
his breast with new ambition to extend
his modest kingdom's boundaries and add
thereto the lands of hostile realms. His star   250
and mighty Scipio's pledge of aid gave weight
to expectation. As the fowler, seeing
out of his snare a little bird take flight,
straightway laments the downfall of his hope
of slender profit, whereupon perchance,
from some unlooked-for corner of the sky,
a nobler bird appears with outstretched wings
and cheers his heart as thoughts of greater gain
make him forget his loss, so in the breast
of that inconstant lover the old care   260
made way for new desires. The conqueror

of love is love and lust by lust is vanquished.
That night new visions filled the prince's dreams:
no longer came the face of his beloved
to his mind's eye, nor her remembered stride
nor lovesome glance; he heard the notes no more
of her soft sighing voice; instead he saw
a throne and towns and cities bravely girt
by sturdy walls and hills and flowing streams
marking the frontiers of a wider realm.   270

Now rosy-colored day upon the east
yokes her swift car and bright Aurora drives
from Heaven every lingering shade of night;

*The
fleet
sails for
Rome*

the fleet awakens to a trumpet blast
and sails are spread to catch the favoring breeze.
The Roman youths assemble on the shore
to see their friends depart and bid them bear
homeward a message to a brother, sire,
or friend or sister, so the morning air
is charged with sounds of eager voices calling   280
in varied notes. And Laelius, by the mast,
saluted first the tranquil waves, then bade
the pilots set the sails, and his command
the sailors greeted with a joyous cry.

*Syphax
bids
Africa
farewell*

But from the midmost bark sad Syphax gazed   285
for the last time upon his fatherland
and on those shores where he was born and bred;
longing he looked and wept his silent tears.
Then when his swelling sorrow broke the bolts
and loosed the doors of speech, he voiced his pain: 290
"O land the gods abhor, land long oppressed
by evil stars, what curse brought to our fields
that queen long since from Sidon fugitive?
What passion to our hearts, what recent scars
of battle did not she, a woman weak
and timorous, bear with her, so rousing us
to lust for war and thirst for blackened blood?
Wiser and safer had we been to keep
within our fathers' kingdom, holding it

in peace. This vast sea Nature had disposed   300
to separate two races, each to dwell
on opposite shores—and we, upon its waves,
have sought our ruin. Say, what have we won
in violating Nature's elements
with our defeats, in trials with the gales
and raging seas? Does not accursèd Spain
lie far from us? What quarrel do I have
with you, Trinacria, pouring forth black smoke   *308*
from molten veins? Would that Sardinia,
that plague-infested isle, whither we bore   310
our ensigns and our arms, had been submerged
beneath the main. Ah no; we were ashamed
to dwell in peace in such a spacious realm!
O fairest Africa, hills of my sires,
I shall not look on you forever more.
Now I am haled off to an alien land
where I shall find my grave. Who would believe
that one born on the edges of the world
would find his burial place beneath the sod
of Italy? My life has known no rest   320
but only cares incessant. So dire Fate
decreed for me and so the gods have willed.
May they, who gave you power and willful heart,
to confound everything, exact due price,
O Hannibal, since you are the true cause
of my sad downfall, and the root as well
of all the final ills that fall upon
the hapless land of which you are the son.
    "Ah, would that lightning, dealing just deserts,
had blasted you when first you stood in prayer   330
by the ancestral shrine. 'Tis he, great Jove,
who should have been thy target; to what end
are vengeful bolts hurled down on harmless oaks
or rocks? Ah youth, ill-omened for your land,
your race, yourself! And you, his sire, abhorred
by the immortals, bearing seeds of war,
much better had it been had you begot
no evil offspring but had rather passed,

a mournful father, down among the shades
and never seen this fury unrestrained.   340
Your own mad lust to satiate your sight
and sword with all the world's blood was denied
to you, but your dire son came forth to send
offerings a-plenty to a savage sire.
Now shall you justly grieve. Ah, but extreme
of anguish, what torments I must endure
caused by that son of yours who now pollutes
lakes, rivers, pools and lands and seas with gore!
Perchance I shall not see with living eyes
his final agony, but I shall see   350
his spirit join the ranks of slain and stand
among the encircling Furies. You, my spouse,
who treacherously strove to cast aside
your consort and recked naught of our defeats,
shall go before me, all unwillingly,
to Tartarus. I'll look once more on you
in solitude and see shame on your face,
for, if my eyes deceive me not, that vile
seducer tarries still upon the soil
of our dear fatherland and thinks no more   360
of you." No further did he speak but bowed
his tearful face to hide it in his lap.
He felt no fear of reefs nor Eurus raging
forth from the cave of Aeolus nor yet
of any monster of the watery deep;
nay, for he longed for death and silently
prayed that an adverse blast might bear his chill
insensate corpse once more to Libya's shore.
So might a tiny acre's jealous lord,
seeing no hope of harvest for himself,   370
pray for a fruitless spring for others too,
with rain and hail and crop-destroying winds.

Scipio   Meanwhile, somewhat unburdened of his cares,
presses   Scipio made haste with ramparts to secure
his   the hills of Tunis, crowning them with towers,   375
campaign   and bade a ditch be swiftly dug to gird

the wooden walls. Thus all at once he camped
in sight of Carthage, laying waste the fields
the peasants had abandoned in their fear.
The townsmen too, by sudden terror seized,   380
cried out in panic that their only hope
lay in recalling their great general.
Quickly they sent forth heralds to disclose
the public state and bid him to return
to final battle and the anguished end
of all his folk under the doom of death.
And other emissaries were dispatched
on swift ship to Liguria to demand
of Mago that he forthwith quit that shore;
for should they not return their land was doomed   390
to final ruin. And though his savage heart
was sorely vexed since now at last he too
had felt the wounding thrust of adverse war,
to Mago it seemed prudent to obey
his fatherland's injunction; he too feared
the foe was readying the final charge.

*Carthage
sends
envoys
to
Scipio*   Also, that wingèd words might earn for them
some respite, to the Roman camp they sent,
drawn from their senate, thirty envoys, armed
with treachery to beguile the Roman chief.   400
The first of these, with tears and deep-drawn sighs
proffered his discourse: "Mighty general,
whose peer the world has never known through all
the years of time since the primeval age,
see how much evil a few cruel hands,
guiding the folly of misguided men,
have brought upon our country. In our plight
we look to you for preservation of
our nation's weal, which madmen would confound.
If it be noble to forego revenge,   410
if yet it shall be proved the better course
(accepting, not rejecting, our appeal)
to have increased the vast domain of Rome
than to have razed a mighty city, aye,

if conquerors in their hour of victory
may to their own advantage call to mind
an ancient friendship rather than be moved
by present wrath—why, then, forgive, we pray
your vanquished suppliants. Succor their estate;
offer your hand to us who die, and raise   420
a fallen enemy. So much the more
you may reproach our shame. To make a friend
of an offensive foeman is the best
part of a victor. Nay, I'll put aside
such specious pleading. Our unhappy state
reminds us that we may not here invoke
the name of friendship. Let it then suffice
that men afflicted seek security
and guilty men ask pardon. In the name
of your own gods, your mighty Thunderer,   430
O Roman, we, expecting punishment
and pain, beg your forgiveness. I shall not
deny our crimes, nay, openly the truth
must be confessed to you, great general.
Tempestuous Hannibal it was who shaped
our fond delusions; it was he who fanned
our greedy appetite for power supreme
to folly and so drove us on to seek
what now, too late, we sadly realize
were better left unsought. That he should die,   440
crushed by the burden of his crimes, were just.
Be that his fate. But with benevolence
look on our lot. If we perceive a townsman
is our true foe, then you, who call yourself
our enemy, be our true citizen."

He spoke and knelt before the victor's feet,
who raised him up and solemnly replied:

Scipio's
reply "I would remind you that I am not come
to Libyan shores as one to treat of peace
but as a conqueror, sworn to avenge   450
old injuries. What Fortune promises
my arms, what victories I may expect—

these things are known to all. And yet your end
I view with pity, nor can I deny
my generous spirit. Further, that the world
may know the wars of Rome are justly waged,
with love of peace ne'er absent from our breasts,
we spare even those unworthy. Now fix well
within your minds these terms of truce and learn
from the great slaughter you have suffered how   460
to keep faith, fear the gods, and honor pacts.
No more than twenty ships for the state's needs
shall you maintain in port; without our bidding
you shall no more wage wars; your armies stand
at our discretion; henceforth shall Spain be
from your allegiance severed and at last
be safe from your attacks, and every isle
that lies between our shores shall be at peace,
from Libyan Mars set free. You shall strike off
your prisoners' chains, and from your captives' feet   470
(your conquerors now) you shall remove the fetters.
Henceforth shall no deserter from our host
find safe asylum with you. Carthage must
recall her generals from Italy
and withdraw all her troops. Three days we grant
for your decision. If your choice be peace,
dispatch your heralds, that the Roman folk
may voice approval and our senators
give legal sanction. If you will not, then
you will have had a few untroubled days   480
and by my favor three nights unmolested."
Thereto he added, mindful of his men,
demands for corn and heavy tax of coin.
      Thus charged, they joyfully accept, as if
no terms of peace could be too harsh for them,
having no hope left in their armament.
Their people, grumbling and with cheating hearts,
give their concurrence. As the mariner,
of little faith but mortally afraid
of watery depths when tempests blast his bark   490
and hope is dead, will with his perjured vows

burden the sea-gods and with tremulous voice
thrice call on raging Nature and invoke
Thetis the queen of waters or the spirit   *494*
of wrathful Nereus from the briny deep,   *495*
pledging rich gifts to temples, promising
fulfillment of great tasks, and when the gales
abate and he perceives the sheltering port,
then put aside in shameless perfidy
or quite forget such inconvenient vows,   500
so the Phoenicians with concessions buy
a meed of time, awaiting the return
of Hannibal from his far-distant camp.

Hannibal   He, meanwhile, with a store of trials beset,
too re-   was on the tip of Italy detained,
ceives   where rise the rugged peaks of Bruttium,   *506*
emissaries   and marked the sly deceptive turn of Fate.
Thither to him the city's heralds came.
One, the most skilled in eloquence, spoke forth
and thus addressed him: "Pride of Africa,   510
sole bulwark of your country and the world's
last hope, take pity on your fatherland,
afflicted by harsh Fate with dire torment;
mark how the sisters with their hostile glance
promise our ruin. Already would our walls
be clothed in flame, had not your fair renown,
though you were absent, shone as from afar
upon your fellow citizens. I fear
that even as across the vast expanse
of ocean we were borne to you the roofs   520
sheltering our fathers may have felt the torch.
For on the brink of imminent collapse
we left our city, shrouded in despair.
It is for you to save the state and prop
the shaken city that with trustful cry
invokes your name across the sea. Attend
her supplication and return or else
confess yourself the cause of our defeat.
Even now, if prescience fails me not, your brother,

returning to the coasts of Africa,   530
drives on his fleet. It will not serve. No band
of brothers nor your martial sire himself,
whose shade unvanquished now departed dwells
in the celestial spheres, could aught avail
in our untoward circumstance. The gods
know not a wrath so mild nor do the hands
of unforgiving Fate with thumb so tender
spin out our destiny. On you alone
depend the life, the weal, the fame, the hopes
of our afflicted country." And in tears   540
he clutched and clung to that unconquered hand.

His   While he heard out this querulous harangue
response   the chieftain wrung his hands and bit his lips
and writhed as does a serpent when a song
compels his will and magic incantation
forbids his flight; then he contorts his form
and twines and twists himself in knots the while
he hisses. And the captain struck his brow
repeatedly and raised his moistened eyes
to Heaven and with frequent, somber glance   550
looked toward his troops, companions one and all
in every venture. Sadly then he said:
"The destiny of Carthage and my line
I have long known; my brother's severed head   554
advised me of what jealous Fortune held
in store for me. And now I seem to see
before my eyes my city's sorry state,
her ill-starred ruins. O Carthage of my heart,
what man has brought us down and made as naught
our many triumphs over Latin blood?   560
Ah, but of hidden foemen too we have
been long aware. For has not our recall
been sought as often as the payments due
our soldiers or new levies to refill
our thinning ranks have been denied? Now hate
is patent and the purpose planned is clear.
They call me back. Perforce I must obey,

though most unwillingly. No foreign foe
confronts me here. Nay, Rome, it is not you,
so often at my mercy, nor this land,   570
with all its muster of Ausonian strength,
that brings me down. My fellow citizens
have triumphed. 'Tis their envy and their schemes
that drive me forth from Latium, and no power
of martial virtue. Mighty Scipio
may not count to my shame this flight of mine
which to perfidious Hanno may be charged   577
and to the senate, by his schemes beguiled.
That man to whom my house, my wealth, my fame
are odious could by no other means   580
destroy them than by mingling public woe
with my destruction. So with the collapse
of the sore-stricken state he lays me low,
involving all in one catastrophe.
Ah, foe of Carthage that he is and Rome's
avenger!" And so, rabid with excess
of grief, he raged as does the wounded bear
with bristling chest and muzzle dripping foam.

The   In Italy's remotest part the town
massacre   of Croton lies, once far renowned and now   590
of Croton   a wretched port bearing a noble name.
Here, sited to salute the morning light
of Phoebus, stood a temple consecrate
to Juno, rich in the embellishment
of precious pictures that with Grecian art
great Zeuxis had created to endure,
by all men cherished and revered. Here stood
the austere image of the goddess-queen
for which five lovely maidens, in the nude,
had served as models for his brush to yield   600
a distillation of the beautiful,
as if the painter, having failed to find
in one sole body all the graces sought,
had drawn from many the one perfect form.   605
Within this port for some time now had lain

concealed the Punic fleet, with everything
prepared for swift departure. For, well-schooled,
the leader of victorious hosts had marked
Fate's oscillations and 'gainst every chance
prepared himself. So with his hastening troops   610
hither he came, resentful of the world,
the deities immortal, and himself.
Not yet had his cruel heart, insatiate
for Latin blood, made its last sacrifice
to the infernal powers. O great throng
of miserable wretches, whither, say,
does Fortune lead you? When he sees that fear
spurs not their courage, that they all eschew
his gory camp and ships disposed to flight,
forthwith in wrath inhuman savagely   620
he burns the multitude of aged folk
and helpless children who in fear have sought
protection of the altar. He slays all:
the weak, the naked, the unarmed alike:
the sanctuary reeks of tepid blood
and cries of terror rise up to the roof.
Thus impiously he stains the sacred gates,
defiling Juno's image held in awe
even by Phoenicians, and the semblances
of other honored gods, and the vast hall   630
echoes with fearful moanings loud and deep.

Hannibal   Content with such libations to the spirits
leaves   that rule the sea, this scorner of the heavens,
Italy   this savage chief, this victor boards his bark,
casts loose the blood-stained cables and vacates
unwillingly the fair Italian shore.
In tearful silence from the open sea
he looks upon the fast-receding land
and moves his head with threatening mien, the while
still deeper grow the furrows on his brow,   640
then, darkly muttering, breaks into harsh speech:
"Ah Italy, ah Rome, thou haughty head
of all the world, what favoring Fortune, say,

wins thee this swift and unforeseen release
from my firm grasp? Say, god of gods supreme,
whoever you may be—my foe, for sure—
as my long labors end I ask you why
in one brief moment you undo my work.
Ah Jove, false champion of Ausonian kings,
say who has lent you power to cast down   650
my many glories in one single day?
If your ill will towards me has always been
so firm, why strove you not with me at Cannae?
Aye, would that in that press you had come forth
against me! Truly then the Thunderer
might with his bolt have strengthened his right hand,
and Vulcan, in our blood you might have dyed
the three-pronged weapon under Aetna forged
anew. His daughter might have brought her sire   *659*
her shield's protection, and the Gorgon head   660
of Pallas been his breastplate—and the gods
from every hand have come to take his side.
You, Mars, through battle clouds might well have driven
your chariot and, Phoebus, you thereto
might have discharged your quiver's mortal load,
and on that day might Hercules have thrust
his ponderous strength to fight beside his sire,
yet there our Fortune would have swept aside
Jove and his sky-born kin. O Bomilcar,   *669*
dear comrade, faithful counselor, say why   670
I spurned your rede on Cannae's fatal day!
Why did I not display such boldness—I,
long tried in war and hardship—as is shown
by conquering Scipio, a youth unschooled,
who dares, while Italy lies trembling
under death's shadow, to invest our walls?
I, though victorious, yet did hesitate
to break through conquered gates. Who was it, say,
that hindered me from leading from that field
my bloodstained army straightway on to Rome?   680
Who reft from me the feast I had prepared?
'Twas Jove himself, by treachery, not strength,

blinded our eyes to what the future held.
Had vision there been granted us to see
through Fortune's veil this time, then yet to come,
no god of heaven or earth or of the deep,
nor all mankind united, could have served
to turn aside our charge. Nay, 'twas our faith,
our own self-confidence that made for thee,
O Rome, a rampart. Nothing hadst thou saved   690
by arms or walls or guarded fortresses
had we not dallied. And with how much blood
the ocean waves and the Tyrrhenian tides
have since been stained! What multitudes of dead,
O Tiber, has thy ruddy current rolled
into the deep! How many chariots,
how many golden-armored senators
I've seen undone, how many rooftrees fall,
charred by vindictive flames, what myriads
of folk in one sole day of slaughter slain   700
while fear manned every tower at my approach!
What cries, what groanings, what laments I've heard,
as sweet as sweetest music to my ears!
No exercise of war do I regret:
I've seen proud cities' walls with arms arrayed,
I've forced great captains many a time to skulk
in hiding. Had I then, great Jupiter,
been sane, I should at once have recognized
in bolts and storms the tokens of your wrath.   709
Why should I call to mind the bloody streams   710
of Trebia and Ticinus at one time
warming their waters with a crimson flood,
from opposite hilltops springing, to be joined,
each after lengthy course, to testify
to my renown through all the centuries
as Po unites them, bearing both along
into the Adriatic? Need I here
recall the carp of Trasimenus, swollen
with blood of Italy? Enough, enough
we have achieved to win enduring fame.   720
Henceforth the annals of Ausonia

will bear with them the fearsome memory
of Hannibal, the name of Hannibal
unfading shall be writ on every scroll
that tells the tale of Latium. Fame supreme
awaited but a little further toil—
but Hanno, mighty leader of our state,
envies my honors and the guilty gods
grow jealous too."

               Thus sadly Hannibal
took leave at last of the Italian shore   730
in the fourth lustrum of his stay, and ne'er   *731*
with greater sorrow did a man desert   *732*
his fatherland or his most cherished friend
than he sailed homeward, for in truth he felt
himself an exile, summoned to return
by order of an alien, hostile folk.
So, laden with such heavy thoughts and full
of vain regrets, he drifted from the strand
and soon was lost to view. Bright Phoebus then
fulfilled his circle under Spanish seas,   740
and night and distance soon obscured the sight
of the abandoned coast. In troubled rest
the chief indulged his weary limbs. Meanwhile
the pilot charged with guidance of the fleet,
eyeing the faithful Bear, the well-known stars,
called up the mariners whose task it was
to man the helm and hold fast to the course
set by the loadstone and the iron and thus
in zealous care to pass the sleepless night.

The fleet   Leaving the coast ill-famed for squalls and storms   750
sails destructive of stout barks, they entered on
homeward the open sea. And Boreas by fair chance
filled out the sails and struck the canvases
with favoring breath. And soon from out the wave,
as stars waxed pale and fled the coming dawn,
fair day arose. Upon the starboard beam
the toe of Italy's extended boot
appeared. 'Tis there where clashing seas forbid   *758*

the juncture of the severed hills that Scylla,   *759*
avid for sailors' bones, and cruel Charybdis   *760*
inspire a double terror. Well aware
of lurking perils, straight they turn their prows
eastward and plough the seas to port. With peak
smoke-plumed and rising heavenward above
the sulphurous waters, Aetna looms close by,
crowning the land the Cyclopes of old
made fruitful, now become a fit abode
for savage tyrants. Syracuse draws near
with its famed coast line. Now they cleave the sea
whereon, long years ago, the Argive fleet,   *770*
urged by the Furies to wars far from home,
perished. The general, the while he stares
upon those walls that bear the still-fresh scars
of recent strife, is moved to thought, remembering
Marcellus, who, by storming them, achieved   *775*
a triumph, ere he was undone by foul
betrayal. Far away the cape of Pachnus
curves softly; passing it at length, impelled
by oar and breeze, the fleet sails onward as
sunshine and day depart, and, as Fate wills,   *780*
taking the shortest course, they cross the sea
by night, leaving Trinacria astern.
While Cynthia, lingering, through the dark shines forth   *783*
and lights the somber wave, amidships sits
the ever-vigilant leader, pondering
the dubious fray to come, the end obscure.

Hannibal's   One, standing near, broke in upon his thoughts:
plans   "O mighty leader, e'er by us beloved,
disclose, I pray you, what you purpose now;
I am one sent as an ambassador   *790*
from your homeland, from your own native town
that watches anxiously for your return.
Therefore deny me not. Will you at once
seek to join battle on the Punic fields
and draw forth our array, or will you first
by entering within your city's walls

bring hope and comfort to her citizens?
Or have you in your mind a better plan
for our salvation and security?
Say, what end, think you, have the Fates decreed   800
for our endeavors, what shall be our lot?"
He answered: "Nay, in such a swirl of chance,
what god can give sure counsel? Who can show
the better course? Homeward, since Hanno bids,
we turn once more. Perchance those cherished walls
again I'll enter ere I try my fate,
for I would first assess the people's mood,
their hopes, their state, their valor, how they stand.
But if the Roman youth should occupy
the middle ground, then is my purpose fixed   810
to try the battle's issue, well prepared,
whatever be the outcome, to accept
what God and Fortune give." And strongly moved,
he said no more.

          An ancient counselor,
standing close by, raised up his hoary locks
and eyes to Heaven above the boundless sea
The trials and thus intoned: "O gracious Jupiter,
of Car- and father Neptune, all ye deathless gods,
thage a suppliant invokes you. Spare, I pray,
recalled Libya from dreadful ruin and avert   820
all mischance. Lo, my lengthy span of years
has taught me much, but now my soul is filled
with fears and I grow timid 'neath the weight
of age. In what grave peril we stood once
when Roman columns cut their hostile path
through stricken Africa and dared assault
the ramparts of our glorious Carthage! Then
their captain was the noble Regulus,   *828*
on whom a doting Fortune lavishly
bestowed such favors that no shred of hope   830
remained to which the afflicted folk might cling.
What weak and tardy succor—Bágrada   *832*
may bear us witness—did we then receive

from our ally, the serpent. For the beast,   *834*
transfixed by Latin darts, fell to the earth
and perished 'neath a hail of javelins;
the sod of four full acres scarce sufficed
to cover that huge monster where it lay.
Yet did our Fortune, all but overthrown
by such adversity, send timely aid   *840*
from the far frontiers of the earth in our
distress, albeit undeserved, for Greece
from faithful Sparta sent a general.
Methinks I see again Xanthippus' face   *844*
with its grave dignity and measured thought
when, Hannibal, I look on you and hear
you speak. You then were but a newborn babe.
But why should I retell the tale? By craft
alone of that great chief 'twas granted us
to conquer our own conquerors. The camp,   *850*
the soldiery, the generals of Rome,
and all her panoply we swept aside
and bound their leader in a captive's chains.   *853*
Ah me, what would I say—what memories,
O Hannibal, does this dark ocean bring!
For it was here (unless the shade of night
deceives my vision) that a treacherous fleet
feigning to bear Xanthippus to his home   *858*
drowned him beneath the waves. I see him yet,
a weary swimmer in a vast expanse,   *860*
his arms more feeble with successive strokes.
Gods, what a vision! Wicked, ingrate souls—
what was their aim? For thus the fleet destroyed
the sole creator of its victory.
I filled the thwarts with oarsmen all in vain
and, sorely grieving, watched him fade from sight,
and therefrom drew sad presage for myself.
Of the ensuing, aye, and final ill
I hesitate to speak; yet it displayed
a vengeance fitting the immortal gods.   *870*

Xanthippus   A few years later that same impious fleet   *871*
avenged   encountered—not too far from where we sail—

the Latin ships; there I myself beheld
our massive slaughter, the wide sea aflame,
the boats in headlong flight, the living bodies
mingled with corpses and the waves suffused
with blood and ghastly flotsam, oars and sails
and halyards reft and barks a-foundering,
wounded and dead past counting and deep moans
mingled with ocean's roar and dreadful sound—   880
an awesome clamor such as might recall
the strife of Erebus and Tartarus.
No favor did the immortals grant to me
save, as the fury of the battle raged,
to see Xanthippus o'er the sea upraise
his eyes and mien and, as he called on Mars
unbridled, fire stout ships and spread abroad
consuming flames upon the ocean waves
and from the heavens rain down darts and brands.
Nor did he vanish till beneath the sea   890
the fleet had sunk there where Sardinia's coast
is severed by the main from Sicily.
So in the vengeance of Xanthippus died
our freedom. Now at last an end to wrath
and cruelty; let his soul rest assuaged;
for one fault let one terrible revenge
suffice. Nay, but I here recall old tales
suggested by this scene: the evil crime
and act of justice that this same expanse
of sea has witnessed." Turning from such plaints,   900
southward they sailed; Malta was left astern,
upreared in mid-horizon, while ahead
to starboard shone the shores of Lilybaeum,
whose harbor's depths give shelter to the tomb
of Phrygian Anchises. So between   *905*
the evocation of the deeds of old
and anxious thoughts for what yet lay ahead,
they passed the evening hours, and at last
their troubled brows were smoothed in restful sleep
until from eastern skies a morning breeze   910
sprang up renewed and with its gentle breath

filled out the canvas of the quivering sails.

*Laelius
brings the
Cartha-
ginian
embassy
to Rome*

Laelius, meanwhile, was hastening his return
together with his royal prisoner,
spurred on alike by zealousness to heed
his chief's revered command and by the thought
of fleeing enemies; he greatly feared
the last day of the war might supervene
during his absence. Rumor had spread wide
of hostile emissaries sent to sue   920
for peace and pardon. So, complying with
the Senate's order, Laelius made his way
homeward, even as a lovesick youth in haste
to seek the cherished portal of his flame,
if sire or mother summons him, turns back
with sad and heavy step, misdoubting lost
the long-awaited night allotted love.
The party, disembarked on Baia's shores,   *928*
was led by Fulvius to Rome, for him
Scipio had sent with them. As ancient use   930
prescribed, they might not make their way beyond
the city's gate. Beside the portal stands
Bellona's shrine and there the honored group
of Senators convene. They then admit
the foreign heralds, who, with false appeals
to the immortals, do but more inflame
the temper of the Senate. Having earned
the scourge of hate they yet presume to ask
the terms of peace their fathers had enjoyed.
The breach of public treaty they deny;   940
the root of ill is Hannibal alone,
they claim; all others are absolved of guilt.
Such words are ill-received; one Father speaks
in anger: "If you seek to claim the terms
of ancient peace, then let us hear again
what was the substance of that pact of old."
The plea of age, an empty tale in truth,
covers them all; nay, were their strength still firm
they'd not hark back to long-forgotten years.

So Punic fraud is clear; the Fathers, seeing   950
the words are spoken but to temporize,
dismiss the delegation from the temple.

Resolutions
of the
Senate Three resolutions were proposed, each one   953
with its own sponsor. One was to defer
reply until the consuls, who by chance
were absent, could be summoned to return
and thus assure the proper magistrates,
with Latin majesty, could act. This motion
Livius offered. Then Metellus rose   959
to move negotiations should be left   960
to him alone who was the best informed
on all details, the Roman general.
But harsher counsel, by Laevinus given
won the consent of all: to treat as spies
the foe's ambassadors within the walls
and cast them out forthwith. Wherefore in haste
the mission made return with no reply,
no peace achieved nor treaty. And with them
a guard was sent to the Ausonian shore
lest they might wander from their course to try   970
with Punic art some trick, as was their wont,
employing their hereditary guile.
Next, Fulvius and Laelius were dispatched
to carry to the general in his camp
his country's bidding, which was to press on
with his endeavor, follow his success,
his fortune and his gods, nor let false talk
of peace persuade him to relax his efforts
or dally in his conduct of the war.
Meanwhile the hope of plighted peace had made   980
the highways safe, and likewise o'er the deep
sailors and travelers fared unafraid.

Fate of
a Roman
fleet Thus warranted, a mighty Roman fleet,
laden with arms and men and ample stores
to feed the needy camp, set out from port,
cleaving in double file the ocean's waves.

Propitious Aquilo sped on its way   *987*
from Cálaris one section of the fleet;
the other, heavy laden, putting forth
from Lilybaeum, met with adverse winds.   990
The latter convoy, scattered by a storm,
were tossed among the combers and the reefs:
some ships sank 'neath the wave and some were driven
upon the hostile shore, secure from foemen
but fearing still the raging elements.
Their plight from Byrsa's summit was perceived
by that perfidious and wily race;
whence straightway rose a tumult in the town
and all sped to the forum. There a few,
who honored truth and faith above gross gain   1000
and prized them more than plunder, with their pleas
and prayers implored the multitude to bear
in mind the truce besought in Italy.
But others, burning with dark hate and blind
desire of booty, all incontinent,
brandished their arms. So in the wonted way
the wiser counsel, silenced by the clamor,
goes all unheeded by the mob. With zeal
they man the ships. Gisgonian Hasdrubal
is chosen captain for the wicked raid.   1010
He issues from the port and seeks the ships
that drift abandoned by their crews. Of these
the ocean has borne some away and some
engulfed; but more the savage pirates reach
and seize. The admiral Octavius,
caught in the tempest's center, makes his way
with thirty ships, propelled by wind and wave
and his exhausted oarsmen, and at last
finds shelter in a cave 'neath Phoebus' Mount.

Scipio's   Stunned by the sight of such a monstrous crime
protest   (though Fortune lent him heart and valor such   102C
                as to make light of labor), Scipio
at once dispatches to the treacherous town
three heralds of high station to present

his righteous complaints. An angry crowd
presses around them and a vicious hail
of stones flies through the air. The ugly mob,
intent on violence, cries out; had not
the highest magistrate there intervened
with his authority, the very laws   1030
that rule all mankind would have been that day
defiled by foul and bestial slaughter. So,
beset by enemies and aided by
a small escort, the envoys reach the shore
and seek their ship. And as she stood to leave
secure and as the crew caught sight of camp,
lo, from an ambush, hidden by the coast,
three galleys rush and battle soon is joined
between two foes unfairly matched. Descending
from their encampment to the nearest beach   1040
the Roman columns gather, giving voice
and burning to assist by arms as well
their comrades, but the water bars their way.
Yet heartened by the sight of Roman standards,
the hard-pressed few, their store of missiles spent,
turn their ships' prows about and with swift oars
flee the unequal fight and seek the shore
and safety. Urged on with a mighty zeal,
the ship is shattered on a rock and wrecked
but disembarks its passengers and so   1050
frustrates the avid speed of the pursuit.
Thus, when a wolf has found a straying lamb,
he makes his leap with fangs made sharp by rage
and hunger, but if then his trembling prey
by flight evades his jaws, he presses on,
biting the air and snapping at the breeze
until, all unaware, he comes upon
the fold; then straightway he withdraws in fear
of the strange place, the barking of the dogs,
and the stout shepherd, seated on a knoll.   1060

   So the Phoenicians; Laelius, meanwhile,
dispatched from Rome, led back the band of heralds

*Scipio
again re-
ceives the
Cartha-
ginian
envoys*
who bore the city's harsh, unsparing terms,
and to their terror, bade them all appear
within the Latin camp. Here Scipio
received them. Nor had their offensive acts,
though twice repeated and with triple hurt,
cast kindness from his heart, and he addressed
the embassy benignly: "Though you first
have sought to hold our treaties in contempt,   1070
scorning the oaths sworn to the gods and all
that justice claims, yet you will not receive
from us the payment due your perfidy.
A day of reckoning for your crimes will come;
I shall but follow my accustomed use
in dealing with you, staining in no way
the honor of my race. I'll not adopt
your fashion of good faith. Wherefore depart
in safety. Better will you fare among
Romans in armor in a time of war   1080
than we have fared among your countrymen
garbed as civilians and in time of peace."   *1082*
    Then, puissant in courage and in strength,
he rallied his command. The troubled state
of Libya was a threat. Both chieftains, called   *1085*
from Italy, were even now in passage
across the sea, each following his own course,
and rumor said that the fraternal hosts
would on two sectors of their native shore
at one time disembark.

*Mago
sails for
home*
                            Now Mago, sailing   1090
ill-omened from the port of Genoa,
trusted his wounded body to the vast
expanse of ocean, yet within him planned,
should Fortune so much grant, a swift return.
Up from the sea the hills of cedars rise—   *1095*
in green luxuriant growth this coastline yields
to none—and on the beach the scattered groves
of palms grow verdant. On one side Delphinus
lies hidden in a sunlit grove that, walled

by mountains, ever turns aside the fierce
blasts from the south; its unvexed harbor lies
in dreaming peace. And on the other side
Siestrum with its winding slope extends.   *1103*
'Tis here they look upon the vineyards bathed
in warm sunbeams, by Bacchus held most dear.
Beyond arise steep Monte Rosso's crest
and the Cornelian peaks, famed far and wide
for honeyed wines; to these might well defer—
and without shame—the storied Meroë   *1109*
and the Falernian hills. Whether through dearth   *1110*
of talent or because as yet it lay
The   unknown to poets, that fair land had owned
unsung   no sacred song. To me therefore it falls
Riviera   to hymn its beauty. As they plough the deep,
shoreward appear the island and the port   *1115*
once dear to Venus, and behind is seen
sturdy Ausonian Eryx with its name   *1117*
borrowed from Sicily. Pallas, men say,
would linger in those lofty olive groves,
forgetful of the Athens of her heart.   *1120*
Then rises the Corvinian cape; the sea   *1121*
swells round about it, flashing white with foam,
and combers break upon the shallow shoals.
Amid them, as experienced mariners know,
a perilous reef protrudes its blackened crest,
but all around the cliffs are white and gleam,
seen from afar when Phoebus sheds his rays.
The coastline curves and Macra's mouth appears   *1128*
and towering Luni's battlements. Beyond,   *1129*
mark where the Arno flows serenely down   *1130*
to mingle with the deep. Upon that bank
fair Pisa can be seen. They point it out
and watch it pass and eye the Etrurian plain,
tiny Gorgona, Elba, looming large,
and stony-beached Capraria; to port
Igilium, rich in gleaming marble, fades   *1136*
behind; ahead to starboard comes in view
the peak that takes two names from its twin mines

of ore: one summit is called Plumbium,   *1139*
the other Argentaro. Not far off,   1140
under the sloping mountain lies the port   *1141*
of Hercules, the Talamonian mass.
There Umbro, yet more baneful than the sea   *1143*
to sailors, puts its slender current forth
in churning swirls. Right of their wind-swept course
tree-mantled Corsica is left behind;
on one side in the distance they discern
the wasted hills of gaunt Sardinia
and on the other golden Rome herself
and Tiber's channel to the storm-racked coast.   1150

The   And as the Punic youth thus fared upon   *1151*
death   mid-ocean, there the ever-waxing pain
of Mago   of his deep wound and the clear prescience
of bitter death, as if with fiery goads,
assailed his fever-stricken breast. Aware
that his last hour drew nigh, he voiced his grief:
"Ah, sorry ending to my life of glory!
How blind the soul to its true good and weal!
What mad, tempestuous force of folly moves
a man of mark to struggle to ascend   1160
vertiginous heights! The summit is exposed
to countless tempests, and ascent must end
in ruinous collapse. The lofty peak,
deluding hope of man, is hollow fame
daubed with the glittering tint of false delight.
Our lives are wasted in incessant toil
of no sure issue; only our last day,
to which we give no heed, is fixed and sure.
Alas for the injustice of man's lot:
the brutes in peace live out their tranquil lives;   1170
mankind alone is harried and harassed
and driven through laborious year on year
along the road to death. Nay, Death, thou art
the fairest thing we know; thou dost erase
our faults and dissipate our idle dreams,
quenching our lives. At last I can perceive

how long and fruitless have my labors been.
What countless toils I've faced that I might well
have put aside! Doomed though he be to die,
man still aspires to Heaven, but death reveals   1180
the worth of his endeavor. What served it me
to ravage Latium with fire and sword,
to breach the universal peace that ruled
throughout the world and spread a panic fear
in countless cities? What did it avail
to raise up golden palaces and gird
their walls with marble if I am at last
to die, ill-starred, upon the lonely sea?
Dear brother, what are you devising now,
all unaware of Fortune's plan and of   1190
my wretched lot?"

          And, as he spoke, his soul   *1191*
broke from the flesh and straightway mounted high
to Heaven, whence it surveyed the earthly plain
and Rome and Carthage with its citadel;
and in its passage Mago found a sad
contentment, that in life he might not see
the final ruin, the shame of mighty arms
once glorious, and the sorrow yet to fall
upon his land, his brother, and his race.

Book 7

Now savage Hannibal was pondering
the varied chances of the war to come;
and unaware of his dear brother's death,
he counted on his aid. In his mind's eye
he saw the fleet already drawing near
and that beloved face; he all but heard
the words they would exchange: his brother's trials
in Latin lands, the tale of his own deeds,
and plans for punishment in time's due course
of fellow citizens hostile to them—   10
and Hanno first of all. And every time   11
that mentally he sketched the battle lines,
with horsemen on the wings, he set his brother
in armor to lead forth the first assault.
Oft would his unchecked fancy fire anew
his ancient hope of empire o'er the world;
then would he portion to his cherished sib
a great estate; he should have Italy
and be called king. So with futilities,
ignorant of the truth, he filled his mind.   20
Even so the anxious mother bird in search
of forage for her young goes with a heart
a-tremble with protective love; and while
she plies her zealous wings upon the air,
perhaps already some sly shepherd lad
has stolen all her nestlings and her nest
and every dearest hope of progeny.

As Hannibal was following a course
hard by the coast of Africa, he bade
a sailor swiftly climb the mast and from   30
its top determine where the fleet might land,
and from the summit came his warning cry:
"I see the outlines of a tomb ahead,

142

thither our prow is driven by the wind."
Ired by this omen, Hannibal forthwith
cried: "Turn the helm about and trim the sail.
Change course: make for a happier mooring place."
So, guided by obedient mariners,
the fleet, evading the deceptive shoals,
with plying oars, to Leptis made its way.   *40*

Uncer-   Meanwhile what state of mind prevailed in Rome
tainties   or throughout Libya were hard to tell;
in Rome   conflicting tides of terror and of hope
filled hearts on either shore. When the exploits
of doughty Hannibal and his victories
came to men's minds, the vanquished hopes of Rome
took flight, but when their hearts recalled the face
of Scipio, his tried, triumphant youth,
his valor every risk had left intact,
then hope came back to Italy, and fear   *50*
once more rushed into every Punic soul.
Albeit the Republic had with joy
seen Hannibal and his brother driven forth
from Latin soil, yet knew she other cares   *54*
that gnawed her vitals. And the charge of sloth
was brought against her leaders, who had had
the strict charge of the Senate to prevent
at any cost the crossing of the foe
safely to Libya, and so assure
that neither land nor sea would offer him   *60*
safe passage. Now the twain, with little risk,
unhindered, had departed, so the threat
to Rome remained; it had but changed its site.
For now in their homeland all Punic strength
was gathered and dire ruin and dreadful doom
were imminent. Rome's final hour drew nigh.
As when a lengthy illness that has wracked   *67*
the stricken body suddenly subsides
and leaves no traces on the outer parts
joy fills the heart, but if the invalid   *70*
feels a congestion swelling in his breast

he shudders, fearing graver ills to come,
and waits his malady's return, suspecting
it may have struck the region of his heart;
even so, although the enemy was now
remote, yet fear was still unquenched; in truth
it had but changed its center and still warned
of like or worse misfortunes imminent.
And sharp too was the spur of fear provided
by Fabius, ever present in men's minds;   *80*
for he, deemed prescient of far-off events
and prophet of the future, a true seer,
had publicly at sundry times foretold
that should dire Hannibal go home at last
then would the city face most parlous times
and days of mourning: "Then shall fleeing kings
and timid generals and shepherd bands,
recruited from the pastures, no more form
the foeman's battle lines, but Hannibal,
whose countless victories already fill   *90*
the annals' scrolls, who has dispatched more sons
of Romulus to Orcus than still live
within the city's walls, will take the field,
flanked by a host of seasoned warriors;
beside him will his fearsome cohorts stand,
sharp-honed by winter, war, and rigorous fasts;
and many captains has he whose best skill
is slaying Roman generals. Their ranks
with naked swords will war with Scipio,
to whom of scant avail will be the fame   *100*
of his great name, his beauty, or his clan,
his fabled birth, his converse with the gods."
Such woes had Fabius foretold, and since
he spoke of them while he lay at death's door
they had the weight of last prophetic words
of patriarchal warning. Now recalled,
they filled the city, terrifying all.
And yet throughout the Latin land peace reigned,
by many long implored; Ausonia's face
once more serene did well dispose the folk,   *110*

now joyful, to be thankful to the gods.
For five full days the altars glowed with flame;
for five days were the temple doors adorned
with festooned laurels green and flowering wreaths.

Dire rumors had caused Hannibal to leave 115
Leptis and haste to Zama. Scipio
was spreading devastation far and wide;
full many a fertile field already burned,
fired by the Roman torch. The Punic chief
plans final fray but fears surprise assault. 120

Cartha- He sends well-chosen scouts forth to report
ginian where stands the enemy and what he plots,
scouts and how his camp is armed and how disposed.
in the Chance leads these rangers on an ill-starred path,
Roman and as they walk unwary the camp guard
camp surprises and detains them. They are led
before the leader. He bids his tribunes
to guide them 'round the camp and show to them
the style of arms, the faces of the men
and their deportment, and disclose to them 130
the numbers and the squads of horse and foot.
It is so done and without fear they move,
so warranted, freely among the tents.
They marvel at the rigid discipline
and order that the well-drilled troops maintain
and likewise at their calloused hands, their frames
well apt for toil, inured to heat and cold,
the scars that mark their bodies—all in front—
their proud sharp eyes, their faces that reveal
high courage, and their voices, wondrous deep. 140
When they had seen all things, then Scipio,
with mien untroubled and a gentle smile,
encouraged them yet more, enquiring:
"Say, soldiers, have you now observed enough
of our encampment and our readiness?
Should aught remain, in safety probe yet more
and carry to your leader full report."
In their amazement at such kindly words

addressed to them, they could but ask themselves
if he who spoke were mortal or divine.   150
Then to both men and chargers ample store
of nourishment was offered; escorts too
were given them to guide them on their way
and to provide safe conduct lest by chance
some wandering cohort might encounter them
and fall upon them, deeming them fair prey.

Hannibal   On that same day the Roman general
seeks   did so comport himself, it came about
parley   that Massinissa with his mighty train
with   of horse and foot, received by lusty cheers,   160
Scipio   entered the camp. And naught he had observed
gave haughty Hannibal more cause for care
than the high confidence the foe displayed,
full of great hopes and fearing not the war.
And since the Fates now threatened final ruin
and nearer drew the day whereon the veil
of his dark destiny would be removed,
he thought to test with speech the purpose held
by his opponent and influence him
by wily counsel, stirring in his breast   170
once more the hope of peace. Was he beguiled
by the rare sweetness of the Roman's manner,
or moved by fear of things to come, or worn
by long and tedious toil—or did he scheme
simply to weave with words a web of fraud,
resorting to his old deceitful ways?
Accordingly a herald is dispatched,
requesting parley, and the plea is granted.
Both generals by agreement leave their camps
and close to one another choose their posts   180
so they may come together. Not far off
stands Naraggara, cased in modest walls.
The hill is swiftly seized and fortified
by Scipio as the site most apt for safe
encampment. It provides fresh streams of water
and ample provender for man and beast.

A scant four miles away the rival chief
secures the heights; there no spring gushes forth
with sparkling spray to freshen fallow fields,
and thirst makes hazardous a long sojourn.   190
In sight of both sides then a hill is chosen
with summit clear to view that leaves no room
for ambush or for lurking treachery
as might a thicket or a woodland cave.
(For prudent Scipio has not forgotten   *195*
Marcellus and his colleague done to death.)
Hither with matching pace from either side
the armed battalions come in strict array,
and at a like point from the hill they halt.
Both leaders at one time divest themselves   200
of arms and then advance on noble steeds;
each has one chosen follower to serve
as witness, henchman, and interpreter.
So on the hill they meet, the most renowned
of heroes or of rulers that all time
had e'er brought forth or ever would conceive
under whatever sky. 'Twas such a sight
as if the Titans, drawn in battle line,
stood to renew their impious attack
upon the gods. Mark there great Jupiter   210
put down his fiery bolt and issue forth
with Mercury beside him; towards him strides
Typhoeus with his aide, an ill-shaped gnome,   *213*
while from afar the sons of earth observe   *214*
their meeting as the wrathful host of Heaven
in stillness watches from the other camp.
See Phoebus with his arrow at the notch
and Pallas brandishing her awesome aegis   *218*
in silent menace; all the earth is shaken
and flames flash through the fiery skies above.   220
Such awe and such anxiety possessed
all who looked on as the great chiefs drew near.
No names of earlier heroes, though far-famed,
shall pass my lips. Fortune will not deny
that she has never seen on any field

two greater chieftains than met on that day.

Their   Each eyed the other outwardly unmoved;
meeting   and a brief silence reigned as both in awe
felt mutual wonder swell in their high hearts.
Marking the cruel face and dire mien   230
of the blood-thirsty leader, Scipio thought:
"Here then before me, Jupiter, stands he
at whose appearance marshalled legions quake,
the terror of all Italy, the prop
and citadel of Carthage. Here he stands,
the conqueror of Spain, who, crossing Gaul,
subdued the Alps impassable to man
and in the teeth of Nature cut a path
through snow-capped peaks. So many has he crushed
of our battalions, slain so many chiefs,   240
and stained so many rivers with our blood!
'Twas he who, with the battle lines drawn up   242
in open field, could overwhelm my sire,
aye, and my youthful self. Nor did our swords
nor any fear of us cause him to quit
our tremulous sill; it was the grace benign
of the Immortals and the storm they stirred,   247
propitious for our city. And I blush
to think we owe our safety not to strength
of arms nor any valor shown by us   250
but to a saving tempest and its blasts."

Thus pondered Scipio. And Hannibal
within him wondered: "So then, this is he
whose fame at such an early age is spread
through the far reaches of the globe, whose birth
the credulous world attributes to the gods;
aye, and his virtue justifies the thought.
This then is he who, with his father's blood
still sodden, unafraid, returns again
to that same field so boldly to avenge   260
the slaughter that he raises from defeat
the vanquished and drives me a fugitive—

after so many battles—forth from Spain
and renders vain my every enterprise.
This man, when others contemplated flight,   *265*
changed their resolve. Alone he steadfast stood
while all around him men were seized with fear.
This man, whose fields no army dared defend,
now mocks our citadel. With eloquence
he turned away from us the king on whom   *270*
we'd set our highest hopes and then in war
o'erwhelmed him, binding him in captive chains.
Me too, ere yet he saw me, he cast down
and now has driven me out of Italy.
What more to say? I vow, in very truth,
I must fear him or no man in the world."
Such thoughts they harbor as their glances meet.

Hannibal
speaks

Then Hannibal spoke first: "If destiny   *278*
had cursed me with a star malevolent
so that, after so many battles won,   *280*
so many hosts destroyed, so many men
in combat slain, I must now come alone,
unarmed, to sue for peace; had fickle Fate
made you the victor, I the suppliant,
I would rejoice that she had saved for you,
above all men, such glory, choosing you
to vanquish me; a worthy conqueror
yielding to such a hero. And unless
my prescience fail me, never will you know   *290*
a greater victory than that Hannibal,
to whom so many triumphs over you
kind Fate dispensed, to whom the Roman chiefs,
so often vanquished in repeated wars,
all yielded, now to you alone himself
must yield, subjected not by force of arms
but merely by the virtue of your name.
Shall I feel pique or wonder at the jest
of Fortune that permits the son to end
the train of wars I opened with his sire?   *300*
For he, in all the fullness of his years,

a conqueror, a leader skilled in war,
yet bowed to me, a youth, and was brought down   *303*
in his own Latin land. Conversely now,
you in the flower of youth will vanquish me,
a general who has ever borne in war
triumphant ensigns, valor past reproach,
and a stout frame by hardship steeled. And this
in my own land, without a wounding thrust.
Most dearly is peace cherished, I avow,   *310*
by nations that have never known defeat.
Not Sicily nor wild Sardinia's heath
nor all Hispania's plains are recompense
for the great fleets and swollen armies lost
and all the blood poured forth to no avail.
How easy is it in repining words
to fault past actions which must still remain
beyond our power to change! The lust of greed
led us in folly on our evil path.
A-hungering for alien lands, I'm now   *320*
imprisoned in my own. Excessive hope
and a proud heart intolerant of my peers
deluded me. And Fortune smiled a while,
but then the traitress, with malicious mien,
fell raging on me when the stakes were high.
Aye, with her various turns (unless it be
she still deceives me) she has taught me well:
he is not wise who puts his trust in her.
Wherefore the love of peace, guiding my acts
with stronger reason, has persuaded me.   *330*
But your age, more impulsive, and your long
propitious fortune give me grave concern;
for both are foes to peace and calm accord.
I well remember my own ardent youth
and what I was at Trebia—pray allow   *335*
me to recall those days—and Cannae too,
and I suspect you are as I was then.
Your youth in flower and the bright revenge
of an illustrious sire, auspicious wars
in Spain and Africa, and Fortune fair   *340*

and never faithless to your cherished aims
have all uplifted you. I've marked it well,
and well I know by proof how passion swells
for conquest and how sweet is victory,
the dearest of delights—if it is sure.
But say, what god in whom you can place trust
has promised it to you? Nay, give me heed:
if we twain put no check upon our wrath,
then flesh and steel and hearts and arms of men
will clash in ranks opposing, face to face.   350
And further, he whom you now look upon
unarmed will be another man, with heart
and mind quite changed, nor shall he use this tone
of voice nor utter words proposing peace.
Therefore change your resolve and do not scorn
to speak of peace. You may with truth affirm
that victory is sweet—ah, but the hope
of victory is allied to anxious care.
'Tis peace that is the fairest thing of all,
towards which, if you reject it not, a way   360
lies open and secure. Consider well
all things, and when prosperity exalts
your state, then vigilantly scrutinize
both past events and what is yet to come.
Ponder not only what a favoring Fate
has given and may give, but probe as well
with mind attentive what the whim of Chance
may yet impose. No reckoning is sure
save when, as hope approaches, caution too
be noted in her train. Aye, victory   370
may be your captive, but what increment
falls thereby to your glory? One more triumph
after a thousand: But should Fortune here,
so long benevolent, abandon you
then would you perish and your thousand toils
be rendered nil and your fair hopes would die.
Your counselor and enemy are one:
let hate be stilled; together let us make
a resolution useful to us both.

And if no danger threatens, let your care   380
for a great reputation give you pause.
Higher it cannot mount, now hold it fast.
To guard a lofty name is no small task;   *383*
would you put to the hazard of one day
so many shining deeds and honors won
o'er such a span of time? Say, shall one day
undo so many years? To curb one's fortune
and end the course while she is yet your friend—
this is true wisdom. Curbing Fortune's course
takes nothing from the sum of your exploits.   390
Nay, rather, if you let the reins grow slack
you tumble headlong in the dust. I might
elaborate my counsel, for a rich
abundance of examples comes to mind.

The re-   How great was Cyrus! Yet in blind pursuit   *395*
versals of   of Fortune past all bounds he came to grief
Fortune   and fell ignobly from a lofty throne;
the crowning ignominy of his end
was that he perished by a woman's hand.
Pyrrhus likewise waged most successful wars   *400*
and stood to earn great praise had he returned
victorious to his realm; might too have kept
Rome's friendship, for his kindly soul, I think
made him well worthy of such honor. But
when he no longer could control the reins
and hold his course, to utter ruin he fell.
Had he but followed on the middle path
he might have spread abroad through all the years
the glory of Epirus. And recall
how once he terrified all Italy;   410
crowned in Trinacria, famous in the north,
he seized the throne of Macedonia.
But ignorant of when and how to halt,
this hero, this great monarch of renown,
by men unvanquished, perished 'neath the stones
cast by a mob of Argive womenfolk.
A Roman case may move you even more:
here in this very land fair Fortune made

your Regulus the peer of great commanders; 419
but when he strove to mount up to the stars, 420
down fell he headlong and with bitter end
concluded all the glory he had won.

"I tell the tale of others and would fain
omit my own. Such as I am and was,
the victim of ambivalent Fortune, you
behold. You will not find in all the world
one who more visibly exemplifies
the plaything of flirtatious fickle Fate.
Discreet withdrawal from her fond embrace
is prudent; trust not in her blandishments. 430
Will you put faith in her who ne'er is still
but with incessant whirling ever spins
her faithless wheel? Sightless herself, she blinds
all those whom she embraces, raising none
with treacherous honors up except for those
whom she intends to hurl to utter ruin
from highest elevation. You are moved
perhaps, remembering the broken truce,
to mistrust Punic faith. Put down that fear.
The hour of peace has come. And you, 'tis said— 440
unless the tale be false—did once despise
a pact contracted in our grandsires' time 442
as being sponsored by unworthy hands.
Think you, if Fate has so maliciously
brought us to earth, that we have also lost
respect for honor? Nay, the gods do not
with such ill-omened eyes look down on us.
I will confess that not to every man
would I subject without a second thought
the public weal and welfare of my state. 450
But we who come to speak of peace today
are men whose charge will be to bear the trials
of battle or assure a tranquil peace.
I grant that I, proposer of the war
until the Fates forbade it, strove amain
to win it. By that very token know

that I shall likewise keep an armistice
or terms of truce decreed at my behest.
Needful is peace although inglorious
to us; for you it is a thing of splendor.   460
Well may the victor set the terms and price;
yet suffer me with my voice to inflict
upon the guilty such a penalty
as our offense deserves. Hesperia
be yours and all the regions of the earth
most far remote, Aeolia's triple realm,
Sardinia and all islands that are found   *467*
in the Tyrrhenian or the Libyan seas.
Possessing these, to wider conquests go;
approach the distant poles; with flashing sword   470
cut through uncharted lands, crush haughty kings,
so may your ever-conquering ensigns move
into the north and west and gird the east.
We, in our Libyan boundaries confined,
shall see you masters of all things and ruling
empires far-flung and held in reverence   *476*
on land and sea, for so the gods have willed
and Fate all-powerful."

                 In solemn tones
he spoke, and when he ended his discourse

Scipio   thus Scipio in his turn made reply: 480
replies   "Full sure I was that any promises
given to me would by your coming be
at once reversed, for Carthaginians
would hardly wish to honor any truce
nor law of nations nor a sacred bond
under the gods, unless constrained by fear.
Nay, sooner this stout steed would wing his way
up to the stars, this sturdy charger rise
to upper air, and Heaven come crashing down
into Avernus than true faith would be   490
your comrade. But just vengeance of the gods
pursues the guilty and an impious race
must feel its scourge; though Justice seems to limp

yet she o'ertakes the culprit in his flight.
God from on high has long remarked your crimes
and perfidy—though, Hannibal, to you
God's very being is an idiot's tale.
How often have the ocean's waves befouled,
by charred and bloody flotsam of lost fleets,
pounded encrimsoned shores! What dreadful count   500
of fighting men, all slain and scattered far
upon the main, what galleons destroyed
in shock of combat, what unnumbered keels
forever vanished 'neath the stormy brine!
Aye, and the votive shields, the temple doors
polluted with dark gore! And you would still
deny there is a god? So little time
has canceled from your heart the memory
of the Aegadian islands? Twice ere now   509
against us you have borne felonious arms,   510
under which provocation we were forced
twice to engage you, moved by just concern
for loyal allies. First 'twas Sicily
that good faith bound us to assist, and then
Spain summoned us where your immoderate
fierceness had blazed and wrought horrendous ruin—
a hard and shameful thing to think upon,
for there to the imperiled folk Rome's help
came tardily; henceforth Saguntum's name   519
must signify a time of infamy.   520
But God, the very God you mock, decrees
for your aggression apt reprisal. Well
you know the issue of the former war
attests as much, and so 'twill be with this
that we wage now, unless it be that God
weary of dealing justice. If since then
we suffered hurts (too many, I confess),
it may be that the Great Avenger chooses
to test and purge his faithful. Of what's past
I'll say no more. Now if it be your care   530
that peace harm not your fellow citizens,
it is my purpose that they shall not reap

fair fruit from foul deceit. To you it seems
small matter to have broken terms of truce
and shattered hope of peace; behold, again
you seek for both, and on indulgent terms.
You, whom your earlier perjury reveals
unworthy of such treatment. Well I know
you have no sense of shame. Now I, forsooth,
must learn of Fortune's wheel and how it spins,   540
how hazardous is lofty destiny!
Captains and kings I'm bidden to recall
dashed by that wheel from mighty eminence,
and I am glutted with such great examples!
Full well I know our flesh is doomed to die
and our souls live forever; I know too
the many torments that await wrongdoers
and the enduring grief for evil wrought.
The virtuous win glory here below
and in the heavens everlasting bliss.   550
Have you yet more, sage doctor, to dispense
to a receptive pupil? Pray, no threats:
I know the risks I face and I concede
you are a leader tried and puissant.
Knowing as much, the greater is my hope
of martial fame. Nor am I unaware
of mocking Fortune's sway o'er mortal things.
And yet there is no strength to vie with that
of God Supreme, whose practice is to lend
a helping hand to righteous warriors.   560
However, let us not draw out the day
in verbal dalliance. If our recent terms
still please you and if right amends are made
for the fresh outrage suffered by our fleet
and legates, why then, be it as you say.
And, that you may not think me ignorant
of what my promise means, let me make clear
I know this peace is a great boon to you.
How far your fate has turned against you, well
you may observe yourself. If, while the storms   570
of war thundered your fame through Italy,

you had, a milder enemy, proposed
a peace, then would it have been arrogance
excessive to refuse. But now, undone,
cast out of Italy, you are by fear
compelled to beg for peace; most rightfully
your suit could be denied. And yet, to show
that we are neither troubled by ill chance
nor by success exalted but, unchanged,
abide serene in every circumstance,   580
and that posterity may know our wars
were not occasioned by a thirst for plunder
nor moved by hate, but born of love of peace,
if truly you seek peace then you shall have it.
But why these empty offers? Well you know
by my own hand and at a bloody price
Spain fell to us. The other lands you see
are all our conquests; your pretentious boast
of giving us what you have failed to hold
is sheerest nonsense. You'd be generous   590
with what is ours. If you have anything
to add to former pacts of peace we've made,
then give it freely. If these terms appear
too harsh to you, disdainer of true peace,
unfit to wear the toga, then prepare
your harness and your weapons to wage war."

    So Scipio ended and with quivering spear
pierced the brown earth. The parley ended thus,
each chieftain having spoken. Even as when
two bulls, after long combat with locked horns,   600
their spirits charged with wicked rage and lust
of battle, will draw soundlessly apart
in order to renew their ponderous charge
with greater force; then, bellowing, will fill
with bestial roarings all the grove around,
while heifers watch and stir each combatant
to fresh onslaught—like passion could be seen
glow in the glances of both generals
as they returned, and in the inflamed breast

of each of them like battle-ardor burned.   610

*Prepara-
tions for
battle*   When they rejoined their armies standing near
they gave the order to prepare all hearts
and arms for war again, and to the skies
rose up the eager clamor. You might there
have seen the sparks of wrath and valor rise,
kindling the fires of war. Harsh threats were heard;
eyes blazed and faces flushed with martial rage.
It was as when a pair of husbandmen
agree in unison to set the torch
and fire the stubble of far-reaching fields: 620
lo, sudden blaze bursts forth with crackling
of brush on either hand. And, as each chief
returns to camp, a joyous chorus rises
like to the hum of bees that welcome back
the exultant monarch of the hive. A throng
swarms straightway round them, eager to observe
and seize each morsel of the news they bring.
One rumor makes the rounds of both the camps:
the final day draws near and on that day
the prizes and the penalties of war   630
will be far different from those they've known
in earlier frays when fields were lost or won.
The victor here will rule the earthly orb
through ages yet to come, the vanquished side
will be annihilated. Mad with fear
and faint of heart stands Carthage on the verge
of swift collapse. Though not yet stricken down,
she trembles helpless before total ruin
decreed by all the Fates inexorable.
The Romans have no open road to flight,   640
no friendly refuge, hemmed in as they are
by waters of the sea; to them is left
no scope for oarage save the open sky.
Terror spurs one side, hope incites the other;
and, in obedience to each chief's command,
a fearsome clamor of discordant sounds
all intermingled rises from both camps.

One man-at-arms looks to his javelin,   *648*
another whets his sword, while yet a third
makes sure his darts speed swiftly from the bow.   *650*
Mark there a horseman don his helm and smooth
its fluttering plumage; mark another check
his eager steed with murmured words the while
he clothes him with protective battle-dress.
Yonder another stoops to shoe his steed
with iron, hammering the piercèd hoof
'midst showers of sparks. One weights his graven shield
and fixes well upon his ample chest
and shoulders mail and light but sturdy plates;
another laces greaves upon his thighs   *660*
and with bright armor, gleaming as might gold,
encases knees and limbs, prepared for strife.   *662*

The court   Since now, O Muses, I must here approach,
of Heaven   albeit with meager gifts, a greater theme
               than aught before, your favor I invoke.
               If ever faithfully I've cherished you
               and courted you, if ever fittingly
               I have invoked you, pray inspire me now
               and nourish me on Helicon's sweet streams.
               Thirsting I roam Castalia's lonely ways,   *670*
               impelled by love of fame and hope of glory.
                  The day, in dreadful preparation spent
               by both encampments, fades and the bright stars,
               as night falls, shine from the high heavens above.
               Then through the ether comes a matron, rich   *675*
               in her attire, still in her prime and held
               in reverence. The towered crown is fixed
               upon her sacred head and in her hand
               she bears the sceptre, but her hair flows free
               as she moves onward with an anxious stride.   *680*
               Towards her another matron, somewhat older,
               with visage darkened by the noontime sun
               advances, dour and threatening of mien.
               Her robe is drawn about her; she too bears
               the sceptre and the awe-inspiring marks

of royalty, and in her heart she scorns
all mankind and the gods and Heaven's king.
Together they attain the midmost heights
where Scorpio holds fast within the clutch
of claw and tail the ruddy glowing star   690
of fearsome Mars. Both reach the gates of Heaven
at the same moment, moving with like speed.
At their approach the gods stand all amazed
and all the stars suspend their rapid course

Carthage   Before the highest throne the older dame
speaks   stands and speaks forth: "Outrageous wrong I bear:
Lo, I, decreed undying by the Fates
and long time hostess of the Queen of Gods,   698
must undergo assault by Italy.
Nor do the many wounds she bears avail me—   700
not even the thrust she took on Cannae's field,
a day to be remembered and a blow
I should have reckoned fatal, if the ways
of war could merit faith. Oh harsh decree
of the immortals, cruel to the just!
May Heaven hear my righteous lament
and heed my utterance of truthful words.
Nature, I grant, was generous to me,
but ye, O merciless immortals, show
me naught but envy. She in kindness gave   710
to me the fairest shore of the wide sea,
adding, as 'twere a gem, a pleasant port
with climate mild as from the western pole
Favonius wafts a soft and gentle breath,   714
commingling with Zephyr's sweeter air.
Before me, on the facing shore, I saw
the frigid ice and felt behind my back
the searing, all-consuming heat. I took
delight in my abode 'twixt two extremes,
a site most fortunate. Unless I err,   720
to one who looked upon it, it would seem
the glass of Paradise. And thereto add
the many noble sons, the many honors

propitious Mars bestowed, the countless feats
and the resounding glory of our chief—
it would not shame you, Mars, to call him brother.   726
Him, so the story runs, the jealous Fates
once stealthily bore off. What great designs
he undertook, how high he thought to raise
my name! alas, unhappy man, consumed   730
by such great filial love. But there are more,
and to say naught of others I may claim,
Praise of what a true hero is my youngest son!
Hannibal This I avow, ye gods, and may my words
be free of mordant envy: the high house
of Jove has ne'er produced a greater man.
What ardor in the breast of any mortal
has equaled his since first Prometheus brought
the spark of fire, from high Olympus reft,
to plant it in the depths of mortal hearts   740
and so illuminate mankind? What strength
of spirit he displays, what steadfastness!
How prompt to challenge perils! Truly, if
the burden of the flesh did not confine
his soul in durance of mortality,
he'd dwell among the gods and hold high place
upon a glittering throne. Since what I say
befits one man alone, there is no need
to cite his name; nay, by his mighty deeds
all men throughout the world know Hannibal.   750
The stars will stray from their appointed rounds
and summer snows will bury in their drifts
the Ethiopian hills and winter, warmed
by Boreas, will free the Riphean crags   754
of ice, ere fertile earth bring forth again
another like to him. It is not love
maternal that here speaks; 'tis but the truth.
Forgive me, all ye gods, but I do fear
lest envy and blind favor harm my son.
Look, Jupiter, upon the Latin lands;   760
mark you the fields of Italy bestrewn
with those who tilled them. See her rivers stained

with her own blood, while in lands far remote
her heroes lie in graves unmarked, unknown.
Throughout the whole vast realm my Hannibal
has wrought such havoc; mountains he has cleft
or joined with rocky avalanche. Some god
must press upon him now; what mortal lives
to take up arms against him? Lo, a boy   769
comes forward to confront our battle line—   770
and here is shame, ye gods! But not that boy
nor all Ausonia can affright me—no,
nor she, my fortune's foe, who stands here mute,
counting her joys in arrogant delight.
Her and the boy and thereto that boy's sire,
the scourge of all the earth, we overcame
in one affray. With like benevolence
no fairer fortune e'er embraced our cause.
Now, strengthened by so many triumphs, what
have I to fear, save for the gods? Do you   780
defend my honor, turn aside all ill.
Unless that child, who even to my heart
brings fear, be thwarted, I shall surely die."

Rome   When she had done, the other in her turn,
makes   with modest visage worthy to revere,
her plea advancing, put her crown and sceptre down
and prostrate fell before the Thunderer
and spoke: "O universal Power supreme,
if by your grace your Rome may flood with tears
your sacred feet and move you with just prayers,   790
O father of the gods and all mankind,
beneficent creator of all things,
succor your people, spare them, ease their burden.
How fierce this southern blast, how hot the flame
that swept Hesperia with its ruinous rage
is well known to the world and better known
in Heaven. Nor shall I deny the truths
outrageous and insulting hurled at me
by that virago. Italy's fair fields
are white with bones and far through alien lands   800

are scattered tombstones where our leaders lie.
And everything the rush of war can bring
upon a wretched world I have endured.
You, Father, from your lofty throne above
have suffered it to be. And I confess
my crimes deserve as much. But now regard,
I pray, more kindly the afflicted folk;
if I am not yet purged of my misdeeds,
then let your right arm deal the flashing bolt
and strike this hated head of mine and blast   810
Tarpeia's citadel. But from our walls
keep Hannibal! Already, it would seem,
you have recalled him and I have come here
to render thanks for such a gracious gift.
I feared, I do confess, the frenzied rage,
the snares, the treacheries and wily words
of that most odious leader. He, in truth,
whom here his impious dam would raise to Heaven
and in her folly likens to a god,
is wont in warfare to resort to fraud   820
and sly deceits, preferring them to valor.
To him I could ascribe the many deaths
of my brave sons—but grief estops me. Ah,
how dreadful is her savagery, how vast
the count of crimes on which she comes to gloat!
To have undone so many mighty chiefs
so wickedly! But now for sure has come
the hour of valor, unless the Fates would treat
with burning hate our flowering hero whom
she calls a boy. Avert this, Heavenly Father;   830
be pleased to grant an anguished mother's prayer:
an end to treachery. Let honest arms
be marshalled in array; in open field
let battle join. And if a mother's love
deceive me not, then shall you look upon
most wondrous clash of arms and countless wounds,
to rival Cannae's sad inglorious day.
I know him godlike, having no regard
to vulgar rumors of his birth divine,

but for the sharp perception of his mind   840
which pierces to the heart of human things.
Let Carthage with her shameless diatribe
seek to rouse envy, let her venerate
as gods her vandals. I am satisfied
with great-souled Scipio, that prince of men,
whose peer no age has seen nor ever shall.
I dare affirm that truly I believe
divine intelligence inspires his soul;
and further I maintain no mortal man
can rise to fame unless the Deity   850
deal with him kindly. Further I shall not
retard the stars. Take my son's part, I pray,
or as a just, impartial judge, forbid
all treachery. If there be none 'tis sure
that we shall triumph. Hear my rival vaunt
that Juno was her guest—a boast she trusts
will move the gods to favor her. She's mad
or else deluded. To conceal herself
beneath such cloudlike screens has been her way,
nor will she change. On my Tarpeian hill   860
stands the fair temple of the Thunderer
wherein we offer incense and our prayers—
prayers of true piety, I hope. There you   863
can teach us sacred rites and will, unless
the voice of destiny that reached my ears
on Heaven's threshold spoke me false. So let
your hallowed breast receive this pleader's suit.
Immortal Sire of men, who art the sole
and highest hope of righteous hearts, I've heard
that all dominion over land and sea   870
and all that ocean girds beneath the sky's
wide canopy was promised to the race
of Latin blood. But who save Thee alone
can give assurance of such majesty?
Nor do I seek a kingdom here; for those
who merit it, let freedom be assured;
I pray you only: save this head of mine
against this foe who hungers for my blood.

And if my prayer be worthy, even though
you spare not me, forgive my progeny   880
whom a new faith, mayhap, in years to come
will make more pleasing in your sight." With face
bedewed with tears, she ended her discourse
and clasped the immortal feet, to which she pressed
repeatedly her warm and suppliant lips.
The king of the star-crowned Olympian mount
smiled for a while in silence as he heard
the prophecy of ages yet remote.
Then, as he showed himself disposed to speech,
the awe-struck ether shook, the sky was stilled,   890
and over Earth and Chaos silence fell.

Jove's   "No mortal wit," he said, "avails to learn
verdict   what future years may bring: celestial laws
decree the secrecy of Heaven's plans.
What rumors you have heard of times to come
have reached your ears within the gates of Heaven;
beyond they may not spread, unless perchance
some ardent soul rise hither, purified
by fire and water; then some glimmering,
as through a narrow cranny, may shine forth.   900
So much, persuaded by great piety,
I may grant to such zeal. Enough of that.
Of all the deeds now done beneath the sun
but few in truth are those that please my eyes.
Virtue, a stranger on the earth, has found
a refuge here and makes complaint of men,
among whose myriads she can scarcely find
one to befriend her. Should your regal purple
persuade me, or your gold? Nay, mark these vast
and shining heavens! Say, what need have I   910
of eastern pearls? Another Orient
delights me with its radiant wheeling stars,
and here I joy in my attendant choirs.
How then should mortal bodies please our eyes,   *914*
or fragile limbs or forms that fade and flee
like shadows? Mine are things eternal, fair,

and splendorous for aye, undying treasures,
and glory of immutable empire.
Virtue alone, in short, of mortal things
delights me with her sheen, as does the pure   920
condition of the soul which I scorn not
to call my temple. But on earth below
I rarely find a welcome. Here attend
and learn your destiny. On every hand
through centuries to come expect great toil;
a common ruin awaits both your tribes.
Which party Fate condemns, which Victory
will smile upon is not to be foretold,
save that the side of justice may expect
my blessing, while the other will have cause   930
to tremble. Since the dawn of things I've given
to righteous men their merited rewards
and to the wicked dealt out many ills.
Today your offspring are your dearest care.

The   The time will come when each will let her son
destinies   wither in bitter exile, far from home,
of Scipio   nor even seek his ashes. Not renown
and   nor glory earned nor filial piety
Hannibal   nor deeds of valor will arouse your love;
               such is the place ambition occupies   940
               in mortal hearts. You do not love your sons—
               only the glory you hope they may bring you.
               Already I've said more than is my wont,
               but one grave matter justifies my speech,
               touching the empire of the world and where
               its capital shall stand. On this yet more
               and in more solemn tones must be set forth.

Jove will   Now hearken well. It is my fixed intent,   948
return to   since now the splendor of the earth is dimmed,
earth   once more among you to descend, assuming   950
               the shape and flesh and bondage which are man's;
               aye, and for love to suffer shameful death.
               And learn, O stubborn and ungrateful souls,
               that though you both alike share in my grace,
               yet shall the victor on the field today

win special blessing; she shall hold for aye
my empire and my sacred seat, for so
my high unshaken purpose has ordained.
Nor shall the time be long ere ye shall see
your hopes fulfilled; know ye that mortal men   960
shall witness the events I promise here
before ten gyres of Saturn's lingering course   *962*
have circled the wide earth. Already I   *963*
am captive to a Maid, whose tender breasts
seem now to soothe me with their flowing milk."
And as with utterance of these words he paused,
all Heaven's dwellers and the angel hosts,
heralds of peace, with zealous wings uprose
and sheltered him. And, marvelling, both queens
departed, each on her own path and each   970
with her uncertain hopes.

                              The eastern shore
The day   now brightened as the day of blood came dawning,
of battle   destined to see the final clash of arms.
Now the war trumpets sounded and the din
of reveille rang through the busy camp.
The generals in either host arose,
and never through the ages had there been
beneath the sky a day more glorious
for Rome, nor ever yet on any field
had armies with such well-paired leaders joined,   980
nor so well matched in strength, in art, in hate.
Their care was not so much for present things
as for the years that far beyond them reached,
for what the issue given by Fortune here
might signify for home and fatherland
and race and clan and progeny to come.
Scipio   Now on the open field great Scipio   *987*
marshals   marshals his forces in precise array:
his forces   with his Numidians Massinissa stands
on the right wing; he mounts a Spanish steed,   990
his crested helmet marks him out, his robes
of royal splendor flutter in the wind.

The Latian horsemen under Laelius—
with breastplate gleaming he bestrides a mount
Apulian, swift as bird in flight—stand firm
on the left flank. The youthful veterans
of Rome, all clamorous for combat, fill
the center. O'er the legions he commands,
with his great stature mighty Scipio towers,
splendid in gleaming purple, shining gold   1000
and bronze, more splendorous still for his great soul,
and most of all for his abundant hope,
surpassing all. Even so, when Phoebus beams,
his comrade stars his brightness cannot bear,
and gentle Lucifer's clear rays grow pale
and wan Cyllenius fades, while round about   *1006*
all other stars take flight nor dare to wait
the coming of the sun. Now Scipio
rouses their valor and their confidence
as he reviews his men, and sparks of fire   1010
blaze in his eyes and all who look on them
are dazzled. To the standard-bearers he
addresses words of cheer, then he harangues
the cavalry, and everywhere his speech
infuses courage into anxious hearts
and fires the timid and uneasy souls.
With exhortation and persuasive plea
he heartens all, reminding every troop
of past exploits and deeds of valor done
by them or by their tribe; he calls to mind   1020
the names and victories of their ancestors.
He praises some and some he gently chides:
with friendly goad he moves the sluggardly;
he shows how close is glory to be grasped,
how near the final fruits of war; likewise
he cautions against risk and warns of shame.
So with these varied counsels he inspires
courage in all. He hastes from group to group
with tireless zeal and of this crowning day
wastes not a moment. When at last he sees   1030
that all has been made ready and his men

are strong in courage, from his saddle set
upon a snow white charger full of fire,
the glorious hero speaks:

"If Jupiter   *1034*
were moved to show you all the fire that fills
my heart, then every one of you would blush
for the anxieties you may have felt
as to the outcome or the will of Fate,
which has sustained us through this testing time.
In all my life no vision has appeared   1040
so clear before me. I see victory
and glorious triumph. I can sense the clamor
of frightened foes, their wavering battle lines
and aimless movements. Courage too I see
and frightful carnage, swollen by disease
and bloodstained trails and piles of slaughtered men
strewn on their native fields. Their chief I see
cast down his arms and take to craven flight,
seeking a place to hide. Would all had heard
our talk of yesterday; well had they marked   1050
his weary, broken spirit. In no way
is he the Hannibal of old; his name
alone may yet strike terror. If 'tis he,
then now the once-resourceful leader quakes
at sight of long-familiar arms; he knows
new hands now wield them at the firm command
of a new general. Here meets he not
the consul all too rash of Cannae's field   *1058*
nor him whom the clear omen of the gods   *1059*
and all previsions of the future warned   1060
'gainst joining battle, had he reasoned right.
Nor is Sempronius come to take command   *1062*
over this host. With me shall dust nor heat   *1063*
nor blinding sun nor wind avail him aught;
nor shall he plot an ambush in the fog
on marshy fens nor yet mount his attack
upon a foe made weak by numbing cold
against which warm sweet oil protects his men.

With me he needs must bear the sharp-edged sword
against the breast, and pierce with hardened lance   1070
the foeman's flank and meet his answering thrust.
Such things he fears—how often in their fright
they've sued for peace, how often faithlessly
broken their pacts; contemptible in fear
and hateful in deceit! For this affray
offer in joy your hands and arms. Myself,
I shall be first to meet the odious foe.
Among them terror grows; they think of flight;
of this I am assured by all the gods,
the prescience of my heart, my hand so keen   1080
to bear my blade, and the invincible
and ardent zeal that rises in my breast.
Call to your memory the fields of Spain
so swiftly overrun, my youthful feats,
so many kings engaged, and Punic fields
laid waste by flames unquenchable. An age
now riper asks of me more virile deeds
and confidence in greater victories.
What yet remains for me is to destroy
this scourge of war, this Hannibal, the root   1090
of all our ills, and gain the glory born
of this high enterprise. Whatever signs
the gods gave to our fathers as they sailed
to the Aegadian isles, they give us now,
and even more. But loss of time for me
was ever torture, most especially
when great things are at stake. Terror, begone!
Our victory is certain; follow me!
Put down all doubts. Let him who would return
in happiness to home and yearns to see   1100
his land, his children, and the cherished face
of his beloved wife, know that the road
to Rome lies this way." So, appearing more
a victor than a man about to fight,
he ended his discourse. And with one voice
with joyous faces and with eager shouts
the troops applauded him not otherwise

than with their wonted clamor. They would march
behind him as if in his snow-white car
he were ascending the Capitoline.   1110

Hannibal's   Hannibal too, now that he sees the hour
array   approach, decisive for this time of trial,
turns from his elephants and mounts instead
a charger fleet; in aspect fierce and wild,
he seems like Polyphemus when he bursts   *1115*
from his Aeolian cave in frenzied rage,
or like a comet rushing in from space,
bearing sad omen to our universe.
He too draws up his lines. With mind to drive
the foe to panic by a monstrous show,   1120
he puts the elephants in front; upon
their backs are turrets placed; they look like hills
with wind-tossed crests or lofty citadels
on rocky summits set. This shield he spreads
across his entire army. As shock troops
behind them he deploys Ligurians
and Gauls, well reinforced by Moors
and Balearic levies. After these
he sets his African and Punic forces.
The third rank is composed of Bruttians,   *1130*
poor wretches, for the greater part constrained
to serve him. He envelopes the wide field
with two vast wings, containing in their sweep
the Roman columns. On his right he bids
his Carthaginians to confront the men
of Italy, and on the left he puts
the rebels of Numidia, all afire
to join in battle with their hated king.   *1138*

He exhorts   When his battalions are arrayed he too
his men   exhorts them, speaking now with his own voice,   1140
now through interpreters, since his array
includes mixed races of divergent tongues.
With zeal as eloquent as Scipio's
he strives to rouse his men; he plays at once

the parts of man-at-arms and general.
The first rank and the standard-bearers hear
his orders; he reviews the left and right
and rear; he mingles harsh and gentle words.
"If rightly I perceive my destiny
our victory is certain," he proclaims,   1150
"but victory alone will not suffice.
Once did we think to utterly destroy
a haughty foe and all the Roman race.
Now may your ancient valor live again,
remembering Trebia and Cannae's plain.
No man comes forth against us here whom you
have not defeated on a thousand fields
whereon your columns bathed in Roman blood.
No man stands there in all the hostile host
from whom you have not reft a sib or sire.   1160
Their very leader, hardened now by years,
and his own father, glory of his land,
feared these same swords and stained our battle flags
with blood and turned in flight—to meet our spears.
Nay, can it be that, far from fatherland,
he fights with better auspices than we
who stand before our citadel? The gods
will scarce be so unmindful of our dear
and cherished Carthage as to let our walls
suffer assault by those who could not stand   1170
and save the lofty ramparts of great Rome.
Their madness brings them hither. Mighty Fate
provides this spectacle for Punic eyes.
As once we filled our measures to the brim
with golden rings from bloody fingers hacked   *1175*
and joyously sent homeward the report
of our exploits, so now with equal joy
victorious Carthage shall see iron chains
circle the pale throat of the Latin chief
and Roman masses driven like herded kine   1180
through the fair city, garrulous Laelius too.
You'll see the weak and fickle king who left
our host—and whose proud yoke I call the gods

to witness, ye Numidians and Moors,
ye shall shake off today—take to his heels;
for Massinissa leads no loyal troops
but captive slaves. In hatred vie with them,
ye Gauls; go forth and meet the foe of old
with fresh-honed blades; let this field expiate
the wrath long nourished in another clime.   1190
Ligurians, whom I mark here in my train,
following my lot, whom toils on land or sea
have ne'er subdued, I bid you: now fall to.
I pledge you, if a merited reward
awaits the victor, no mere savage vale
nor zone penned in by craggy rocks shall be
your portion; but instead the teeming fields
and the rich meadowland of Italy,
while Rome, your terror and your torment, falls
into mute impotence. Ye of my host,   1200
so dear to me, my fellow citizens,
need no incitement. Here we must prevail.
Look on your fatherland quaking with fear
of the foe's torch and cursed javelin;
look on those long-familiar walls which gave
your childhood shelter, wherein you have borne
your dignities and wherein lie the tombs
and ashes of our fathers, with the praise
of their great worth cut in eternal stone.
In your arms, in your valor our dear land   1210
puts all her trust; defend her in this hour;
defend your wives and precious children; guard
your timid mothers and your grandsires gray
and venerable in years; be yours to keep
your forebears' sepulchres inviolate."

The
battle   Ere he had done, while yet a rush of words
is joined   stood to lend ardor to his eloquence,
lo, horns and bugles from the Roman camp
blared loudly and a mighty uproar rose
from out the foeman's ranks and swelled and filled   1220
the air of Heaven. Hearing the great noise,

the birds checked flight, the serried ranks were stunned,
and in their terror the war elephants   *1223*
turned madly, throwing their own battle lines
into confused dismay; the wings fell back.
Benighted mind of man, blind to the truth,
by your own schemes beguiled! The very beasts
which the prevision of a prudent chief
had carefully arrayed in the first line
to shield the host, there caused the opening shock,   1230
the first disaster. Such uproar it was
that broke off Hannibal in mid-harangue.
So might by chance a clap of thunder sound
and interrupt a singer, or so might
a lightning bolt flash from the riven sky.
Breaking the cadence of his vibrant voice,
he says no more but raises up his gaze
to the dark welkin. Neither does he flinch,
this fiery battle lord, so often tried
in countless turns of chance, whose arms so oft   1240
have known the ebb and flow of combat. Nay,
he marks the enemy as he comes on
and stirs his troops to courage, mocks their fears
and wavering hearts and turns his angry steps
ahead. As when a boar, beset by hounds,
turns bristling with his sharpened ears upraised
to meet the mad beasts and the hunters' spears,
and straightway hurls himself upon their thrust,
so Hannibal in fury rushes on,
invoking his famed sire's warlike name.   1250
Against him Massinissa stands, alert
and full of warlike valor. He perceives
the Carthaginian wings in full retreat
and pierces through the foeman's frightened ranks;
wherever the stampeding beasts give scope
he straightway charges. Trusting in his lead
comes Laelius, judging well the time and place;
pours through the mass of men-at-arms and slays
whoever stands, and harries those that flee.
And like a lion when it seeks out prey   1260

to feed its young and falls on trees and beasts,
great-hearted Scipio with flashing blade
drives deep into the Punic host. His men
all look on him with awe, and from on high
Jupiter marvels. Bright the hero's arms
gleam with their burnished gold; his purple cloak
casts radiance around him and the sun
is moved to wonder if the universe
now holds a splendor rivaling his own.
Then the true foemen clash, as blood-stained arms   1270
of Carthaginians and Romans meet.
A passionate fury, fierce and pitiless,
moves the two races and their generals.
Never in all the world was shock of arms
more violent, no battle in all time
fought with more bitterness. This war is waged
for no reward of lucre; here are men
who strive with their own blood to quench the flames
kindled by their own hate. But one desire,
one purpose, fires all legions: to assuage   1280
their righteous indignation, although death
may be the fee. The taunt of Roman pride
or Carthaginian perfidy is hurled
with every thrust. Invectives are exchanged
and biting taunts, and even as they're voiced
the throats that utter them are slashed and stilled.
The annual tribute, harsh and burdensome,   *1287*
imposed on the Phoenicians is recalled,
as is the massacre, perfidious
and cruel, on Saguntum visited—   1290
or any other insult frenzy spawns,
inflamed by ancient hatred, and dictates
to either combatant. The sum of all
outrages suffered, dreadful actions done
through years of strife, here blend in common wrath.
Sword strikes on sword and armored breasts collide,
and death to death is joined and wound to wound.
For them it is a pleasure to go down,
entwined in tangled entrails, 'midst the shades,

and there perturb the ghosts with wild outcries   1300
as warriors invade mute Erebus.
Ah, madness! How much better for each race
to bide in peace in its ancestral lands!
Alas, ambition will not have it so,
nor arrogance of unperceptive will,
nor that undying appetite for gain
which sears men's souls and goads them on to wars.

and   So clash the raging lines, nor does the thought
moves   of country most impel them; each believes
to its   that when he strikes a foe, 'tis his own hurt   1310
climax   that he avenges, or a fallen sire
             or brother slain. It is the hate of old
that makes so keen their spirits for the fray.
The leaders, goaded by the ready spur
of wrath more recent, urge on their commands
with high raised voice to conflict, showing them
where lie the fairest dangers and thereto
leading their charge. For truly fair it is,
when life is promised to the fatherland,
to picture death in honor on the field.   1320
The concentrated rage of passion joined
to clash of arms combines with dying groans
in dreadful harmony. A stream of blood
already deeply flows and floods the fields
with its polluted current; now it swells
to cover all the corpses of the dead
and bear them rolling in its furious train.
A mountain of slain men and chargers rises
so high as to create a barrier
between the armies. Surely, no such fright   1330
shook those Aegean mariners of old
when suddenly uprose a newborn isle
hard by Therasia (which a learned seer   *1333*
marked as a portent of the might of Rome
and Macedonian ruin) while in shock
the simple seamen clutched their swaying thwarts.
Meanwhile, dismayed by adverse turn of war,

the Carthaginian support of horse
slips from the field. The victors, pressing on,
hunt down the fugitives. The heaps of slain   1340
hinder the scattered Romans in the chase;
some, seeking a precarious foothold, climb
upon the summit; others, all dispersed,
strive to advance over the slippery ground.
On such a surface standard-bearers flounder
and squadron-leaders too; the aimless troops
might well have changed the battle's favoring tide
to swift disaster, in defeat defiling
the glory of the day, if Scipio,
ever resourceful, had not marked their plight   1350
and given orders to regroup. The men,
hearing the well-known trumpet call resound,
no longer stray but, as the signal bids,
obediently reform their ranks. The hosts
again join battle, in a second joust,
with vigor undiminished, even as when
tempestuous Auster musters all the clouds
spread through the sky, and for a little while
the fierceness of the storm is checked and stilled,
only to thunder and break forth anew   1360
and pelt the earth with mingled rain and hail.

Intrepid Scipio had thus withdrawn
from where the mountains of the slaughtered rose,
and with their forces and their standards ranged
in proper order, both the armies joined
again in battle on the level plain.
*The
stakes of
battle* I dare believe that with anxiety
God must have watched that contest 'neath grim Mars,
that mutual slaughter of two warlike breeds
unvanquished both, and pondered on the end   1370
of such horrendous and relentless strife.
For on that day, in truth, Fortune herself
on that one field of all this vast wide world
was weighing who should have the privilege
of rule supreme, which power should prevail,

which hold the sceptre of the universe.
For if by chance Fate's final verdict had
favored the Punic army, who could doubt
that godless Carthage, mistress of the globe,
would have enjoyed the ultimate command,   1380
and to this day the name of Rome would bear
no meaning? For the land of Italy,
corrupted by barbarian colonists,
would have beheld its ancient noble stock
suffer sad alteration in its blood,
and all the world would be called Africa.
For truly, if the unarmed Greece of old
could so impose her name, more easily
victorious Africa could do as much.
But merciful Puissance, Heaven-born,   1390
supports the just and endows Italy,
distressed through many long and anguished years,
with this great champion who courageously
takes up the burden of so fierce a war;
not only present perils he averts
but will prevail o'er trials yet to come.
With him her champion, Freedom has been saved
for his own age and through the future years.

Scipio's   Now in the heavens' mid-zone the kindly sun
charge   reined in his steeds and downward looked in awe   1400
on such untrammeled fury. Scipio,
unwearied and with limbs resistant still
'gainst toil and heat and wounds and burning blast
of wind-whipped sands, strove with his faithful troops
to risk the final tempest where a wedge
of foemen thickly clustered offered hope
of finding confrontation, face to face.
As when the streams of fire from Aetna's top
down-rushing sap the mountain's quaking flanks
and on their course hurl rocks and devastate   1410
the woodlands, while the sulphurous vale resounds
on every side, so with like impetus
and equal fierceness Scipio struck down

all who would stay him, crying as he ran
incessant exhortations: "Men of Rome,
I bid you conquer here or die. With me
attempt the final charge. Onward! The path
ahead leads us to Rome or else straightway
to Heaven." Shouting such commands, he charged
into the soldiery of Hannibal.   1420
The latter fearlessly sustained the shock
of his assault. Both leaders there exchanged
the thunderbolts of war; and eye to eye
stood Scipio and Hannibal in arms.
Mars from the heavenly heights cast down his glance
and marveled that the lowly earth could claim
two such great masters of the art of war.

Magnitude   I dare to hope that lying Greece henceforth
of the   will cease to vaunt the names of her old chiefs
conflict   or prattle of unwarlike Asian folk   1430
subdued and Ganges brought beneath her yoke.
Let Parthian kings be still, let Persians boast
no more of their mean phalanx, nor let Troy
dare to compete, nor all of Priam's house,
lauded so long by Greek and Roman bards,
nor any king with flowing, scented locks
and robed for combat in Assyrian silk.
In this affray no Indian army fights
with purple mantle over shoulders cast;
here is no mob of bowmen who discharge   1440
their futile arrows and then turn and run.
Here swords are wielded by the youth of Rome,
well-trained in war, made sturdy by the strength
of their own Italy; opposing them
the Punic columns stand, to whose might Spain
and, better, Latium can testify.
For have they not a thousand times and more
with sword and all the tools of war cut down
the dauntless and unconquered men of Rome?
Between these two the fighting is pursued   1450
with rivalry unmatched, with passion rare.

One host, to speak the truth, excels in strength,   *1452*
the other in its swift agility,
but one deep hatred spurs both armies on.
At length the Carthaginians, tiring, yield
a little, whereat Hannibal, enraged,
cries out: "The battle standard that you hold
I gave you, scoundrel, not to lead retreats.
Halt there—'twere better to abandon it
and leave its shreds and tatters with the foe.   1460
By all the gods, say, whither would you fly?
You follow the wrong road; turn back. 'Tis here
you'll find the enemy. Nay, is it thus
that you remember Carthage? Thus, you think,
you'll find your way back home? Nay, wretch, you err:
it is the path to exile and to prison."
So speaking, fearless, all alone he rushed
upon the foemen's ranks and so revived
his wavering troops, moved now by spur of shame
and love of their commander. Keener strife   1470
ensued; the massive slaughter was renewed.
Against the hostile phalanx Scipio
was first to charge and deal death all around:
"Shall I see treachery in such endless fray
snare Virtue? Nay, I think the gods will not
be so unmindful of our piety
of old. Forward, my lads, with steadfast heart
and sturdy hand. The fight is all but won."
So he addressed them, fearsome, with drawn sword.

The Car-   At last the enemy retired in fear,   1480
thaginians   slowly at first and then with quicker pace;
routed   respect for their great leader could not serve
to keep them longer in their ranks. And now,
back from their long pursuit of fugitives,   *1484*
came Massinissa and brave Laelius
to fall upon the weary enemy
surprised by this assault upon their rear.
So flight grew past control, beyond all check;
and naught availed to halt the Punic rout:

not love of fatherland or thought of honor 1490
nor Hannibal's great name nor frenzied pleas.
Seeing his army broken and dispersed
and all his men in frightened flight, he feels
Hannibal at last the clutch of panic. He too turns
a fugitive his swift steed to the rear and all in tears
leaves the lost field, and, cursing as he rides
all mankind and the gods, he makes his way
to nearby Hadrumetum, where he rests *1498*
behind the shelter of its friendly walls.
The Carthaginian Senate summons him, 1500
wherefore he quits the town. And when he comes
within the ramparts of his shaken city
he does not seek the forum nor the shrines
of public worship; rather does he choose
to slip off furtively to his own hearth
in black despair; there, in the darkling gloom
that shrouds its inmost part, he hides away.

Book 8

The sun, impatient to inform the folk   1
of the Antipodes of the events
he'd witnessed on the earth, urged on his steeds
and hastened to the ocean with all speed,
while Scipio, as yet not free from bonds
of lingering cares, could not but meditate
on the collapse of that ignoble race,
the time and place, the acts and the design
and every circumstance of that last hour,
calling to mind in silent reverie   10
the conflict's crucial stages. When at length
the slanting sunbeams and the twilight hour
persuaded the exhausted soldiery
to think of rest, he ordered a retreat
and granted to his well-deserving troops
a time of surcease and a night's repose.
Withal he deemed it wise to thrust at once
into the foeman's camp; himself he led   18
a stout detachment past the barriers,
unguarded now, of the Phoenician host.   20
They found vast booty: scattered all about
lay countless precious objects, for the foe,
driven to sudden flight, had justly weighed
what price to put on treasure and on life.
The raiding force lays hold with avid hands
on Carthaginian gold, long since amassed
in bloody forays over land and sea:
all that Hispania, under Libyan rape,
has yielded to barbarian avarice;
all that was stolen from Sardinian mines   30
and all the impious extortions reft
from shrines of Sicily; all tribute sent
from out the zones of scorching noonday sun,
and from the dusky Ethiopian clans;

the plundered riches of Numidian kings
and Moors and other tyrants through long years—
aye, and the tributary gold once paid
by lands of Italy—such blood-stained wealth
now greedy Africa regurgitates.
What are the fruits of so much plunder? Nay,   40
one thief despoils another. Cross the wide
and perilous seas, demolish citadels,
bring towers crashing down, and let the plow
make mockery of ancient walls—one foe
possesses in the end your booty reft
from all the world and thereto adds your spoils.

*The
victors
review
the
combat*
    At length, his host now wearied, Scipio
withdrew his standards and as evening fell
returned to camp. His orders were to keep
the captives and whatever prize might serve   50
for glorious and magnificent display;
all other booty was apportioned out.
Each had his share and so the savage breast
of every man-at-arms was satisfied.
Later, from Atlas' summit the fair star
of eve appeared and, scattered through the bright
expanse of heaven, points of light shone forth;
then on a grassy knoll the happy band
of victors lay them down to seek their rest.
Above, in highest place, sat Scipio;   60
beside him, on a verdant couch, the king.
Their bodies, worn by labor and the stress
of battle, craved repose. When they had supped   63
and satiated hunger's pressing pangs,
Laelius, most eloquent in pleasing speech,
began: "Having been granted by the Fates
the sight of such a glorious day, I vow
henceforth I'll follow gladly where they lead.
Nor shall I ever grieve that I was born,
since I was honored to live in your time,   70
O valorous leader of Hesperia,
to whom alone, and well, our common weal

has been entrusted. Of one fairest hope
I was defrauded, I confess: when I,
returning as the field was all but won,
observed how Massinissa smote the rear
while you charged hot upon their battle line,
I said within myself, now Hannibal
cannot elude us. I can only wonder
what guile, what path afforded him escape;   80
his flight amazes me. Of course, for them
these parts are more familiar, which, no doubt,
saved many of the enemy this day."
Then, interrupting, Massinissa spoke:
"This day, in truth, will rightly be acclaimed
by all posterity in years to come,
while yet the glory of Ausonia's fame
shall in men's memory live. But Laelius,
believe me, for I well know Hannibal,
his nature and his mind, I gravely doubt   90
that he will ever yield or be o'ercome
by arms or art. His single eye, methinks,   92
is worth a thousand; I have called him oft
the Argus of warfare, and none can fail
to recognize his genius and his skill.
For all that, this one day has overturned
his lifetime schemes and marred the tactics planned
against this crucial peril. I had thought
that I already had him in my clutch,
a prize for Rome, where he might share the cell   100
of odious Syphax; with attentive eye
I look about me—and he slips away
to safety by some path well known to him.
Those massive mounds of corpses, I am sure,
and those great lakes of blood would have increased
in bulk and flood had neighboring citadels
not offered shelter of their friendly walls
and darkened alleyways to fugitives."

    Then Scipio in his turn: "All I have seen
or heard of in my life, I will admit,   110

seems trivial when I think of Hannibal.
Yourselves have seen, dear friends, how skilled he was,
how ably he deployed his soldiery.   *113*
'Gainst me, in the first rank, he set himself,
opposing Carthaginian men-at-arms
to Latin levies, while Numidians,
rebellious, Massinissa, to your rule,
he set against you, mindful that those troops
were moved by fear and hatred of their king.
Mark where he shrewdly placed the Italians too,   *120*
well knowing they had been constrained to serve
with him. And in the van he put the beasts
of India and the Gaetulian herd,   *123*
deeming the sight of them would terrorize
the Roman army; such had been their shock
in countless past affrays. But Fortune, kind
to us, removed this fear; I was myself
concerned to find some tactics to avoid
their dangerous charge or to devise a plan
to blunt the impact of the beasts' assault.   *130*
I chose at last to leave the front ranks thinned
so that the elephants might easily
pass through the files and as they passed disperse
and with less fearsome progress make their way
with harmless fury. But, great Jupiter,
with what calm fortitude he stood unmoved
when he saw both wings shattered! Fearlessly
and often he revived his flagging troops
and thereby shook my confidence. I've heard
it was his boast that in the catalogue   140
of warriors renowned he would stand third
in all the world through all the centuries.
Great Alexander he would call the first,   *143*
and Pyrrhus after him, and then himself.
But for my part—and I shall not allow
malice or hate to overshadow truth—
the greatest of them all is Hannibal,
unless we would deem it a mightier thing
to put down Porus or Darius than   *149*

to have o'ercome so many of the best   150
of our own captains, or unless we count
the conquest of a weak barbarian folk
more notable than 'twas to decimate
a Roman battle line. So much for deeds
alone of mighty generals. Should I
compare their characters? I would not here
unveil the frailties of the king; let him
behind his shield of glory ever stand
renowned among the nations. But let's grant
our bitter enemy his well-earned lauds.   *160*
What hero was there ever readier
to take up battle, or in times of risk
more wary? Who more temperate in food
or drink—or even sleep? I must admire
a thing I've often heard. 'Tis said that once
a war of dubious augury was launched,
then Hannibal, incessantly alert
and planning in his heart some brilliant thrust,
would never once sit down to eat a meal.
Nor is it necessary to recall   170
his competence in arms, his skill supreme
in arts of war; how oft he made his bed
upon his shield or the uncovered earth;
recall his scorn of tinsel finery,
his love of fiery chargers. And how great
his strength to bear extremes of heat and cold,
and weary marches, hunger too and thirst!
Nay, but how much a soldier may inspire
his leader and the chief likewise his men!
First was he always to make the assault   180
upon the foe and last to leave the field.
Such matters we have all long known by proof.
If only in that breast a better nature
had placed a spark of truth and piety,   *184*
then I could wish he had been sired and born
under our Roman sky. I'll not hear praised   *186*
a leader governed by a blind excess   *187*
which all should shun and is the very death

of men who hold high office. Who can praise
banquets befouled by blood or corpses born   *190*
amid the feasting? Or the reckless dives
in heat of summer into ice-cold pools?   *192*
Who could admire barbarian indolence
and luxury and strange and new delights   *194*
of Persian style or purple garments woven
of clinging silk? Enough; by no such ways
did Hannibal display himself so strong
as to wreak havoc throughout Italy
in fifteen years of war." Such were his words.

Then Massinissa in a modest tone   200
briefly rejoined: "If you will pardon me,
O generous arbiter of your own deeds
and prompt admirer of competitors,
I'm bound to contradict your sentiments.
If you accept what has come down to us
concerning lives of famous men of old,
that conqueror of all the earthly orb,
great Alexander, when he had subdued
all nations, reached the East at last and there
ended his happy fortune and his life.   *210*
But Hannibal, as you have seen today
was overthrown in shorter space of time
and with much greater violence. The king
brought all of Asia underneath his yoke
and won all that he strove for, vanquishing
cities and chiefs and nations beyond count."   *216*

and main-   But Scipio replied: "Nay, I would say
tains his   he rather seems to me like to the wolf
argument   that has in safety ravaged a rich fold
yet dares not face the lion's angry gaze   220
that eyes him from afar. You know, great king,
how Alexander conquered every land
that he invaded, but he did not strip
their ancient glories from the Greeks. We know
with what great force he moved to subjugate
Asia and Arabs, poorly skilled in war,

and powerless Bactria, but, mark you, not
the northern lands where, since they were so near,
he might well have begun, nor Punic realms,
nor Italy, the head of all the world,   230
nor Spain, nor Gaul—all these he left untouched.
Omitting them, what conquests would you count
as worthy of high praise and eulogy?
Conceding that where'er he turned his steps
he was victorious, yet I would contrast
against his triumphs over eastern kings
and all the carnage wrought in India
the four great battles Hannibal has fought   *238*
'gainst mighty Latium. Shall I offer you
a true and famous witness o'er the years?   240
The other Alexander, who held rule   *241*
over Epirus (uncle to the Great
and no less bold in spirit), when they thought
to share the world, invaded Italy.
There did he meet his end, and when he saw
his body pierced by an Ausonian spear
and death drew near, he uttered these last words:
'What contrary destinies, alas, befall
my nephew and myself!' As 'twere in play
he has with scant resistance overcome   250
a womanish tribe; a more exacting Fate
has brought me, waging war against armed men,
to this last pass." With foemen such as these
has Hannibal fought fiercely through the years
and with what bravery you all know well.
As for the mighty king's enduring name,
fair Fortune, ever well-disposed to him,
his constant faithful comrade to the end,
even as she gilds his public glory, hides
from those who would probe most assiduously   260
all evidence that might disclose the truth.
One side of two-faced Fortune lies concealed:
how great the Macedonian might have been,
faced with adversity, we cannot say.
His early death, his too-brief years have won

this favor for him. Fortune grants no boon
more fair than to bring life and happiness
on one day to a common end. If you
but weigh the times allotted to both chiefs,
then surely you will see that Hannibal   270
spent more years vanquishing his enemies
than Alexander lived. At the same age
the great king died, say, who in the whole world
in his own time had conquered Hannibal?
Had he still young gone down among the shades
then, from a bright resplendent chariot,
he would have looked upon bleak Tartarus
nor needed any easy triumph won
over the Persian or Arabian hordes.
Conversely, had the great king spun his days   280
to reach his later years, what oracle
deserving credence could have guaranteed
that lengthened future? Would a propitious Fate
have blessed the old man as it did the youth?
Would loyalty, rare even in prosperous times,
have bided with him as his years increased?
Especially if, as he was often wont
to threaten, in old age, he had essayed
new wars in Italy and Africa?
     "Night counsels sleep now and I shall conclude: 290
having regard to what I have set forth,
Hannibal seems to me more great in war
and more illustrious than Alexander,
aye, and if Fortune cannot either give
or take away true fame, then on this day
he has won for himself more worthy honor
than did the other with his victories,
however much the Grecian scribblers
may make a great commotion of his name,
offering in evidence their empty screeds."   300

     So he concluded and his listeners
stood by attentively. One soldier spoke,
an older man and graver than the rest:

"There is no doubt that he whom you call great
must be the greatest. For no trivial things
arouse your admiration; you are not
one who would praise the merely commonplace.
Yet one thing I would ask: if Hannibal
calls himself third, what rank thinks he reserved
for valorous and famous Scipio?   310
And I'd know too where he would place himself
had he—the gods forbid—by turn of chance
led a victorious army from this field?"
    On this, sage Laelius remarked: "Should one,
ranking the stars of Heaven, put first
Lucifer, then Arcturus, then the chill
Boötes and the other lesser lights,
think you he'd be forgetful of the sun?
Not so; the sun stands by itself, alone,
whence comes his name. And I can well surmise   320
the answer given by that artful chief
had he, in yesterday's affray, borne off
the victor's prize: he would have called himself
superior to Macedonia's lord
and Pyrrhus and all other generals
that fame has glorified throughout the earth.
He scorned, mark you, to count himself as fourth,
nor deigned to mingle his bright light of day
with gleams of lesser stars." The rest approved
his verdict in their hearts; and by their nods   330
and murmurings made agreement manifest.
So in such colloquy the better part
of night passed by, and there was little sleep.

    Ere yet their words were done the evening star
had sunk into the wave and the full moon
had crossed mid-heaven. And then, finally,
bone-weary, each and all found resting spots
on the green slope, as when a swarm of bees
suffers assault beneath the open sky
and showers of slain pour downward to the earth,   340
then the survivors fleeing from pursuit

seek out a refuge where they crowd around
their king and hum and murmur their acclaim,
till finally their wearied bodies yield
to dewy sleep, and all is hushed and still.

Laelius
dispatched
to Rome
Scarce has day dawned anew when Laelius   *346*
once more is bidden to take ship and bear
the glorious tidings o'er the sea to Rome
and to the anxious Fathers. And he cleaves,
a most propitious herald, the salt waves,   350
and favoring Auster fills his widespread sails.

Panic in
Carthage
So with the Roman camp. But oh, what grief
and terror reigned in Carthage; what a weight
of anxious care for the affrighted senate!
The people, shaken by calamity
so swift and sudden, press around the halls
that house the senators, imploring aid
in these dire straits and asking remedies
to heal the sad state of their fatherland.
Dismayed, the troubled senators convene;   360
it is as when a ship upon the main
strikes on a hidden reef and, shuddering,
threatens to break apart, and through the night
the frightened pilots anxiously confer
in the bleak darkness, seeking to contrive
some desperate solution. All agree
on one first step, which is to ascertain
the mind and mood of Hannibal, to learn
if the stout heart of the great general,
tested and tried through many years of war,   370
has failed, confronting such a perilous pass,
or if his spirit still abides steadfast
in this dark hour and leaves hope yet alive.
On his part he, at first reluctant, yields
to the repeated pleas of senators
and folk alike. Wherefore in shame
and sad dejection he at length comes forth,
leaving his hiding place, in aspect like
a high-born spouse who through no fault of hers

has been defiled, and, conscious of disgrace,   380
utters no word and seeks to pass unseen
and fears her husband's presence and the sight
of faces of her kin. Even such he seems.
When in the forum, shaken with alarms,
he took his stance, a mighty multitude
straightway thronged round him, curious to see
the general whose name for many years
had reached their ears from far-flung battlefields
and wars in lands remote. And all the folk
together with the Fathers crowded 'round   390
and choked the crossroads with their pressing throngs.
Looking upon his fellow citizens,
he felt his bold and noble heart once more
within him swell. He bade the crowd be still
and then, with dolorous mien, addressed them thus:

Hannibal   "If I have lived a single day of life   396
in despair   beyond the measure fit and fair, I vow
the fault was mine. For some time I have sensed
(though without voicing it) that I have striven
against the foeman under hostile gods,   400
but Glory's smile and the blind lust for fame
impelled me on through all vicissitudes.
Let the same gods whom I have felt my foes
bear witness here: in every enterprise
my arms, my art, my hand were well employed,
nor was devotion to my lofty charge
ever deficient. Nay, it was the gods
that made my efforts vain. And now I stand
defeated utterly. No shred of hope
is left me. Wherefore sue as suppliants   410
for peace from Rome. This is my best advice."
And having said as much, he then withdrew
to his retreat and would no more come forth
to meet the light of day. There shame and grief
and anger joined with fear to rack his soul.
And when his widespread fame and lasting hate
of Rome had made his tarrying unsafe,

he planned a secret flight. In daylight hours
he made repeated visits to the forum
and mingled with the throng; at set of sun,   420
dispatching chests of treasure to the shore
conveniently close, he left the walls
as might a casual stroller. When at last
a stormy night enshrouded the heaven's vault,
he furtively embarked and spread his sails
and took his leave with many a parting curse
cast at the ill-starred and unhappy strand.

His   When, from afar, he sees from out the deep
flight   the shape of Italy emerge, he sighs,
remembering how his destiny was forged;   430
then he resolves once more to test the faith
of kings and his own sword, and to renew
fierce warfare and once more to waste the earth
with fresh and furious storms. The Syrian lands
and all the sea-towns of the Hellespont
were at that time in ferment. There for long
Antiochus had reigned. He held his seat   437
at Ephesus, the center of the strife.
His fleet patrolled the sea; his cavalry
ruled the wide plains, but for his enterprise   440
he lacked a leader to command his arms.
So Hannibal gives order that the prow   442
be thither pointed and the rudder turned
and canvas set to make the swiftest course.
Soon they pass Drepanum and, sailing on,
Panormus' well-known beach and curving bay;
then, Zephyr favoring, they glide between
Vulcan and Lipari and look with awe   448
at the black plumes of smoke, the fearsome flames
that rise from the twin peaks. Such sights they flee   450
and friendly currents speed them on their way.

Between Trinacria's fields and Italy
a bay extends, so placed that mariners
who view it from afar are oft deceived

until experience has rectified
their first opinion: one would deem the shores
are not divided but compose the coast
of one land only and the two peaks stand
close joined together, as indeed men say
they stood of old. And thither by design   *460*
or chance the helmsman of the Punic ship,
Pelorus, steered his bark. The wily chief,

Pelorus   fearful of treachery, trusting no man,
slain   had the unhappy pilot put to death,
though guiltless and deserving no such end.
The leader, when he learned of his mistake
regretted bitterly his savage act
and there on that Sicilian hillside gave
the body honored burial and raised
a tomb above it, with a monument   *470*
and altar. Now the mountain keeps and will
forever keep the memory of his name.
Free of these perilous straits, the impious bark
ploughed onward through the deep, and first ahead
is Cephalonia sighted, then the isle
Zacynthus, moderate in acreage.
To port a narrow passage could be won
if the Corinthian isthmus, a high sill
between two seas, would give way to the waves.
More justly than his predecessor here   *480*
the pilot might well fear the punishment
for faulty steering. So he turns the helm:
the strand of Methon comes in sight, where once   *483*
it chanced that Philip, Macedonia's king,
had lost an eye in battle. To the mind
of Hannibal the memory returns
of his own widowed brow, the loss, the pain,
and Methon seems that dark Italian marsh.
Keeping their distance from the rugged cliffs
that rise from the Achaean, they sail on   *490*
and skirt the point wherefrom a fertile coign
puts forth its precious vines. Here Knossos lies,   *492*
with beaches open to the eastern winds.

Hard by the countless islands studded o'er
the sacred sea he holds his steady course
and quickly comes to Ephesus. Once there,
by presentation of his bold designs
he stirs the fiery heart of the fierce king.
As when a cloud hard-driven by urgent winds
fills sundry zones of Heaven and, laying waste   500
the fields with hailstones, thunders far and wide
and flashes from afar and downward pours
its torrents, in such fashion to the east
was Italy's invader driven at last.
What tumult he brought forth, what carnage still
that savage chieftain vowed his sword to wreak
should Fortune favor him—for he feared naught
save to betray his pledge made to the gods—
I shall not tell; should I pursue that course
I should perforce abandon my true theme.   510
That task of honor I shall freely leave
to my successors' talents; they may treat
of eastern fortunes (fusing Libya
with Asia) and the exploits of two brothers.   *514*

Scipio   Scipio with his craft and Heaven's aid   *515*
moves on   now strives to bring about the final end
Carthage   of cursed Carthage; his intent is fixed
to follow whither Fortune leads nor waste
the time the Fates have granted. He commands
Octavius with his legions and his standard   520
of victory to march forthwith by land
up to the savage city's very walls.
Himself, he makes his way to Utica
where Lentulus, from Italy dispatched,
has come to anchorage with many ships.
There Scipio, uniting the two fleets,
the old and new, sets forth on ocean's path
towards Carthage, for he deemed the vanquished foe
might, as a last resort, turn to the sea—
if Fate permitted aught of their spent strength   530
and spirit to remain, if any hope

in arms, however scanty, still survived.
Already he stands close and nears the port
flanked by forbidding shores, and now the waves
about his ships, the caves and rock-faced cliffs
resound with the war clarion's strident blare;
the very air is shaken by the sound,
and past the walls, within the town is borne
the terror generated by the blast.
A ship bedecked with verdant olive fronds   540
and bearing suppliants draws near the fleet,
asking for peace and pardon. To such pleas
one stern response is given; they are told
they must turn back to shore and there await
the Roman general and his troops. Meanwhile,
close under the detested city's walls
he brings his ships and from close vantage scans
the lofty fortress. Marking the great towers
of solid marble soaring high above
the portals and the harbor's iron gates   550
with ramparts rimming all the range of wall,
he marvels, deeming that he looks upon
a second Rome. In truth the city stands
well-guarded by the sea's protective arms
that gird it round and further reinforced
by site and walls. Did not the narrow strand
behind thrust back at times the salty waves
'twould be an island. Far below, the wide
expanse of harbor lies serene and still.
The gates are well-secured with massive chains   560
and frequent towers stand along the shore.

  Surveying with a calculating eye
the task before him, Scipio weighs the risks
and marks his best approaches: where the land
is easiest to reach and by which way
the harbor may be entered, from what side
the hated citadel may best be stormed.
Even so the husbandman who would uproot
a rock or oak-stump harmful to his field

of grain goes circling around the spot, 570
considering how best he may proceed
in order to remove the obstacle
in such a fashion as to do no harm
to his fair field, his neighbor or himself.
   When he has filled with panic the whole city
and caused the sea to echo with his oars,
the skies above with all his trumpets' din,
the very air with rustling of his flags,
in manner menacing Scipio withdraws.
The hill of Mercury and Apollo's mount, 580
amazed, observe his movements and the folk
must shudder as they look down from the walls;
the mothers alternate their frightened wails
with fervent prayers—just as the anxious bird
who, when she sees the shepherd climb to rob
her nest, makes shrill complaint and, quivering
with beating wings and fluttering in fright,
moves to the higher branches. So were they.

   Once back in Utica he joined his force
with troops Octavius had meanwhile brought, 590
then to the walls of Tunis made his way
and anchored 'neath a sheltering point of land.
From there he marches; but he goes not far
before a messenger suddenly appears
with tales of an approaching foe. The son 595

Vermina's
attactk
frustrated
of Syphax, called Vermina, has come forth
in unpropitious hour to avenge
his father's fate and fall. Of his own will,
with tardy succor—worthy of less scorn,
if he had come that day by purest chance— 600
he leads impetuously onto the field
masses of horse and foot, all unaware
of Hannibal's defeat. And Scipio
does not command his troops to take up arms
nor build up ramparts nor retire to camp,
nor does he bid their standards lead them forth;
unmoved they stand, with arms and hearts prepared

to loosen bridles and destroy the foe
with their swift onslaught. But he bids them set
an ambush, and they readily obey.   610
Into an enclosed valley the young prince
marches with all his men and there is trapped.
He stands to fight and hastily deploys
his strength as best he may. Then comes the clash
of battle joined and slaughter and affray,
and groans of anguished pain. Since no retreat
the site affords, the youthful leader's host
is massacred; hardly a man is spared.
The prince alone, upon a swift-paced steed,
slips through the Roman net and, hapless wretch,   620
makes for the wasteland of the hostile hills.
Ah, better had it been for him had he   622
been buried 'neath the slaughtered piles of slain,
had Fate permitted, than have lived to bear
his miserable father company
in Alba's prison cell or shared with him
his Tiburtine interment far from home.

So Scipio leads onward o'er the road   628
already chosen his victorious files
with burdens of great booty: arms and steeds   630
and gold-embroidered tunics, helmet crests
all gleaming, and yoked chariots; even so
a torrent, blocked by some small obstacle,
will first exceed its banks a little, then,
swollen with victory, obliterate
aught that retards the fury of its flood,
and finally, brooking no impediment,
turns to pursue again its former course.

When news of young Vermina overpowered
and the sad issue of his enterprise   640
was spread abroad in Carthage, every soul
trembled with fear; a lesser shock renewed
the pain inflicted by the major blow.
So, when a ship is shattered in a storm,

the hapless mariner, tossed by the waves
and far from land, puts all his faltering hopes
on the frail oar to which he clings. When that
is reft from him by the malevolent sea
it seems a second shipwreck, and once more
he mourns his death: such weight the final hour   650
adds to a minor stroke of adverse chance.
The Carthaginians send to sue for peace
and mercy thirty worthy citizens,
well-chosen for their dignity and age:
their aspect indicates their high estate.

So 'twas in Libya. News of the war's end   657
had not yet come to Rome, still ill at ease.
The Fathers, whom the Punic rebel's fame
gave cause to fear, were troubled, and the folk
in terror and dismay could not ignore   660
Portents the many portents of the gods: the sun   661
in Rome high in mid-heaven faded and grew dim,
losing its splendor, while the earth beneath
shook and yawned wide and swallowed in its cleft
entire vineyards: then, before men's eyes,
subsided, leaving a tremendous gulf.
The Tiber, bearing in its raging flood
uprooted trees, broke through its barriers
and with a deluge never known before
alarmed the city. On the Palatine   670
a sudden shower of stones came pelting down.
So, in accordance with the Sybilline
prescription they sought out the hidden cause.
As they were bid they offered sacrifice
to all the gods; girt as the rite required,
the high priest called on mighty Jupiter
and friendly deities and then implored
the aid of threatening Juno and thereto
Latona's astral offspring. And he sought   679
with a sleek bull to mollify grim Mars,   680
the father of the empire, and likewise
his sister; aye, and Leda's sons, the Furies,   682

Chaos, and Earth, the mother of all gods,
if truthful be the myth; and river nymphs,
mothers of streams, and Nereus their sire.
So sumptuous offerings to all he made:
the altars smoked in emulous piety.

*Claudius
sails for
Africa*
When it appeared that the immortals' wrath
had been placated by these solemn rites,
then straightway the new consul, Claudius,   690
left Rome and set forth on his journey towards
the coast of Africa. The wretched man
was prey to mad ambition; he believed
that but one course would win him lasting praise:
to have the Fathers give him equal rank
to that of Scipio, that he might use
like power of command in the great war.
The people disapproved; yet he prevailed,
wooing the Senate with incessant pleas.
(How often it falls out that failure shows   700
ambition's vanity! By what great toil
men win to honors for which they should blush!)
So, as the champion of knights and plebs
he hastened to present himself as peer
and partner of great Scipio. In truth
Nature herself felt shame and barred his way,
stirring to indignation sea and air
till the resentful elements aroused
the ocean with tempestuous violence.
Even as they quitted the Laurentian shores   710
with favoring winds, the doughty mariners
singing the while their old sea-faring tunes
against the ocean's murmur, with the oars
propelling the sharp prows through the salt waves—
lo, suddenly, churned by a sudden squall
the angry waters rise and, breaking out
from their Aeolian cave, the brothers rush   717
and, blustering, lash the sea and air and sky.
In vain the sails are set against the blasts;
the dark blue combers whirl and seethe; the fleet   720

is scattered far; hither and yon the barks
are driven at the mercy of the storm,
nor do their prows have hope of any port.
Here Boreas tears the halyards and the sheets,
there, from the south, comes driving rain to drench
the canvases and mighty waves arise
to race across the watery expanse
and break at last upon Ausonia's shores.
The mastheads sink to touch the ocean's floor;
as often as the waters brush the clouds   730
and hurl their brine 'gainst the Tyrrhenian hills,   *731*
so often in their alternating rage
they climb, engulfing the long Tuscan shore.
On ocean's floor dry patches are revealed
where dolphins shudder on the naked sands
and keels are shattered on the frequent rocks.
Night shrouds the sky, save for the furious flash
of lightning, and from every coign of Heaven
pour thunderous bolts; the seething seas grow black
and briney mountains rise up from the deep.   740

and
meets
disaster

Alarmed by vision of his dubious fate,
the heart of Claudius trembled in affright:
and now he cursed his impious desires,
regretting he had sought out such grave risks,
and gladly would have chosen to eschew
the clash of arms with all the fair renown
appropriate to Scipio and his rank;
better, himseemed, had he remained at home
and in his family's tomb found his last rest,
renouncing all a warrior's lasting fame.   750
Even as he pondered thus the rough east wind
swept from Calabria's hills to smite his fleet.
His ships, harassed by storms, are first espied
by Populonia, then by Elba's clifts,   *754*
wreathed by the salty spume, and harried on
past Corsica's threatening reefs, until at last,
propelled by furious seas and lashed by gales,
north of Sardinia the ill-starred wretch

is borne. There many of his barks, the prey
of the victorious main, sink far from shore,   760
and many more are hurled 'gainst cruel rocks
or broken on dark reefs. The stiffened corpse
of many a mariner is shattered there
and some are borne back by the hurricane
to the Etruscan coast as if they sought
solace of burial in Italy.
But panic-stricken Claudius himself,
with a few ships snatched from the jaws of death
and the rapacious sea, comes safe to port,
as by a miracle, in Calaris.   770
Here winter found the consul still intent
on striving to repair his fleet, his soul
still terrified with thoughts of perils passed.
Nor was he destined e'er to look upon
the Punic coast nor hear the din of war
alarm his timid ears. With the year's end
and expiration of his consulship
back to his city he returned—but as
a private citizen, with all his ships
and crews destroyed in his vain enterprise.   780

   Meanwhile the happy news of victory
has come to Rome. The temple doors throughout
the city are thrown wide; the Romans throng
to every altar, offering solemn thanks
and grateful sacrifices to the gods.
Far from their borders has the foeman fled;
the heavy yoke is lifted from their necks;
defeat and terror have changed their abode
to dwell within the walls of savage Carthage,
the root and source of their long agony.   790
That dreadful chieftain, vanquished on the field,
lies prostrate: all their fears are at an end.
But now the project of a man of power
stirs up the folk and gives the Fathers pause.
Cornelius Lentulus, consul-elect,   795
desires to glorify his high command

The
plan of
Lentulus
(to be assumed while yet in Libya
the war continues) and therewith his name
and consulship. For thus he calculates:
should fighting end and peace be made at once,   800
the honor of it would redound to him,
and should hostilities yet be prolonged
their end, already close at hand, would be
a simple thing for him to bring about
and great would be the glory he would gain.
So, leaning on the labors of another,
burning for honors he does not deserve,
he plans to reap a bounteous harvest sown
by hands not his. Ah, fatal lust of fame,
accursed plague of mankind, say how oft   810
have you not injured Latin pride and power!
And here I briefly put aside my theme,
obedient to the impulse of my pen,
and ask of you who in your colloquies
equate what Rome has wrought with deeds performed
by alien hands: say where on earth is found

The trials
of Roman
generals
a nation with like spirit—and like foes?
Speak of great peoples, kings, and mighty lords,   818
yet, without prejudice or envy, say
what kings or rulers have achieved so much?   820
Your champions of other nations knew
no rival to beset them; envy's bane
did not afflict them in the midst of trials,
and their pursuit of glorious exploits
was not retarded by an idle year.
No enemy at home could interrupt
the term of their command, nor did their folk
forbid them to break camp. No senate's word
recalled them as they stood to win a war,
nor yet refused to reinforce their host   830
with horse and foot and ships, nay, nor withheld
a merited reward for work well done.
Great tyrants rule their kingdoms as they choose
with no direction of another's will:
at their own time their wars begin and end,

and as it pleases them they take up arms
or lay them down, so they are free to plan
their own campaigns and lead their standards forth.
No predecessor's sluggishness or sloth
requiring reparation by the sword   840
did ever trouble them in their fatigue
throughout a weary year. They never knew
disaster brought upon them by the act
of a rash colleague leading sullen troops
into dire perils plainly seen by all.
They planned their stratagems all unconcerned
by thoughts of a successor. Spur of fame
did not oblige them to accelerate
their pace nor change their course and rush headlong
to their undoing. And let no man seek   850
to quibble with me over Virtue's name,
if he but carefully distinguish it
from empty shadow nor extol the prize
won by another as it were his own.
Know ye, by far the sweetest thing of all
is glory, and if once its appetite
takes root within the heart, with powerful goads
it drives the strong and rouses noble minds
and fires generous spirits. Who could doubt
that such a leader, free of such concerns,   860
would swiftly have brought haughty Carthage down
to her deserved defeat and final ruin
under the heel of Fate? For Scipio,
men say, when he returned from war, would oft
sadly lament that Byrsa, tower and town,   *865*
would have been burned to ashes and therewith
the hated homes, the clan, the race, the gods,
the very name of Carthage—had not, first,
blindly ambitious Claudius and then
rash Lentulus taken it upon themselves   870
to spare the lofty walls of the doomed town
poised on the brink of ruin. Assuredly
for Scipio's grandson the gods planned to save
the long war's end, the name of Africanus.   *874*

Aye, well I know how far and whence I've strayed:
I come back to my theme. When Scipio reached   *876*
the citadel of Tunis, to him came
disconsolate envoys; on their knees they fell
before him, trembling with fear. With voice
of suppliants in sorrowing words they mourn   *880*
their errors, their ill fortune and the rage
of maddened Hannibal, their harmless land's
true bane. They sue for pardon once again.
But Roman ears are closed by memories
of faith betrayed, the countless instances
of Punic treachery, and the new truce
recently breached in flagrant insolence.
Council is held; all feel the same desire
to punish fraud with sword and vengeful flame
and hear no talk of peace. And yet this view,   *890*
unanimously held, was tempered by
consideration of the arduous toil
a lengthy siege would cost, whose glorious end
would little profit them, for rumor spoke
of a new leader soon to take command.
But little did the lure of fickle fame
and titles serve to sway the lofty mind
of Scipio nor his firm character.
Nay, rather, as one seeking higher things,
he raised his eyes to gaze on Heaven's stars   *900*
and Virtue's austere beauty. He gave ear
as well to all his trusted councilmen
whose hearts recoiled at the harsh verdict. Thus
it pleased him, while the suppliants' tears poured forth,
to grant the peace and end the cruel war.
In such wise might a cunning steward pluck,
for fear of night marauders, from the bough
the unripe apples; so the countryman,
anxious to thwart the serpents, will make haste
to clear the roosts of fowl and, emptying   *910*
the nests, remove to safety the young chicks.

Next came the envoys back again to ask

for greater favors. Scipio replied:

He rebukes
Cartha-
ginian
envoys

"Impious race, have you not learned at last,
after so many dire calamities,
that in the Heaven above there dwells a God,
avenger of all wickedness, to whom
all crime is odious and who regulates
all mortal things? O savage race, the foe
of every virtue, though you have but late   920
and through misfortune learned your lesson, now
begin to act as humans and renounce
at last your insane lust for doing ill.
Must it forever be your greatest joy,
ye tricksters, to deceive and practice fraud?
Though your destruction were well merited,
yet shall we hold in check our righteous wrath
and spare the undeserving. As thus far
you stand, so shall you hold your state,
nor see your walls cast down, nor shall your land   930
be seized by conquerors. Aye, liberty
shall be your lot, who rightly should be slaves.
We ask for Hannibal, that root of war
and source of fury. Abandon him and serve
better than ours your own tranquillity.
To cling to him would kill all hope of peace,
for in his heart are born the seeds of strife
for which you've paid so heavily in blood.
O long afflicted folk, who have so oft
made mockery of gods and men, forsake   940
that man and so avenge the countless dead
of Italy and your own fatherland.
And further, by surrender of this man,
this one wrongdoer, you will liberate
from everlasting fear two lands, two peoples.
No more shall elephants, those beasts of war,
be tamed and battle-trained in Libya
and you must yield us those already schooled.
Further, let fitting honors make amends
for public insult offered our envoys   950
in violation of their staff of peace.

Ships taken on these shores must be returned.
All other matters may be easily
disposed of, following the terms I first
laid down when, in the name of peace, you came
to mock me; even as a fairer Fate
would not abate our rigor, one more harsh
shall not mean your destruction. Now convey
these dictates to your senate and your folk,
and if you find deception ever sweet— 960
well, try your luck again." So Scipio
concluded and they heard his words in fear.

Carthage
accepts
the terms
and sends
a mission
to Rome

    Then in the frightened town a tumult rose
as jostling throngs pressed 'round the envoys. Long
raged passionate discussion and debate.
But finally all the Roman general's terms
found sad acceptance; such was Fate's decree.
Just so the anxious bird, while clinging fast
to the thick thorn bush, spies the hawk above,
and, daring not to move from where it sits 970
in desperate terror of the hovering threat,
suffers the fowler's noose and grasping hand.
    So to the town of Romulus went forth
one more Phoenician mission; at its head
went Hasdrubal, called Haedus by surname, 975
an enemy of war and friend of peace,
a worthy man whose aged countenance
won reverence; a man of different stamp
from those who favored savage Hannibal.
He was escorted—as the Roman chief 980
had ordered—by three knights of Italy.
But at the city's portals Lentulus,
perverted by ambition, barred their way;
hungry for war, the consul would have shunned
a peace with honor. But his efforts failed;
Bellona welcomed in her sacred fane 986
the Fathers and the foe's ambassadors.
So, in the presence of the Senate stood
the legates, in their majesty of age;

their hoary locks fell twining on their necks,   990
framing each venerable countenance
all shadowed with a sad solemnity
that touched the heart. In silence they came in.
Then they began, affirming they had come
as friends of peace, and not in word alone,
but with true hearts sincerely seeking peace.

Hasdrubal's And Hasdrubal continued: "If the gods,
plea   when properly implored, never deny
forgiveness for wrongs done, then I must be,
O conscript Fathers, whom renown equates   1000
with the immortals and their sacred ways,
assuredly encouraged by high hopes.
I will confess that wearisome old age
has made my long life tedious to bear,
especially when I saw that golden youth   1005
purposing further wars. I was afraid.
I could foresee disasters imminent,
but long I held a curb upon my tongue
and in my fear said naught. But now my years
have made me bold. I call on Jupiter   1010
and all the gods and Carthage once so proud
to be my witness. And I dare surmise
that even hither frequent rumors came
to tell how often I dared to oppose
that youth's designs and plans; how often thus
I risked grave perils, even death itself.
The venerable Hanno yet survives,   1017
my comrade and my witness, he than whom—
Hamilcar will indulge me—no man born
in Africa was greater nor more wise   1020

The   When that fierce youth so worked upon his sire,
account of with wheedling words, that he won his consent
Hannibal's to join him in the war he waged in Spain,
misdeeds
and swore—O portent dire!—that fateful oath   1024
upon the altars—then it was that first
we were distressed, for we perceived the spark
of peril lurking in his heart; yet still
we were indulgent of his tender years.

And then his father died (ah, would the Fates
had snatched the son while in his mother's womb,   *1030*
an embryo pernicious to the world!)
and he, with fearful schemes already planned
and mindful of his solemn oath, prepared
his own assault upon Hispania;
the foolish folk applauded him; the mob,
seeing him like his sire in voice and mien,
admired the father's valor in the son.
'Twas then we stood against him, but we failed.   *1038*
He went to Spain and quickly learned the use
of evil power and death-dealing arms.   *1040*
That tiny spark brought forth a mighty flame,
and you have seen what fires have spread abroad
to ravage the Ausonian world. And now
the errant flame returns to its own hearth
with conflagration such as we now see.
You have scant reason to believe my words,
yet here I swear—the gods my witnesses—
that I did grieve of old for all your ills
as much as now I mourn my country's wounds,
for I have always seen the fatal chain   *1050*
of evil move in sequence preordained
to Libya from Latium; that fierce blaze
I knew would leave your shores and come to ours.
Forgive me, Fathers, if I here recall
that ill-starred day for which we now have paid
so dearly with our blood: when messengers   *1056*
brought to our avid city the fresh news
of Cannae's slaughter, we—we two alone—
with melancholy voice and somber mien
marred the display of universal joy,   *1060*
for great-souled Hanno too foresaw the woes
we have experienced. A hostile Fate
dragged our ill-omened folk along the road
to rightful expiation; destiny
had closed their sorry ears to helpful rede
and veiled their eyes with a deceiving shroud.
Be merciful, ye Romans; God and Fate

have done what human strength could not achieve
and stripped us of illusion. But I blush
to blame the immortals. We all erred. The fault   1070
each one of us must own. Yet I avow
the folk are innocent; the true cause lies
in the ferocity of one mad heart
and in the force and fury of grim Fate.
Aye, though they call me pitiless and severe,
yet I absolve the people. Some I must
condemn for real offenses; I concede
fraud has enslaved a few vainglorious souls.
Swollen with pride, these braggarts like to boast
before the folk of their forefathers' deeds   1080
and point to where their statues stand in stone
on crumbling pedestals, and with cheap words
revile the deeds of others and present
themselves as leaders of a raging mob.
They feel no shame in making silly jests
anent your origins; your sires, they say,
were rustic yokels and you are a tribe
of shepherds. Here, mayhap, they speak the truth,
for, as Mars is our judge, ye hold as sheep
great warrior kings, unvanquished hitherto,   1090
and all their folk seem destined to become
so many timid flocks. But all the world
well knows the seed of your new race and how
you spring from Mars whose true paternity
your valor and your exploits demonstrate.
Where now is that obnoxious crowd? Concealed
in what dark shadows is it lurking, numb
with craven terror? Why come they not forth,
those facile orators, once more to dupe
with false assurances the hapless folk   1100
and all the credulous and gaping throngs?
Ah, would they but return and look again
upon their fatherland, then might we seize
and bind the culpable in well-earned chains—
and let this old man castigate that youth.   *1105*
No whit more joyously would Scipio

as conqueror ascend the Capitol
in splendid triumph than my hand would drag
our fettered leader by his villainous neck
before you here—and I would count myself   1110
thus to have won the fairest spoils of war
from the most odious foeman of my land.
Believe my words, that man of treachery
with all his heart hates Hasdrubal as much
as those he calls his foes; to march before
your car of triumph would gall him no worse
than to stand here before me to be judged.
In dark of night he slipped off through the gloom;
he could not bear to meet our eyes, well knowing
he is the source of all his country's ills.   1120
So furtively he left us, well content
with exile self-imposed from his doomed land:
aye, for the criminal rightly stands in fear
of his compatriots' justice and thereto
their frowning anger and their clutching hands.
And were he apprehended, it is true,
he would be crucified at once: his corpse
would feed the vultures as 'twere felon's flesh,
unless instead it were cast in the sea,
a fitting food for sharks, or yet again   1130
a righteous judgment with a passionate zeal
might change his human shape and make of him
a Libyan monster of repellent form.
Nor would your claim have been denied though he
is answerable to both nations and the world.
I would myself have yielded him to you,
alive or fragmented in bleeding bits
or with a head half-gnawed.

"Wherefore, we pray,

Hasdrubal
pleads for
clemency   let our good will suffice; the folk of Carthage
with one voice and most willingly embrace   1140
the terms that please your leader. See our writ,
declaring every clause acceptable.
It is the noblest revenge to spare

a prostrate suppliant. No victory
is greater than to discipline oneself.
The happiest of men is he who knows
himself content and cleaves with modest mien
and soul to moderation. This may seem
a rigid rule to those who know it not;
such men are rather moved by present spurs   1150
of trivial pleasures, wont to overwhelm
those who are not true masters of themselves;
but your hearts which are constantly appeased
by endless triumphs must find their delight
in pardoning your enemies. No less
by mercy than by strength of martial arms
will you enlarge Rome's rule. Now we have need
of your compassion; we put down our arms
and plead for clemency. Let suppliants
be spared your wrath; let it suffice that you   1160
have had it in your power to do us hurt.
As conquered folk we are your lasting fame;
as foeman spared your greatest glory. If
perchance the punishment and pain of those
who well deserve it is appropriate,
meseems that what the mindful gods have willed
and Scipio has ordered should suffice.
If aught remains, yet, do you, conquerors,
spare those you've vanquished and let your revenge
find highest satisfaction in the sight   1170
of agéd Hasdrubal, pleading for mercy."
No more he said; his venerable brow
revealed his silent grief. On every side
his comrades, prostrate on the portal's sill,
with tears besieged the senators; the hall
re-echoed with their sobs. So might, bereaved,
a father witness his son's burial
nor shed a woman's tears but in his heart
within him mourn, the while the mother lies
with hair disheveled, ravaging her cheeks,   1180
and floods the air with tears and piteous sighs
and lamentations suited to her sex.

*The
Senate
sanctions
the peace*His words had mollified the Senate's wrath,
and as he spoke, more readily they heard
with hearts less hard the old man's righteous plea.
One senator, still bitter with the thought
of Punic treason, spoke: "By what gods, say,   *1187*
would this new peace and treaty be assured?
For you have broken every former oath."
Then Hasdrubal with humble mien uprose   1190
and answered: "By those very gods we swear
who so much hated all our perjuries
that with a different fidelity
we shall observe this peace." His utterance
estopped objection and restored new calm
to all the faces of the senators
and to their hearts and minds. In harmony
they gave their sanction to the peace. Whereat
Hasdrubal spoke again: "Now may the gods
reward you rightly, Romans, who withhold   1200
the punishment our madness has deserved
and cast a righteous anger from your hearts.

"Now I would speak, not to an ancient foe,
but to our new allies and lords, and ask
a favor of you. Now that we stand here
within your walls, it is our ardent wish
to look upon your captives and to meet
your citizens. It would much solace me
for my long journey hither; such a boon
would be an honor, aye, and a reward   1210
for this task given me so late in life.
In truth I'd gladly cross the widest sea
to gaze on Rome, the whole world's capital."

*The
envoys are
shown the
sights of
Rome*His wish was granted and in reverence
he entered the great city. Such amaze
he knew as did the Trojan youth of old   *1216*
(unless the tale be false) when suddenly
he felt himself borne off from Ida's top
to walk 'mid straying stars on Heaven's paths
and from on high look down on Ilion's groves.   1220

First are they welcomed by the Appian Gate   *1221*
with marble threshold, whence they may perceive
the Palatine with ancient walls disposed
in a huge circle. On that hill was built
Evander's palace; on that famous site   *1225*
first rose the newborn city. Here the guide
points out the traces of the early town
still visible to an experienced eye.
Here dwelt the mild Arcadian spirit, here   *1229*
took place the greatest wonders of all time: 1230
the finding of the books, the works of love
wrought by Carmenta, prophetess benign   *1232*
to be revered through all the years to come
for her endowment of the Latin arts.
Between two hills the visitors now stand;
the Coelian on their right, the Aventine
raising its lofty summit on their left:
they mark the citadel that towers high
above the cliff, the yawning cave beneath.
Here they attend to hear the story told   1240
of Cacus and the toils of Hercules   *1241*
and the oxen bathed in the Etrurian stream,
narrated in fair words that charm their ears.
And here likewise the multicolored pier
of the Sublician bridge recalls the deed
of stout Horatius, and that site, far famed   *1246*
for its equestrian statue, turns their eyes
upon the frowning maid. And they admire   *1248*
the altar of the sun, the golden fanes,
the shrine of Mother Earth; then timidly,   1250
as if their path led them to Heaven itself,
they make their way up the Capitoline.
When they learn that a human skull was found
by those who first dug deep upon that hill,
the Carthaginians are moved to curse
the ancient omens of their motherland,
for there an ox head had been brought to light   *1257*
to signify that they were doomed to bow
their necks beneath a shameful yoke, condemned

to suffer heavy labor. Next they see 1260
Jove's temple, than which none was built more fair;
the census lists concealed beneath the rock;
and the famed threshold over which have passed
a thousand triumphs; they observe the arms
reft from the foe, the gleaming chariots,
the golden diadems of mighty kings;
sceptres and armlets, precious collars torn
from foemen's necks and jewel-studded reins
and ivory saddles, all in order ranged.
And when their glance encounters their own shields 1270
and shattered ships and Punic battle-flags
and breastplates, trophies of the former wars,
grief overwhelms them and their tongues are stilled.
They wander on, pausing to mark the bird 1274
of silver whose outcry of old gave warning
of Gauls preparing their assault. They move
ahead to look on heroes stout of limb
and stately matrons by the folk revered
for their comportment, spacious mansions too,
and arches laden with war's divers spoils, 1280
triumphal emblems past all reckoning
and battle scenes on solid marble graven
and splendid tombs. And they are shown as well
the aqueducts, both those that arch the air
and those beneath the ground. Suburra's vale 1285
displays the home of the Caesarian clan
to which pertains the highest sovereignty
and lordship of all things. Though wearied now,
they leave the valley and resume their way
over the Esquiline, across the hill 1290
to which the willow gave its name, and climb
the summit of the Quirinal, whereon
two naked giants stand before their eyes—
a celebrated work that men assign
(so keen is competition for renown)
either to famed Praxiteles or else
to Phidias. Here the Phoenicians quake,
seeing the palace of the Scipios

with its high walls and mighty towers and standards,
all too well known in Libya, and the proud   1300
majestic countenance and awesome name.
There they turn left and draw near to the gate
now called Flaminian, facing Tuscany;
returning thence, the Campus Martius
and its adjacent river welcome them.
Here the vast plain extends, with memories
of a long sequence of great matters which
it erst had witnessed; it could tell who first   1308
achieved the honor of the consulship,
with what deep wound the virtuous matron pierced   1310
her breasts; to whom was liberty entrusted;
and with what ax the pitiless sire struck down
his sons. There too they hear the tale retold
of tyrants banished from the town they've wronged—
and carefully take note. Then, on their left,
the spacious temples sacred to Minerva
and all the gods are shown them—saved to serve   1317
a higher purpose in the future. Next
they cross deep-flowing Tiber's stream and touch,
on its right bank, Etruria's frontier.   1320
The guide points out to them the massive tomb   1321
of Romulus and, as they walk along,
shows where a whirlwind bore Quirinus off   1323
to dwell among the stars; he tells them how
the hero overwhelmed the senators
with such a tempest that the very sun
paled in affright. The vision he recalls
of Proculus and the Caprean Marsh,
but says naught of the criminal senators.
Descending to the margin of the stream,   1330
they mark the hill where stood the ancient home   1331
of Janus and close by the temple raised
to Saturn. There they learn the origins
of the Ausonian kings, the Latin stock,
and likewise all the famous heroes' names.
Here Italus, once king, to Italy   1336
gave first its name. The visitors are told

of Picus, his good comrade, and the line 1338
of ancestors and the new people's home. 1339
Below, they listen, rapt, to the account 1340
of the long contest waged against the kings
returning in their might from Clusium. 1342
They mark Porsenna's camp and seem to see
Scaevola bending towards the flickering flame, 1344
inflicting anguish undeserved upon
his errant hand. By the twin bridge they cross 1346
the Lycaonian isle. They scarce believe
the marvelous thing they hear: how such a mass 1348
was made of booty plundered from the king
and by the raging folk cast on the stream.
Once more upon the fields of the left bank,
they ponder on the house of Fabius, 1352
the melancholy fall of that great clan,
and Cremera, that dark and fatal flood.

Descending from the Capitol at last
they halt their weary march and suddenly,
as they recall and think on all they've seen,
a great awe falls upon them. So, benumbed,
for long they sit in silence. Then word comes
that they may see the captives. In long files 1360
The envoys the trembling wretches stand, with swollen cheeks
meet their and tangled locks of long-neglected hair
captive falling on naked backs, their aspect marred
com-
patriots by a foul squalor, yielding a rank stench.
They shuffle slowly, linked by iron chains,
and heavy manacles deny to them
the consolation of embracing those
whom they hold dear. The visitors exchange
fair words with them, the while the clanging chains
ring through the air, and tears of pity born 1370
stain every cheek. The captives fain would know
how fares their city, what will be its end,
and to what gods a conquered folk may look
for succor. Just as when a new shade falls
to join the spirits of the nether realm,

fresh from our world and burdened with his griefs,
and round him throng the ghostly presences
eager for tidings the recruit may bring:
one asks how fares his son, another seeks
for news of a dear wife or aging sire,   1380
and yet another tearfully inquires
about a brother or a cherished friend,
and all would learn of matters and events
of common interest in the world of men:
who holds the sceptre now, and who the power,
how goes the war, how long may peace endure;
and anxious jaws gape wide and bloodless lips
move soundlessly in eagerness to know—
even in such fashion does the squalid crew
of captives press around the visitors   1390
and harry them with questions. When all's done
and tears have ceased to flow, then Hasdrubal
pleads that for some of his compatriots
a ransom may be paid. The conquerors,
desiring to deny him no request,
invite him to submit a list of names
of his own choosing. He writes down ten score;
a gracious Senate orders them transferred
from grim captivity to Libya,
if they but swear to keep the terms of peace,   1400
a free gift offered to their fatherland
and with no ransom asked. And so 'tis done.

Hasdrubal   Then Hasdrubal again looks on the walls,
salutes   once hated, now so dear, and in these words
Rome   proffers a eulogy to cherished Rome:
"O city pleasing to the gods, sole head
of all the world, pride of the universe,
unrivaled cradle of illustrious men,
and thou, O nation great in arms, the home
of the immortals, best of things on earth,   1410
O Rome, farewell. I follow willingly
whither the Fates may call these ancient limbs,
for all that earth may offer of her best

I now have seen." Then, leaving Tibermouth,
he sails in triumph to his native land
and with him go the files of prisoners.
Indulge me if I dare here to equatc
the earthly with the heavenly, man's things
with the eternal, and the trivial
with the sublime: even so Almighty God   1420
descends from Heaven to loose from ancient bonds
the captive souls, and shattering with his voice
the gloom of Tartarus, bears home with Him
a train of sad and pitiable spirits
exhausted by their torments long endured.

On his return, with mild and peaceful mien
Scipio receives him. Folk and chiefs alike
approve the peace. With the gods witnessing,
before the shrines the treaty pact is sworn;
a sow is sacrificed; the leaders' hands   1430
unarmed are joined. Later, in Italy,
after the Senate Fathers have approved
the action of their general, the terms
of peace agreed upon will be set down
in books, as old ancestral law decrees,
and duly ratified by solemn oaths.

Scipio Content at last to have brought to an end   1437
takes his lengthy labors, Scipio prepares
leave of to take his leave. But first he makes awards:
Carthage his soldiers win his praise and generous gifts;   1440
Cirta and all the lands that Syphax held
he gives to Massinissa, rightfully
extending the frontiers of his old realm.
He further, as was fixed in the accord,
condemns the vanquished to indemnify
the king, his good ally, and pay to Rome
the stipulated tribute. After that,
he deals out punishments, with penalties
each suited to the case. More leniently   1449
he treats the slaves, whose nature, he believes   1450
explains their faithlessness and cowardice.

But any freeman who has fled his post
must die forthwith: the general spares none
who have in times of grave emergency
besmirched their honor, been false to their word,
or failed to keep their military oath.
If any such be Roman, Scipio
remorselessly bids him be crucified,
and if a Latin, then his craven neck
is severed with the ax, as he deserves.   1460

When all these things are done, the general
makes his way shoreward, to the beach's edge,
preparing to set sail. The Punic Senate
with an attendant and admiring crowd
of suppliants escorts him to the strand.
And there, for the last time, already poised
for his departure, lofty Scipio
addresses them with mild and gentle words:

His ex-   "Be ye content with what is yours and live
hortations   mindful of the immortals; let not envy   1470
to the   blind you with fury, driving you to arms.
Cartha-   Within your ancient frontiers a vast realm
ginians   is left to you and all your laws remain
confirmed, as is your state, in liberty.
Though it be glorious to rule the world,
obedience to the just is more secure.
For a long time to come—believe my words—
you are assured of peace, while on our backs
a heavy burden of continuing toil
must press and bring us many griefs and cares.   1480
Whoever draws his sword, where'er he be,
or fires new war by angry words or arms
must be our enemy. It is a grave
and weighty duty to stand vigilant
against the trespasses of all the world,
but you will have enduring peace and calm
free from all strife. If you but scorn it not,
you'll find in us a true and steady shield.
I am myself the living pledge between

our Senate and all Carthaginians. 1490
So learn at last to live your lives in peace:
take peace into your hearts and let the sword
be absent from your minds; let it not be
that Fortune has, inflicting such distress,
twice failed to teach her lesson. Try no more
the pathways of the sea. Lo, I remove
great perils, painful trials, and endless toil,
for I shall burn your fleet which carried you
and all your fury to the widest shores
and was the origin of your downfall, 1500
persuading you to assault Italian lands
and teaching timid men to cross the waves.
If what I do seems harsh, I pray put down
your passions and consider well this thought:
a limb of evil fatal to your health *1505*
has been lopped off. Let it suffice that you
possess an empire of a vast expanse
and the frontier of a divided world.
To seek for further cares is mankind's curse;
repair your own estate and turn to us 1510
for counsel. Put anxiety and fear
of Hannibal behind you. Let him go
abandoned to his own resentful wrath.
If lingering doubts remain anent the course
the Fates have charted for your commonwealth,
give ear to what your elders tell you here."
So ending his discourse, he clasped their hands,
but on one side illustrious Hanno knelt
and on the other Hasdrubal, and both
embraced his feet. Then the whole fleet was
    launched. 1520

Burning   But Scipio halted briefly in his course
of the   and gave his orders that the Punic ships
Cartha-   should all be burned. And such a mighty blaze
ginian   lit up the waves as ne'er was seen before,
fleet   nor e'er before had Thetis felt alarm
lest her far-rolling combers be consumed,

not even when the son of Phoebus snatched
the reins he yearned for from his father's grasp'
and fired with the spreading flames the sky
and all the world beneath. Nay, Neptune feared   1530
this conflagration more than any seen
in ages past; neither the Punic fleet
by Roman torches burned in the first war   *1533*
nor yet the ships of Athens long ago
gutted by Spartan fire at Syracuse
had spread so wide a blaze upon the deep.
The hapless citizens in sad amaze
bewailed their loss as if all things they loved—
their wives and children and the citadel
and all their temples—nay, Carthage itself   1540
were burning in those soaring crimson flames.

Book 9

Over the tranquil sea the Roman fleet
sails onward, bearing Scipio. No storm
stirs up the waves to fury; winds are stilled.
One would have said the waters recognized
the victor, while, no less serene, the sky
displayed a placid countenance. And thus
the perilous sea and all the elements
most graciously indulge the general.
The shores of Africa fast fade from view:
the ships sail on, what time the mariners,   10
singing of victory, ply sturdy oars.

Amidships on the deck of Scipio's bark
sat Ennius, witness and companion too   13
in the great enterprise. Lost in deep thought,
he said no word until the general,
approaching, roused him with this fair request:
*Ennius
exhorted
to speak*
"Will you, sweet solace in my many trials,
forever hold your peace? Nay, speak, I pray;
wasted with cares incessant all our hearts
are weary, as you see. 'Twas e'er your wont   20
to lighten them with pleasing words. Do now
so charm us. You have but to loose your lips,
since great Apollo gave you at your birth
the heavenly talent which has won you fame,
and goddesses, while you were still a child,
immersed you in the sweet Castalian spring   27
of sacred Helicon and led you forth
to the high hills, bestowing on you there
the pen and voice and spirit of a bard."
So charged, the poet raised his head and spoke: 30
"O youth, O flower of Italy and pledge
of godlike stock, what would you have me say
to please you? As I silent sat and mused

223

within me, I reflected that the years
before us never brought a soul to light
better exemplifying noble worth
than our own age has witnessed and henceforth
no mortal will conceive a great design
who will not, as he loftily aspires,
have on his lips your virtuous name. No man   40
preparing to perform a great exploit
will fail to think of Scipio and yearn
to have enjoyed the gracious privilege
of looking on your visage. Greater glory
awaits you past the grave. Envy, 'tis true,
gnaws at all deeds of men, but death destroys
Envy and drives her from the sepulchre.
Your glory has already overcome
that foul infection and securely soars
above the earth and all the evil ways   50
of men to reach, in its propitious course,
parity with the gods. Aye, mark you well—
experience gives me warrant for my words—
the final day will augment your renown:
as day by day your hour of death recedes,
greater will grow the glory you have earned.
With passing years your honor will increase
and in the world's last years your fame will glow.
Since Virtue may not further upward rise   59

He de-   I fear lest it descend. Our eloquence   60
plores the   still lacks the strength to reach the goal it seeks,
state of   since it but recently among our folk
Roman   has sprung from tender roots, for hitherto
eloquence   it has been nurtured by Greek husbandmen
and scarcely known upon our Latin fields.
It was indeed this thought that moved my heart
to indignation: that your peerless worth
would find no proper eulogist. The king   68
of Macedon, when on Achilles' tomb
he saw the great inscription, sadly cried: 70
'Oh happy youth, to whom 'twas given to find
so great a singer of his name!' Indeed

it's no small thing for famous men to know
a poet skilled in use of lofty verse
to sing their virtues and proclaim their praise.
To you, alas, O most illustrious chief,
than whom no rival better might deserve
the voice of Homer, Fortune, otherwise
most gracious, has been miserly
in this regard; you have no bard save me.   80
In some far future century perchance
a poet may be born who will in song
more worthy of you bear to Heaven your lauds
well-merited and chant your great exploits;
to him perhaps Calliope will lend
notes more sonorous and a lyre whose strings
may with a greater sweetness make response
to the mellifluous plectrum." "Say no more:
to my mind neither the Maeonian bard   *89*
nor great Euripides nor any man   90
on whom the Greeks have lavished their applause
can justly be preferred to you. I'd ask
no other voice but yours to sing my praise,
if I am to be lauded in a song.
Nay, rather, what I would request of you   *95*
is further speech; may it be granted me
to learn, through your instruction, how far runs
a poet's warrant, and the ends defined
for things of glory, and what signifies
the laurel which has crowned alike the brows   100
of famous generals and sacred bards.
I pray you, deem me not unfit to hear
of such high matters, for my spirit too
is moved by beauty's sweet allure; my heart,
grown weary of unending war, now yearns
for leisure and agreeable discourse."

Ennius   "No spirit, I avow," said Ennius,
on poetry   "O gracious leader, is so harsh and fierce
as not to feel, 'midst life's vicissitudes,
how sweet it is to hear the Pierian song   *110*

and join the train of those fair goddesses.
Your heart, I am assured, was never closed
nor hostile to the Muses; so ill-starred
Nature would not have shaped so great a hero.
Gross were her error had she not inspired
such love in him on whom she had bestowed
an ardent zeal for fame, for one who feels   *117*
pride in his high achievements must hold dear
immortal poets and their sacred songs.
Now, touching on what you would learn from me,   120
hear these brief words. The warrant of a bard
does not pertain to those who openly
would please the multitude. For, mark you, first,   *123*
one who would plan a poem must lay down
a firm foundation of the truth whereon
he then may build a cloud-like structure, sweet
and varied, veiling the foundation. Thus
he will prepare for those who choose to read
a lengthy, tranquil, and rewarding labor.
So, as the meaning harder is to seek,   130
the sweeter is the finding. All such things
as trials that history records, the ways
of virtue, lessons taught by life,
or Nature's secrets—all such matters are
a poet's substance, not to be exposed
as elsewhere, but to be disguised beneath
a covering cloak, or better, a light veil
which tricks the watcher's eye and now conceals
and now discloses underlying truth.
One who invents what he relates should not   140
be honored by the title of a poet,
nor deemed a seer—but rather called a liar.
This will make plain to you what you would know:
the measure of our labor, our frontiers,
and how much license has been granted us.
As for the laurel crown which graciously
you think me fit to share with you: if war
and talent have alike some glory, then
it may be granted generals and bards

to bind the verdant fronds around their brows. 150
On both the never-dying green confers 151
immortal fame, assuring centuries
of lasting memory. It is for this
the laurel is held dear by kind Apollo,
the god of genius, wonted oft to lead
with tuneful lyre the Pierides in dance 156
in the Cirrhaean cavern where he dwells.
This leaf alone of all fronds Jupiter
assaults not with his bolt; the sacred tree
deserves the honor, rightfully enjoying 160
the clemency of Heaven's king. For Fame 161
stands firm against all blasts—save only time
which undoes everything. Haply this fear
is alien to our glory, which weaves crowns
of verdant leaves that spurn the thunder, plucked
from branches of the holy tree." No more
he said, but Scipio, with a smile, replied:
"So far you please us, but your brevity
offends us. What you say is sweet to hear
but breaks off in mid-course. Come now, speak on! 170
No land is to be seen; the sun has crossed
meridian. Give voice to those fair words
of which your gentle mind has such a store
and bear us willingly with you on long
and pleasant discourse, so we may beguile 175
part of the day and something of our journey."

Yielding to such persuasion, Ennius,
while all all the sailors' murmurings grew still 180
and Scipio and his comrades held their peace,
His cult began: "Alert as is a sentinel
of Homer on watch, I have traced back through ancient years,
as best I might, the tenuous spoor of fame.
At length, spurred on by my inquiring mind,
I reached the furthest shades, the first of men,
whom Time, grown weary of the lengthening road,
had long abandoned to oblivion.
Whoever of those days still shone with light

of merit I felt honored to embrace   190
and cherish as I would a well-loved sire;
and most especially in my heart's core
I gave warm welcome to the bards of old
whom shining genius set apart. Of all
the thousands such, one name I hold supreme:
Homer, I mean, possessed of qualities
I cannot but respect, admire and love.
Often meseems from Heaven he comes to me,
and I am awed to think a mortal man
could have attained such heights or ever known   200
such starry paths, so many climes of earth.
Although his life was spent before the time
of our first king, before the birth of Rome,
yet in my thoughts I've brought him to our age
and shaped an image of him, giving him
true presence in my heart. No day, no night
for me has passed without his company.
Once he made short feasts long and now he makes
long journeys short; from him too I have learned
to traverse on a level path the peaks   210
of craggy mountains; nay, asleep, awake,
whatever I have done by day or night,
I've never been without his comradeship.

His dream
of the
bard
    "Hear me yet further. It befell one night,
while yet the issue of our war remained
in doubt and I lay sleeping in my tent,
he came to me. Who could describe that dream?   *217*
Wakeful I was; around, the war raged on
and peace was nowhere. I was restless too,
for you were late in coming back to camp.   220
To speak the truth, though I was not afraid,
yet with the setting sun my fragile hopes
struggled with doubts. And as the night wore on
I felt a deep concern for what the day
might bring to end such grave uncertainty.
Then in the depth of night—behold, I saw
an aged man draw near, his body wrapped

in fragments of a toga, with a beard
unkempt, his grizzled hair with strands of white.
His sockets had no eyes. That spectral face,   230
hollowed and gaunt, bore a crude majesty,
yet moved my heart to horror. I lay frozen.
Then, as might one whose sight is in his hands,
he fixed me in my fear and in Greek speech
addressed me: 'Friend, my only friend among
the Latins, greetings! Here stands what your heart
and mind have so long yearned for, here behold
Homer as he appeared in living flesh.
Hither I come, fresh from the cell of Dis
but recently unbarred. I've made my way   240
in silence upward through the bowels of earth.'
Prostrate I fell and in humility
sought to embrace his feet. My lips, alas,
brushed but the naked ground; he was a shade.
'Rise up,' he said, 'and join me. Walk with me
as might an equal. While you yet have time
indulge yourself in colloquy with me,
such as you have for many years desired
but heretofore in vain. For you are worthy.'
Straightway I eagerly arose and spoke: 250
'O shining glory of the men of Greece,   251
and Hellas' highest honor, who has wrought
such anguish on a man so venerable?
Who from your sacred brow reft those fair lights,
those guides by nature given? Who presumed
to wreak such injury upon the world?
I would not have believed what I behold;
nay, rather I'd have deemed a glance acute
and potent vision in you were conjoined
with loving mind. Has not your lucid eye   260
portrayed for me the opulent ports that line
the shores of Greece on both the azure seas
enclosing her, the hills, the well-tilled fields,
the caves in hidden dells, the wooded peaks,
the reefs that mark her waters? Can it be
that you, unable to see things at hand,

have given others sight of far-off things?
I marvel at the thought. Behold, I count
the Cyclades strewn o'er the Aegean main;
I follow with my eyes the thousand curves   270
that mark the Hellespont, while you yourself,
who show me all such scenes, cannot see me.'
He answered: 'All that you have said is true
and yet no marvel. What then, could not God,   274
who took from me corporeal eyes, yet give
me others apt for seeing hidden things?
No longer strive, O mortal, to undo
by tedious entreaty God's decrees:
that is mankind's most ignorant complaint.
What God effects is right. Your fleshly charge   280
prevents your knowing all that lies within
the murky confines of your prison cell.
Many there are whose eyes have served them ill,
whose sight has led them from the rightful path
and turned them from an honorable course;
wherefore full many of their own free will
have put down such a burden when it grew
oppressive and injurious to bear.   288
Shall we go on? Spurn not a sightless guide;
you may see much to please you. Be not moved   290
by thought of misadventures yet to come;
under the light of morn the fields will run
with Punic blood as Latium rules the day.'
Cheered by the prophecy, I followed him.   294

Their   "There in the distance I could see a youth
vision of   seated within a valley closed by hills.   296
the poet   I asked: 'O cherished guide, disclose, I pray,
of the   who is it I behold taking his rest
future   under the tender laurel? Lo, he seems
                about to bind his locks with those green fronds.   300
I know not what he ponders in his heart,
but surely it must be, unless I err,
some high and noble purpose.' 'You err not,'
his answer came, 'I recognize the youth

as one of a late line of progeny
whom Italy will bear in times to come.
Etruria's Florence, daughter of old Rome,
unbuilt today but destined to be great
and far-renowned, will from her spacious walls
deliver him to you. So you may learn   310
where that fair town shall stand and flourish, know
its walls illustrious Arno's flood will lave
as toward Ausonian Pisa it descends.
That youth in distant ages will recall
with his sweet notes the Muses, long exiled,
and though by tribulations sorely tried
he'll lure the venerable sisters back
to Helicon. He will be called Franciscus;
and all the glorious exploits you have seen
he will assemble in one volume—all   320
the deeds in Spain, the arduous Libyan trials;
and he will call his poem *Africa*.
How great will be his faith in his own gifts!
How strong the love of fame that leads him on!
At last in tardy triumph he will climb   323
the Capitol. Nor shall a heedless world
nor an illiterate herd, inebriate
with baser passions, turn aside his steps
when he descends, flanked by the company
of Senators, and from the rite returns   330
with brow girt by the glorious laurel wreath.
Already in his heart that green frond stirs   332
so great a love, a reverence so deep
that in the Delphic grove alone he finds
his true content. See how he practices
to fashion garlands of the tender leaves,
already comforted by prophecies
of things to come. Nay, he by aging Rome
shall be more cherished than a late-born son,
fruit of a womb long barren of a mother   340
by death bereft of earlier progeny.
For she, in truth, not having seen his peer
over the span of ten full centuries,   343

will look upon him with benevolent pride
when he receives the wreath and when he leaves   *345*
his garland in the temple and so lays
upon the sacred altar his first fruits.
'Tis he, O Rome, who shall endear to you
the folk of Florence, nor shall you repent
of having founded on the Tuscan stream   *350*
that daughter town. Zealous in study, he
will sing the glories of the men of old   *352*
and trace from their first origins the sons
of Romulus; a faithful chronicler,
in syllables unfettered he will tell
of your great race, its titles and its clans.
Wherein, resplendent and by no means least,
great Scipio will stand, and he who writes
will openly admit indebtedness
to him above all heroes of the past.   *360*
And if the days allotted him suffice
and no new tempest turns him from his course,
then will you see yet greater scrolls unrolled
whereon, with varying colors of his pen
he will inscribe the great events to come,   *365*
aye, down to his own times. Who could tell all
his fertile mind is planning to bring forth?'
My beating heart throbbed with desire to see
this youth and to hold colloquy with him;
wherefore, incredible as it may seem,   *370*
I wished great Homer might bring to an end
his sweet discourse. Already I held dear
the youthful Tuscan, learning he would sing
of you and matters lofty and sublime.
I quietly drew nearer where I might
observe him. There he stood before my eyes,
in youth's full flower, though by cares oppressed.
He held a pen in hand. The verdant turf
whereon he sat was girt by sundry trees
among which limpid brooklets flowed; beyond   *380*
rose craggy mountains fresh with cooling springs.
'Remark,' my guide admonished me, 'the bowers,

the nature of this rural countryside:
'Tis here his genius will be moved to turn   *384*
to such great topics as we have described.
And soon, from divers regions of the earth,
as he goes wandering over land and sea,
he'll put forth concepts nurtured in his heart
throughout the years. And finally, when set free
of all the turbulence of worldly cares,   390
his agile pen will treat of many things.'

    "With wonder and amaze my eyes absorbed
all details of the scene. At last I dared
to speak. Gravely the youth raised up his brow
as if in preparation to respond—
and suddenly the morning trumpet's blast
dispelled my vision. Shattered is my dream
and I awaken to see you in arms
lead from the camp your troops with standards raised,
urging them onward to the battlefield."   400
    While Ennius with golden words beguiled
the watery journey, telling of such things,
already weary Phoebus had come down
to seek refreshment for his panting steeds
in the Atlantic current. So one borne
in a swift chariot across the plain,
his limbs in heavy slumber steeped, marks not
the fading day, till suddenly he wakes,
amazed that his long journey has grown short,
and scarcely can believe 'tis at an end.   410
    To gentle Zephyr, rising from the west,
the fleet spread out its sails; the prows were turned
to starboard. Cynthia through the night relieved   *413*
her brother, keeping watch. The mariners
were free to rest their weary limbs in sleep.
When sound of oars and creaking timbers ceased,
in mild and gentle fashion Scipio spoke:
"Whether such things be true or fancy-bred,
I will confess that they are sweet to hear;
they charm the imagination and the heart.   420

I long already to embrace that youth
who did but recently appear to you
and erstwhile to my father; he is mine   423
by warrant of this double sponsorship.
Whoever he may be I cherish him,
and if an empty name, why then I'll cherish
an empty name." He said no more. Soon all
had yielded to sweet sleep their tired frames.

The fleet   When from the eastern wave the sun returned,
reaches   causing the sails to cast far o'er the sea   430
Italy   huge shadows, the keen mariners espied
the shores of Lilybaeum and acclaimed
with glad outcry Trinacria's welcome strand.
Past Drepanum they sail and onward thence,
skirting one side of Sicily. At last
they set their feet once more upon firm fields
of solid earth and take a path by land
across the lovely meadows. Here my song
lacks strength to tell of Italy's great joy,
the throngs that stream from every part to greet   440
the victors; towns are emptied of their folk
who come to meet the warriors on their way,
singing hosannas for their liberty
so valiantly defended. So at last
the walls of their own city welcome them.
Then comes the day so long and ardently
desired, bearing triumph with its dawn.

And here, Calliope, I summon thee,
though late my prayer: smile on my final toil
and aid me as my song draws to its close.   450
Italy   Ausonia had not seen a fairer day:
welcomes   Aurora, rosy-cheeked, attends the team
the heroes   of Phoebus; he, more joyous than his wont
and fairer far, with words exhorts his steeds,
and now, from Apennines' summit crowned with trees,
smiles down on Rome. The magnates and the folk
rush towards the gates, both sexes, every caste,

all ages, high and low; of every rank
they hasten forth; on either hand the ground
is strewn with gold, and stands and tiers are decked   460
with divers glittering gems. The very streets
are carpeted in purple; canopies
of purple too are spread from roof to roof
to shade the conquering heroes as they march.
On one side lines of elders make their way
towards the first portal, all of gentle mien,
and on the other phalanxes of youth
in festive garments go with them to greet
the general. Within the towering walls
Scipio enters, his aspect serene,   470
borne on a purple-covered chariot, drawn
by chargers white as snow. His countenance
of noble semblance proves his birth divine.
Close following his car come hordes of sad
and grieving captives, with their fettered hands
behind their backs: the Macedonian lords,
sent by King Philip to stir up the war,
their chief Sopater first, the king's own sib,
with mournful tread, and after him, in chains
of iron plods his dismal company.   480
Beyond, behold the moving spectacle
of once-great Syphax; his high majesty
in bondage is a sight most pitiful;
great floods of tears bedew his breast and fall
upon the ground he treads, and as he weeps
his eyes turn towards his noble conqueror's face
and with unspoken bitter thoughts he marks
the manner of the man he scorned as friend.
So shame—unhappy man—comes to increase
the anguish of his ruin. A huge crowd   490
of his cohorts upon his traces comes
with feeble, faltering stride. And next in line
the true transgressors march, the treacherous seed
of Carthage, fettered as they well deserve,
once more to see the walls of noble Rome;
and first among them is the general,

brother to Hannibal. Then files of Moors
and bands of savage Gauls. Look not to find
Italian warriors here, for Scipio
has doomed all such to just and speedy death   500
and left them buried under Punic sod
as foes unworthy evermore to see
their native land or rest beneath its soil.
Ivory and gleaming gold and precious goods
and robes of splendid purple and the wealth
of mighty kings are likewise borne along
as the great triumph wends its solemn way.
Mark too the heavy shields and armor seized
from mighty warriors, standards, fearsome helms
with crests of waving plumes, and captured steeds,   510
no longer mettlesome, and elephants
with heads bowed low, reft from the enemy.
Around these monsters countless children press;
the ignorant crowd, awed by such creatures, gapes
and utters loud expressions of surprise
and wonder that barbarian lands should bear
such huge and ponderous brutes. On either side
the Roman ranks break forth in joyous song,
as is the ancient custom, celebrating
salvation from the impious servitude   520
that threatened them; they cannot satiate
their avid vision as they look upon
their savior. First among them stands the famed
Terentius Culleo, senator of Rome: *524*
a free man, it is said he venerates
his cherished patron and through all his life
has honored Scipio as his liege lord.
Next comes the conquering host, the seasoned troops
with Latin arms, in files of horse and foot,
prepared to meet fierce Hannibal's assault   530
should he appear again before the gates.
Horns and triumphant trumpets far and wide
blare out their raucous notes; the Tiber's waves
and circumjacent groves are terrified;
the dreadful noise shakes Alba's ancient walls,

Argolic Tibur and Soracte's snows   *536*
and high Praeneste's towering citadel.   *537*

Scipio in   At last, in such a triumph as great Rome
triumph   has never witnessed, Scipio ascends
the Capitol and offers there his thanks   540
to the propitious gods. Within the fane
of Jove he stores a mountain of pure gold
and treasures vast and copious to enrich
his country for all time. But for himself
his title is enough; no particle   *545*
of wealth he carries with him to his home.
His sword, beyond all doubt, has cleared the way
for conquests yet to come, assuring Rome
of world empire. With Carthage overthrown,
no nation henceforth will deem it a shame   *550*
to wear the yoke and call the men of Rome,
Quirinus' sons, invincible in war,
the rightful lords and rulers of the world.
Wearing his crown of laurel, Scipio
comes down again from the Tarpeian rock
and traverses once more the joyous town.
Upon the right hand of so great a guide
stands Ennius, his temples also girt
with like triumphal crown, to celebrate
great learning and sustaining poesy.   560

After this twain, throughout the long years since,
others have come, in eager rivalry.
Petrarch's   I too, when fifteen centuries had passed
farewell   through their appointed cycles, greatly strove
to his   with all the means my meager strength allowed
poem   to follow o'er the rough and thorny path
those precious traces and to imitate
with similar crown, like site, and glorious name,
the ancient heroes and their dignities
sublime, lest what the Greek bard had foretold   *570*
of me might prove a faulty prophecy.
Now, Goddess, after all these joyous things,

I dare not call on you to share my song
of savage deeds nor dark events and dire.
Nay, rather turn your face away and flee.
In truth I would flee with you, staying not
to tell sad tales of envy, count the crimes
and faults of senators and errant folk,
nor speak of Scipio's self-banishment
and death, nor of his mournful epitaph,   580
the harsh, resentful syllables inscribed
upon his marble tomb. Let others write
of such grim matters. I purpose now to bring
my song here to its end. I'll not consent
to let the sacred sisters be abased
by dark and gloomy substance for their notes.
My *Africa*, what pain has it not cost
to bring you to conclusion! While you grew
under my loving hands, incessantly
embellished and recast, lo, Death, the churl,   590
has borne away before his proper time
the great-souled Robert from a world that has   592
sore need of him. And now I am deprived
of all that life holds dear. The path I hoped
lay open to your destiny is closed.
What road will you now take, O luckless one?
I shall point out the way. Seek not the halls
funereal tears have ravaged nor the court,
once happy, of Parthenope. Nay, take
your grief where fresh stones mark a recent tomb   600
and there pour forth your tears. When you behold
the little plot that holds the mighty king,
commend yourself to him in death as once
while he yet lived you had been pledged to him,
and with his sacred ashes keep true faith.
His soul returning Heavenward looks down
with scorn upon the inert earth below,
bidding farewell to transitory crowns
and holding mortal deeds of small account.
And yet the king, who now has but a smile   610
for the abandoned sceptre of his realm,

his former cares and taxing toils and all
the errors of mankind that from his seat
celestial he surveys with pity, yet—
unless I sadly err, he loves me still.
Of old he did most kindly judge my gifts.
Now that this star has been reft from our earth,
alas, I tremble lest a harsher age
may fall on you and in blind cruelty
defile your glory. Now that he who was   620
protector of our Muses is no more—
for of our generation he alone
could truly pay to Letters their just meed
of praise—my hopes likewise are dead and gone.
Ah, happy those whom better days than ours
have nourished; would that I—but all in vain
my futile wish. It is impossible
to turn back on our path. Latecomers all,
this new age holds us fast and a cruel Jove
looks down upon us from the poles of Heaven.   630
We must accept our lot and follow on
whither our stars will lead us, patiently,
lest we be dragged along at their caprice.
My life is destined to be spent 'midst storms
and turmoil. But if you, as is my wish
and ardent hope, shall live on after me,
a more propitious age will come again:
this Lethean stupor surely can't endure
His hopes   forever. Our posterity, perchance,
of future   when the dark clouds are lifted, may enjoy   640
glory   once more the radiance the ancients knew.
Then shall you see on Helicon's green slope
new growth arise, the sacred laurel bear
new leaves, and talents will spring up renewed,
and gentle spirits in whose hearts the zeal
for learning will be joined with the old love
for all the Muses will come forth again.
Be you then mindful to restore my name
by virtue of your art; let my renown
return to my grave-site at least, and may   650

my ashes have due honors paid to them.
Among such men my life will be more sweet
and my fame will deride the sepulchre.
Meanwhile I bid you make your cautious way
with careful step, revealing not your name,
through the indifferent years that lie ahead.
Few homes you'll find, alas, to shelter you,
and rare infrequent welcome where you go
throughout the universe. But if your Fates
should happily provide you with a friend   660
of honest virtue, let him be your host.
Seek but a corner of a poor man's hut—
rather than wander lonely through the world,
forever dogged by wickedness—and there
grow old in peace; let wrinkles crease your brow
until you reach the sill of a new age.
Then, when the dawning of a happier day,
kindly to poets, gracious to the just,
shall light the world, renew your verdancy.

   If it has been the fortune of one youth   670
to drag another from the fiery blaze
and bear him safely o'er the rolling deep,
I pray you through the long years of your age
preserve these exploits after I am gone,
and when voracious time has swallowed all,
defy the fleeting days, the circling sun
that burns away the centuries, and the teeth
of bitter envy, ever prone to gnaw.

Notes

In preparing our notes to the text of the poem we have found Corradini's "Adnotata" to his edition an invaluable aid. In addition to the cases where specific acknowledgment has seemed appropriate, we have turned to them frequently, sometimes slightly revising them. Particularly for the references to classical authors we have depended heavily on Corradini's guidance.

For Petrarch's *Familiares* our text of reference throughout is the edition of Rossi and Bosco.

INTRODUCTION

1. Translated from James Harvey Robinson and Henry Winchester Rolfe, *Petrarch: The First Modern Scholar and Man of Letters*, p. 70.

2. Ernest Hatch Wilkins, *Life of Petrarch*, p. 19.

3. Nicola Festa, *Saggio sull'Africa del Petrarca*, p. 7.

4. The works, in Bernardo's phrase (Aldo Bernardo, *Petrarch, Scipio and the "Africa,"* p. 11) "evolved simultaneously." Guido Martellotti in his edition of the prose work, *Francesco Petrarca: La vita di Scipione l'Africano*, discusses their relationship at length.

5. Bernardo, *Petrarch, Scipio and the "Africa,"* pp. 72, 102.

6. Robinson and Rolfe, *Petrarch*, p. 72.

7. Wilkins, *Life of Petrarch*, p. 30.

8. Festa, *Saggio*, pp. 16-17.

9. Ibid., p. 9.

10. Ibid., p. 9.

11. Morris Bishop, *Letters from Petrarch*, p. 9.

12. Aldo Bernardo, trans., *Francesco Petrarca: Rerum familiarium libri I-VIII*, p. 399. See further E. Paratore, "L'elaborazione padovana dell *Africa,*" in *Petrarca, Venezia e il Veneto*, ed. Giorgio Padoan, pp. 53-91.

13. Wilkins, *Life of Petrarch*, p. 119.

14. Ibid., p. 184.

15. The above remarks from Burckhardt, Toffanin, and Carrara are cited by Bernardo in chapter 8 of *Petrarch, Scipio and the "Africa."*

16. *Petrarch and His World*, p. 180.

17. T. K. Seung, *Cultural Thematics*, p. 155.

18. *Petrarch and His World*, p. 181.

BOOK 1

3. first: Two Scipios were called Africanus. Petrarch's hero is Scipio
Africanus the Elder (235-183 B.C.); his grandson by adoption, victor in
the Third Punic War, was Scipio Africanus the Younger (185-129 B.C.).
    8. Helicon: the legendary mountain of the Muses.
    17-18. These lines support Petrarch's statement (see introduction) that
he began his poem at Easter time.
    22. Parnassus: a mountain sacred to Apollo, god of poetic inspiration.
    26. Trinacria: Sicily. The king is Robert of Naples, King of Sicily, some-
times styled "the Wise" (1275-1343, crowned 1310). See introduction.
    32. "If you read . . .": *Legenti* in line 24 of the original is impersonal.
But one may assume, in view of the allusion to the end of the work, which
contains a eulogy of Robert, that "the reader" is the king. Develay, Westin,
and Barolo translate as we do.
    52-98. In this passage Petrarch is recalling, one might say publishing,
his conversation with Robert on the occasion of his examination for the
laurel crown (see introduction). On the exchange Wilkins (*Life of Petrarch*,
p. 26) reports: "Petrarch showed him the *Africa*—it may well be that he
read him some lines of it—and Robert asked that the poem be dedicated
to him. He asked also that Petrarch write something in verse in his honor."
Wilkins's source is undoubtedly *Ep. Met.* 2.10, wherein Petrarch states
that he was stunned by the request to sing of Robert, since he felt inade-
quate to the task, but as for his "Scipiad," it could be sent to no worthier
court than that of the king. See Corradini, pp. 411-12.
    69-72. These lines allude to the epics of Virgil (*Aeneid*), Statius (*Thebaid*
and *Achilleid*), and Lucan (*Pharsalia*). Emathian: Thessalian; a reference
to the battle of Pharsalus in Thessaly where Caesar defeated Pompey,
48 B.C.
    77. Ausonian: Italian. The poets often speak of Italy as Ausonia, after
the name of the Ausones, ancient inhabitants of central and southern Italy.
    88. Parthenope: Naples.
    113. See Livy 21.1.
    142 ff. Corradini (p. 412) is reminded of *Aeneid* 1.16 and 4.628.
    151-54. Rome fought three Punic wars. The first, 264-241 B.C., se-
cured Sicily for Rome; the second, 218-201 B.C., deprived Carthage of
her Spanish provinces and her fleet; the third, 149-146 B.C., resulted in
the destruction of Carthage. The words of the original (lines 110-13)
are almost literally from Florus 2.15.
    156. Petrarch's subject will be the Second Punic War. Some of his
phraseology echoes Livy's comment (21.1.1-3) on the magnitude of the
contest.
    157. After this line (114 of the original) Festa (p. 7) indicates a lacuna.

158. See Livy 27.19 and 20.28.16.

159. star-splendored: "sidereum" in line 115 of the original. Corradini (p. 412) refers us to Petrarch's discussion of the word in *Fam.* 10.4.

168. This is Hasdrubal Gisgonides, commander of the Carthaginian army in Spain.

174 ff. Scipio, having victoriously concluded the war in Spain, returned to Rome in 205 B.C. Elected consul, he won the approval of the Senate for his plan to invade Africa. His expeditionary force, probably thirty-five thousand in number, sailed from Lilybaeum in the spring of 204 and landed near Utica. Scullard (*Scipio Africanus: Soldier and Politician*, pp. 108-15) provides an account of the political and military background.

177. Phoebus: the sun. 184 ff.: Livy 2.7.38-40.

211. Tithonus' bride: Aurora, the dawn; Ovid, *Met.* 9.421.

222 ff. The dream vision here is inspired by the commentary of Macrobius on the "Somnium Scipionis" of Cicero. In Cicero's version (found in book 6 of *De re publica*), Scipio Africanus the Younger dreams of Scipio Africanus the Elder. In Petrarch's version it is the elder Africanus who dreams of his father Publius Cornelius, killed (211 B.C.) fighting against the Carthaginians in Spain, as was the latter's brother, Gnaeus Cornelius. Petrarch's adaptation is strategically sound. He preserves the dream and with it the "aura of sublimity" (Bernardo, p. 128) essential to his hero, who still participates in the vision though as disciple rather than master, and at the same time he leaves the exploits of his Africanus still available for narrative purposes. "What Petrarch needs . . . is a hero whose accomplishment is ahead of him rather than behind him" (Seung, *Cultural Thematics*, p. 143).

246. The woman referred to is Dido.

256. Bágrada (sometimes Bágradas): a river in North Africa, flowing near Utica; now called the Medjerdah.

258. Byrsa: another name for Carthage, from the Greek, meaning "hide." It derives from a legend that Dido, having been granted as much land as she could cover with a bull's hide, cut the hide into thin strips and marked off an area large enough for a city. See *Aeneid* 1.367; Livy 34.62.12.

299. The "lucis inaccessae" of line 223 of the original is from 1 *Timothy* 6:16 (Corradini, p. 412).

300-01. See *Apocalypse* 21:4 (Corradini, p. 412).

317 ff. For Scipio's father's last battle see Livy 25.34. His uncle was killed twenty-nine days later (Livy 25.36).

333. We prefer Corradini's conjecture "Mars" (p. 113, note) to the "Mors" of the manuscript.

339. Celtic: actually, as Festa (p. 13) notes, Celtiberians, but the word would not suit the meter.

342. Petrarch cautions against mercenaries also in *Rhymes* 128.

368. Erebus: a god of the lower world, son of Chaos, here standing for the nether world itself, Hades.

389. Eryx: a mountain in Sicily, now called Monte San Giuliano.

390. Auster: the south wind.

445. Hesperia: Spain.

446. After "mine" Festa (p. 16) postulates a lacuna, following line 318 of the original.

460. Augustine in the second dialogue of the *Secretum* reminds Petrarch of this line.

466. From Cicero, *De re publica* 6.14.

490-91. The Phrygian (Trojan) Penates were carried from Troy by Anchises when Troy fell to the Greeks.

502. Marcus Claudius Marcellus, slain in a skirmish with the Carthaginians in 208 B.C. Livy (27.27.12) says he was over sixty years old at the time. Petrarch alludes to his death in *Rerum memorandarum* 3.5.15.

504. Following this line (362 of the original) Festa (p. 18) indicates a lacuna.

506. T. Quintius Crispinus, commander of the fleet and the winter camp near Syracuse (Livy 24.39.12); for his death see Livy 27.26-28 and 33.

509. The other: Marcellus.

513. Fabius: Quintus Fabius Maximus, the famous "Delayer." After the Roman defeat at Lake Trasimenus (217 B.C.) he was made dictator by popular vote. the first such in Roman history. Wearying of his defensive tactics, the Romans later replaced him—and suffered defeat at Cannae.

518. "Yonder soul" is Fabius. He died in 203 B.C., before the end of the war. See Cicero, *Cato Major de senectute* 10-13, for praises of this hero, an opponent of Scipio's policies.

522-25. Tiberius Sempronius Gracchus, betrayed by a Lucanian ally and slain in ambush (Livy 25.16 and 17). Livy (24.16) relates that in his haste Gracchus rushed into battle without his shield, hence "unprotected."

526. Aemilius Paulus, consul, slain at Cannae in 216 B.C. (Livy 22.44.49)

533. Gnaeus Lentulus: a tribune. Livy (22.49) relates that after the battle Lentulus found Aemilius Paulus sitting on a stone, covered with blood; the tribune offered his horse to the consul.

547. The consul Terentius Varro was the imprudent colleague.

582. Livy (22.49) gives the number slain as 45,500 infantry and 2,700 cavalry.

602. Calpe: one of the Pillars of Hercules, now the Rock of Gibraltar.

613-14. Cf. Dante, *Paradiso* 15.28-30.

634 ff. See Cicero, *De re publica* 6.15.

703. Numa Pompilius (Livy 1.18-21). Virgil (*Aeneid* 6.809) mentions his aged aspect (see below, lines 713-14); Petrarch alludes to it again in the third dialogue of the *Secretum* (Corradini, p. 414).

709. The nymph Egeria or Camoena, wife and teacher of Numa.

714 ff. Tullus Hostilius (Livy 1.22-31). Petrarch alludes to the thunderbolt in *Fam.* 15.9.

716. The "omnem/Militiae artem" of the original (lines 519-20) is a phrase taken from Florus 1.3 (Corradini, p. 414).

718 ff. Ancus Martius (Livy 1.32). Commenting on the phrase "Quartus arat muros" (line 522 of the original), Festa (p. 25, note) speaks of Petrarch's "coinage" of *arare* in this sense; he cites *Aeneid* 5.755, "urbem designat aratro," as a possible source. Corradini notes that Petrarch's phraseology follows that of Florus (1.4) very closely but the poet has not quite understood his authority.

724. Tarquin, fifth king of Rome (Livy 1.34).

727 ff. Again, from Florus 1.5.

731. Servius Tullius, sixth king of Rome (Livy 1.41); Petrarch speaks of him in *De remediis* 2.5.

738. See Florus 1.8.

743. Tarquin the Proud: the seventh king (Livy 1.49).

750 ff. See Florus 1.8.

757. These are the Horatii, the three Roman brothers who fought a duel with the three Curiatii, champions of Alba Longa, to determine which city should be supreme. One of the Horatii survived, slew the Curiatii one by one, and assured the triumph of Rome (Livy 1.24 ff.).

790. This is Valerius Publicola, who succeeded the first Brutus in the consulship (Livy 2.8.1). We may note here that most of the noble Romans in this roll call, as well as those enumerated in the catalogues of books 2, 3, and 8, parade before us in the "Triumph of Fame" 1.

BOOK 2

43. one-eyed: Corradini (p. 416) suspects that Petrarch's "latronem . . . luscum" (line 32 of the original) was suggested by Juvenal's "ducem . . . luscum" (*Satire* 10.158), and remarks that the word appears again in the rather striking picture of Hannibal in the early version of "Triumph of Fame" 1.121-27: "vidi oltra un rivo il gran Cartaginese/la cui memoria ancor l'Italia punge;/l'un occhio avea lasciato al mio paese,/stagnando al freddo tempo il fiume tosco,/sicch'egli era a vederlo stranio arnese,/sopra un grande elefante un duce losco." See below, book 7, line 1115, note, and book 8, line 92, note.

61-76. Petrarch will keep his word; these verses are an outline of Hannibal's argument in book 7, lines 278 ff.

116. Scipio in later life, it is said, went as an envoy to the court of Antiochus and in Ephesus met Hannibal, who was a refugee in the court. According to Livy (35.14.5) the generals exchanged courteous discourse. Charles-Picard (*Hannibal*, p. 10) says that the famous conversation "est sûrement apocryphe mais reflète un état d'esprit vraisemblable."

128-30. See Virgil, *Georgicon* 2.505-07.

141. A thought expressed also in *Fam.* 13.10.

147. Betrayed by the king of Bithynia, Hannibal committed suicide in 183 B.C. (see Livy 39.51).

155. This notion is found in Florus 2.7.

160. Aetolia: a region of western Greece, occupied by Rome in 191 B.C.

162. younger brother: Lucius Cornelius Scipio "Asiaticus," conqueror of Antiochus III of Syria at the battle of Magnesia, 190 B.C. (Livy 37.37. 41).

168-180. Corradini (p. 417) cites Florus 2.7-14 in addition to Livy as Petrarch's source for these lines. Galatia: a region in central Asia Minor.

175. The "sires" of the Romans were the Trojans.

176. Acilius Glabrio: consul with Cornelius Scipio Nasica, a cousin of our Scipio, in 191 B.C. He defeated Antiochus at Thermopylae (Livy 36. 16-19; 37).

177. L. Mummius Achaicus defeated the Achaean League and destroyed Corinth, 146 B.C. (Livy 42).

178. Flaminius: conqueror of Philip V of Macedonia, 197 B.C. (Livy 33. 6-10).

181-86. These clans and *cognomina* recur frequently in Roman annals, although some attained prominence only after Scipio's time. L. Aemilius Scaurus, consul in 115 B.C., was involved in the war with Jugurtha. C. Livius Drusus was co-consul with Scipio Africanus the Younger in 147 B.C. L. Caecilius Metellus, consul in 247 and 241, was famous for his rescue of the Palladium from the burning temple of Vesta; his son Q. C. Metellus served under Claudius Nero at the battle of the Metaurus. Line 185 alludes to the emperor Nero.

187. M. Porcius Cato, the "censor" (234-149 B.C.), of plebeian birth, author of *De re rustica*, was celebrated for the austerity of his life. He served under Scipio at Zama, disapproved of his general's lavish disposition of the spoils, and became his implacable enemy (see Livy 38.54). He was ultimately responsible for Scipio's political downfall (see Scullard, *Scipio Africanus*, pp. 221-23). A later M. Porcius Cato ("of Utica"), a stern republican, committed suicide after the victory of Caesar's forces at Thapsus. See below, line 314 and note.

190. your heir: see above, book 1, line 3, note. Petrarch mentions the adoption also in *De remediis* 3.131.

196. Sulla: L. Cornelius Sulla (or Silla), 138-78 B.C., was the leader of the aristocratic faction opposed to the popular party of Marius. Conqueror of the Samnites in the Social War of 89 B.C. and of Mithridates of Pontus (85 B.C.), he is also famous for his massive proscriptions of the followers of Marius (Florus 3.21). Of the Pompeys the two most celebrated are Pompey the Great (108-48 B.C.; see below, lines 218 ff.) and his son Sextus Pompeius (74-35 B.C.).

197. This is Marcus Junius Brutus, one of the assassins of Julius Caesar.

205. The leader is Caius Marius (156-86 B.C.). In 104 B.C. he defeated Jugurtha of Numidia and took him prisoner (Sallust, *Jugurtha* 87-114). Petrarch mentions him in *Ep. Met.* 1.3 and in *De remediis* 2.5, in both cases defining him as a "rustic."

213. At Aquae Sextiae, now Aix-en-Provence, Marius defeated the Teutons and the Cimbri, invading German tribes (102 B.C.; Florus 3.3). Petrarch alludes to the victory in *Rhymes* 128.44-48.

220. another: Pompey the Great; see Caesar, *De bello civili* 3.86, and Cicero, *Epistulae ad familiares* 5.11.2.

222. Baetis: now the Guadalquivir.

225. rebel: Quintus Sertorius attempted to set up an autonomous government in Spain; he was defeated by Pompey, 76 B.C. See Livy 44, summary.

254 ff. Festa (p. 36, note) reminds us that these lines echo *Lucan* 2.576-94.

261. Maeotis: the Sea of Azov.

262. Riphean: in the northern part of Scythia.

265 ff. Petrarch follows Florus 3.5 *extra*.

266. Saba: Sheba, ancient name for a region of Arabia, including what is now known as the Yemen; famous for frankincense and myrrh.

267. In 64 B.C., after three months' siege, Pompey captured Jerusalem (Josephus, *History of the Jews*, 14.1-5).

276. In *Fam.* 15.7 Petrarch speaks of Crete as "the ancient home of superstitions."

286. one: Julius Caesar. Corradini (p. 419) cites Florus 3.10 and Suetonius, "Caesar" 25, as Petrarch's sources.

313. See above, line 177, note.

314. Pharsalus: a town in the region called Pharsalia; see above, book 1, lines 69-72, note. At Thapsus, on the coast of Tunisia, Caesar defeated Pompey's last partisans, 46 B.C.

315. Munda: ancient Spanish town near Córdoba; here, in 45 B.C., Caesar defeated Pompey's sons.

317-30. The nephew is the emperor Augustus (63 B.C.-14 A.D.). He was made "Imperator" in 28 B.C. See Florus 4.3.11 and 12. This passage is echoed in *Fam.* 23.1.

321. consort: Cleopatra, wife of Mark Antony. For the rattles see *Aeneid* 8.696.

324. Ister: the lower Danube.

333-35. The portals of the temple of Janus, two-faced Roman god of beginnings and enterprises, were closed only in times of peace. See *Aeneid* 7.601-10.

337. See Suetonius, "Augustus" 99.

348 ff. The allusion is to the emperor Vespasian (reigned 69-79 A.D.)

and his son Titus (made co-ruler 71, died 81). Orosius (8.3.8; 9.9) mentions the double triumph; Petrarch alludes to it in *Fam.* 23.1.

347. Tartarus: Hades, also called Orcus. See book 2, line 371.

362. Trajan (98-117) was born in Spain. Septimius Severus (193-211) was an African.

380-83. Of the Roman emperors of the third century Philip may be called "Syrian" and Decius was an Illyrian. Gaul was represented as early as the second century by Antoninus Pius (138-161). In the fourth century came the Greek Julian and Valentinian of German ("boreal") stock. (But the poet may have in mind Charlemagne and his successors.) Petrarch mentions the diversity of imperial origins in *De remediis* 2.5.

395. The spectacle of Roman ruins made a deep impression on Petrarch; see *Rhymes* 53.

400-02. If Petrarch is here thinking of his own times, as seems likely, he has no doubt a specific "strong man" in mind. Martellotti (p. 627, note) believes it may be either the unidentified "spirto gentil" of *Rhymes* 53 or Cola di Rienzi; Stefano Colonna is suggested by Corradini (p. 420).

431. Cynthia: the moon, sister to Phoebus Apollo, the sun.

446 ff. This strain of sententious melancholy is recurrent in Petrarch; see *Fam.* 1.3; *Rhymes* 91.12-14, 244.12, etc. Also the "Triumph of Death" 1.79-100.

467-69. Boethius (2.7) speaks of the smallness of the inhabited globe and of the consequent insignificance of human fame. Petrarch may have had the passage in mind here. Perhaps a little closer is the passage in Cicero's *De re publica* 6.20. Dante's vision from Gemini (*Paradiso* 22.133-54) is suggestively similar. Augustine in *Secretum* 3 quotes these lines to Petrarch.

487 ff. A passage to which Truth alludes in the introduction to the *Secretum.*

499 ff. See Cicero, *De re publica* 20.

514. Taprobane: Ceylon.

525 ff. See Cicero, *De re publica* 21 and 23.

555. See *Secretum* 3, where Augustine alludes to this passage, and the "Triumph of Time" 139-45, especially line 143: "chiamasi Fama ed è morir secondo."

573. The youth is Petrarch. Etrurian: Tuscan.

575. Ennius: Roman poet, 239-169? B.C., author of the *Annales,* an epic of Roman history written in hexameters. Petrarch speaks of him as "rudis" in *Bucolicum carmen* 3.155, echoing Ovid's line, "Ennius ingenio maximo, arte rudis" (*Tristia* 2.424).

589 ff. Augustine quotes these lines to Petrarch in *Secretum* 3.

610. The thought is from Cicero, *De re publica* 6.23. Petrarch enlarges upon it in *Fam.* 14.4.

626. Augustine quotes this verse in *Secretum* 3. See also *Fam.* 1.2. Petrarch's thought follows Cicero, *Tusc.* 1.45.109.

651-53. "Scipio" in Latin means "a staff for support." The "other title" is "Africanus."

664-68. Gaius Laelius, of plebeian stock, was the friend and confidant of Scipio. He had a distinguished career; after serving with Scipio in Spain and Africa he held various public offices, including the consulship (190 B.C.). His son, another Gaius Laelius (line 668), became the friend and confidant of Scipio Africanus the Younger. Petrarch affectionately bestowed the nickname "Lelius" on his own intimate friend Lello di Pietro di Stefano dei Tosetti. See *Fam.* 19.3.

682-85. See Cicero, *De re publica* 6.26.

698-700. The same thought is expressed in *Fam.* 2.3.

702. The story of Scipio's political eclipse and self-imposed exile is told in Livy 38.52–54.

704. An allusion to the inscription Scipio caused to be carved on his tomb. See below, book 5, line 992 and note.

BOOK 3

19. cousin: see above, book 2, line 176 and note.

26-27. An echo of Christ's words, *Luke* 23:34.

36 ff. Scipio's uneasiness is justified. During Scipio's campaign in Spain Hannibal had remained in southern Italy, a constant threat to Rome. Scipio's strategy, which called for dislodging the Carthaginians from Spain, then invading Africa, and so ultimately necessitating Hannibal's withdrawal from Italy, was finally successful but always risky and subject to criticism.

88. Syphax was king of the Massaesyli, "a tribe directly facing the region of Spain in which lies New Carthage" (Livy 25.17.5). He was an ally of the Carthaginians; in 206 B.C. Scipio sent Laelius to him with gifts, attempting to win him over. The mission was well received but Syphax requested a visit from Scipio himself. See Livy 28.17.

108. A lacuna occurs after this line (midway through line 87 of the original). The narrative resumes with the entrance of Laelius into the palace of Syphax. The progress through the ornamented hall has echoes of Aeneas in the Carthaginian temple of Juno (*Aeneid* 1.441–93), and gradually takes on something of the nature of Petrarch's *Trionfi*. The whole passage, a kind of humanistic exercise in its own right, has attracted the attention of scholars; Bernardo (pp. 128-42) discusses their findings and adds his own comments.

111. At this point (line 90 of the original) Festa's text shows a lacuna.

117. Atlas: mythological king of Mauritania, son of Iapetus and Clymene. A lover of astronomy, he studied the courses of the moon and the stars. He was turned into a mountain by Perseus (Ovid, *Met.* 4.632 ff.). Petrarch may have found some of the details here in Augustine's *De civitate Dei* 18.8.

118. seven spinning stars: the planets.

119-20. Saturn.

120-21. Mars.

122. The kinder rays are from Jupiter.

123. The carbuncle holds the place of the sun.

128. Phoebus: the sun. See book 2, line 431, note.

129. Another pair: Venus and Mercury.

137-63. Here Petrarch describes the signs of the Zodiac, beginning with the Ram, who brings in springtime and, for most mediaeval calendars, the new year. The poet sees the Ram as looking back at Helle, daughter of Athamas; legend tells that the girl fell off the back of the Ram into the sea, henceforth called the Hellespont (Ovid, *Fasti* 3.869-70). Taurus is seen carrying off Europa, daughter of Agenor, king of Phoenicia. The "rosy Maiden" of line 147 is Virgo. Lines 152-57 describe Sagittarius, a legendary centaur from Thessaly. The "naked man" of line 160 is Aquarius.

173. The lad from Ida: Ganymede, snatched from Ida by Zeus to be cup-bearer to the gods on Olympus (*Met.* 10.155-61).

175. Saturn was the ancient Italian god of agriculture. He is sometimes identified with Cronus, the ancient deity of the Greeks who, fearful lest he be dethroned, devoured his own progeny.

178. The dragon, guardian of the Hesperian fruit, was slain by Hercules and translated to the heavens by Hera to become the constellation Draco.

182. Neptune's trident gave him power over the waves and sea creatures. See *Met.* 12.580.

188-89. Apollo's changing aspect is an allegory of the passing of time. Petrarch enlarges on the theme in *Secretum* 3. See also "The Triumph of Time" 61-71 (Corradini, p. 427).

193 ff. Corradini (p. 427) sees another allegory in these lines: the serpents signifying the circling years and the three heads the three ages of Roman history, as described by Sallust.

204. The Python was a monstrous serpent generated by the earth and slain by Apollo (*Met.* 1.438-47).

211. Apollo's younger brother is Mercury, the messenger of the immortals, god of traders and thieves, known for his acuteness and eloquence. Line 217 refers to his putting Argus to sleep with his music (*Met.* 1.682 ff.). According to Corradini (p. 427) the youthful bride of line 128 is Philology (following the fifth-century epic of Martianus Capella, *De nuptiis Mercurii et Philologiae*), her "dowry" being the seven liberal arts. Mythologically she can only be Io. The significance of the cock, either mythological or allegorical, is obscure.

221. The three Gorgons are Medusa, Stheno, and Euryale, daughters of Phorcys (see *Aeneid* 6.289). Medusa's glance was so potent that it turned to stone all living things. All around her dwelling petrified figures of men and beasts testified to her power. See Ovid, *Met.* 4.750-81.

224. The ancient: Atlas.

225. Pegasus: the winged horse, sprung from the Gorgon's blood (*Met.* 4.786).

226. The fountain of Hippocrene.

232 ff. That the lovely Venus should have as a husband the mis-shapen and gross Vulcan was a constant source of amusement to the immortals and resentful embarrassment to Vulcan. Petrarch may here be alluding to the love affair between Venus and Mars.

237. Pan, the god of woods and shepherds (*Met.* 11.146-47).

242. The queen is Juno, wife of Jupiter.

246. Iris, the rainbow goddess, Juno's messenger (*Met.* 1.270-71).

248. Minerva, goddess of wisdom. See *Met.* 6.78-83 and passim. Sometimes called Pallas, her favorite bird was the owl, her favorite tree the olive.

255. Cecrops was the mythical founder of Athens, named after Pallas Athene (Minerva). See *Met.* 6.70-71.

257-59. Born of the head of Jupiter, Minerva mocks the shameful birth and lowly cradle of her sister goddess. The reference is to Venus's being born of the "aphros" or froth of Uranus when he was castrated and his genitals floated to Cyprus, traditional birthplace of Venus.

266. The attendant girls are the Graces.

270. the Boy: Cupid, whose arrow wounded Apollo and caused him to fall in love with Daphne (*Met.* 1.452 ff.).

276 ff. Diana: virgin goddess of the hunt; Dryads: tree nymphs; Oreads: mountain nymphs.

280. The shepherd is Endymion..

282. Actaeon was changed into a stag and killed by his hounds after he saw Diana bathing (*Met.* 3.198 ff.).

288. Cybele: mother of the gods (*Met.* 10.104, 696, 704).

300 ff. The description of the underworld is adapted from *Aeneid* 6.

303. Tartarus: another name for the lower world.

304. Proserpina, abducted by Pluto (*Met.* 5.391 ff.).

309. nine dark provinces: as in Dante's *Inferno*.

310-18. In these lines Petrarch brings in all the traditional rivers of the lower world. So too in his *De otio religiosorum* 2. Avernus: Hades.

319. Charon, the boatman who ferries the souls of the dead across the Styx (*Aeneid* 6.326).

328. Cerberus, the three-headed dog, guardian of Avernus (*Aeneid* 6. 417-18).

387. Livy (28.17.7-8) mentions that Laelius brought gifts which the king was glad to receive, but does not specify them.

390. Auster: see above, book 1, line 390, note.

464. Meroë: the legendary Ethiopian island in the Nile.

468-69. The feast of Alcinous is described in the *Odyssey* (8.62 ff.).

Petrarch knew Homer chiefly through the incomplete translation of Leontius Pilatus.

477-500. These lines summarize the various exploits of Hercules: the slaying of the lion of Nemea and the Hydra of Lerna (regions in Argolis), his visit to the lower world, his raising of the Pillars of Hercules, and so on. Festa (p. 67, note) sees Lucan (*Pharsalia* 4.609 ff.) as Petrarch's principal source; see also *Met.* 9.182-98.

481. Haemonia: Thessaly, separating Mount Ossa from Mount Olympus.

482. Erymanthian: Arcadian (*Met.* 2.499).

484. The centaurs were fabulous creatures, half man, half horse. Hercules slew the centaur Nessus for attempting to violate Deianira (*Met.* 9.118 ff.). Geryon was a three-bodied monster also slain by Hercules (*Met.* 9.184).

486. Antaeus: a Libyan giant, killed by Hercules (*Met.* 9.184).

494. Orcus: Hades.

496. Megaera: one of the Furies.

501. Festa (p. 68, note to line 400 of the original) suggests that the youth is Alexander the Great, dismissing Corradini's candidate (p. 428), Pythias of Marseilles, a navigator of the fourth century B.C.

509. Medusa: see above, line 221, note.

517. Perseus. See *Met.* 4.772 ff.

524. queen: Dido. Petrarch enlarges on her history in *Sen.* 4.4; he defends her also in "The Triumph of Chastity" 10-12 and 154-59.

526. Probably Petrarch is thinking of "Byrsa" as the name of the city. See above, book 1, line 258, note. "Carthage" is from the Phoenician "Kereth-Hadeshoth" meaning "new city," new as compared to the older Utica. See Smith, *Geography*, 1:529.

535. The detractor is Virgil.

544. The Philaeni were two Carthaginian brothers who, for love of their country, allowed themselves to be buried alive. See Sallust, *Jugurtha* 79.

556. Livy (21.37) tells of Hannibal's use of "vinegar" to split rock and make his way through the Alps.

590-92. A reference to the naval battle of the Aegates (a group of islands off the west coast of Sicily); the Roman victory there marked the end of the First Punic War, 241 B.C.

598. Tarpeian rock: a steep eminence, jutting in ancient times from the south face of the Capitoline. Roman annals and records were preserved in that area.

604-07. Corradini (p. 430) notes that this comment echoes a passage in Sallust, *Catilina* 8.

620. An allusion to Mummius Achaicus; see above, book 2, line 177, note.

626. Anchises' son: Aeneas.

637. Lavinia was the daughter of Latinus, king of Latium. Aeneas married her and became heir to the kingdom. See *Aeneid* 7.249-85.

644. Romulus avenged his grandfather Numitor, king of Alba Longa (Livy 5.3; 6.2).

660. Curius Dentatus: victor over the Samnites and Pyrrhus (275 B.C.), famous for his valor and simple habits. See Livy, "Periocha" 11; Cicero, *Pro Sulla* 7.23; Val. Max. 4.3 ff.

661. Camillus conquered Veii and freed Rome from the Gauls (390 B.C.; Livy 5.49 ff.). Pauli: the most famous fell at Cannae; see above, book 1, line 526 note.

662. For the three hundred said to have perished in the battle of Cremera fought against the Veiians (477 B.C.) see Livy 2.48-50.

665. Legend tells of an early Torquatus who wore as an ornament the chains of a Gaul he had slain in battle; a noteworthy Lepidus was Marcus Aemilius, consul in 187 B.C., who laid out the Via Aemilia. The names recur, as do those mentioned above, in Roman republican annals.

666. For the Catos see above, book 2, line 187, note. Caius Fabricius, consul in 282 and 278 B.C., conquered the Samnites and Lucanians; he was famous for his spurning of the rich gifts offered by Pyrrhus. See Livy, "Periocha" 13; Cicero, *De officiis* 3.22.86; Val. Max. 4.4.3.

667. The hero is Papirius Cursor ("the runner"), conqueror of the Samnites in 290 B.C. (Livy 9.16.11-13). Petrarch alludes to him in *Sen.* 4.1.

669-70. Livy (7.26.1-8) tells of one Valerius who was aided by a crow in the course of combat with a Gaul; he adopted Corvus ("crow") as his surname.

671. Marcus Claudius Marcellus conquered Syracuse, 212 B.C. (Livy 25. 23).

672. The most famous of the distinguished clan of the Gracchi are the brothers Tiberius Sempronius (162-133 B.C.) and Caius Sempronius (154-121 B.C.); both were tribunes and defenders of the people. Their mother was Cornelia, daughter of our Scipio. But the family was famous too in Scipio's time; see above, book 1, lines 522-25. The faith of the Reguli is best exemplified by M. Attilius Regulus. Captured by the Carthaginians in the First Punic War, he was sent back to Rome to advise the Romans to sue for peace. Instead he urged them to carry on the war, but, having given his word to his captors, he returned to Carthage to face torture and death. See Livy, "Periocha" 19; Cicero, *De officiis* 3.26.99; Horace, *Carmen saeculare* 3.2.

689 ff. For the sacrifice of Marcus Curtius (362 B.C.) see Livy 7.6.

753 ff. Decius Mus, consul, offered his life for his country in the Latin War of 340 B.C. (Livy 8.9 ff.). His son followed his example in the Samnite War of 295 B.C. (Livy 10.28); his grandson did the same in the war against Pyrrhus, 279 B.C. (Cicero, *Tusc.* 1.37 ff.). Petrarch speaks of them also in *Fam.* 6.4.

758. Gabinian: in the style of Gabii, a Volscian town.

792. See above, line 672, note.

804-05. From Livy 2.12.

833. The impious ruler is Tarquin the Proud. Livy (1.47-48) tells of his violent seizure of power and his murder of his father-in-law.

867. The royal youth: Sextus Tarquinius, the king's son.

870. The chaste matron is Lucretia, wife of Lucius Tarquinius Collatinus, a cousin of Lucius Junius Brutus. For her story and its sequel see Livy 1.57-60. Petrarch follows his source very closely.

984. The founding of the Republic dates from the fall of the Tarquins, 510 B.C.

991. Brutus was elected one of the two first consuls (Livy 1.60). He is thought of as the founder of the Roman Republic.

995. Brutus had his two sons executed for plotting with the exiled Tarquins (Livy 2.5).

BOOK 4

11. For these heroes see above, book 3, line 544, note.

52. Achilles.

53. Ennius: see above, book 2, line 575 and note.

54. Scipio.

64. Laelius breaks his thread because discussion of the envy that obscures Scipio's fame would lead to comment on Roman factionalism, inappropriate here.

73. Laura's locks were golden too; see *Rhymes* 198, 220, 227.

103-04. In *Fam.* 1.2 Petrarch pays the same compliment to Scipio.

106. At the time of Laelius's speech Scipio was in his thirtieth year.

124-29. These lines follow Livy 26.50.13.

145 ff. See Livy 26.19.

155-60. See Livy 26.19; Aulus Gellius, *Noctes Atticae* 6.1.6. For the Tarpeian hill, see above, book 3, line 598 and note.

165. See Livy 26.19.

236. Livy (21.46) tells how Scipio saved his father's life at the battle of the Ticinus, 218 B.C. Petrarch alludes to the deed in *Sen.* 2.1.

242 ff. See Livy 22.53. Petrarch returns to the subject in *Fam.* 22.9 and *Sen.* 2.1.

267. This is L. Caecilius Metellus, brother of Q. C. Metellus (see above, book 2, lines 181-86, note). For the episode here related see Livy 22.3.

288. Hercules.

321-24. See Livy 22.53.

328. See Livy 26.18 and 19.

329. The two Scipios mentioned here are our Scipio's father and uncle. See above, book 1, lines 317-455.

338. See Florus 1.6.

348. The Pyrenees were "fabled to derive the name from the Greek word

pyr, fire, from a great conflagration which destroyed its woods and melted
the ore of its mines so that the brooks ran with molten silver" (Smith,
Geography, 2.687).

353 ff. For Scipio's capture of New Carthage (Cartagena) see Livy 26.42-
47.

422. Hebrus: the principal river of Thrace, now the Maritza. Festa (p.96)
detects echoes of *Aeneid* 12-331 ff. in this passage.

460. The two men, according to Livy (26.48), were Q. Trebellius, a
centurion of the Fourth Legion, and Sextus Digitius, a soldier serving
with the fleet.

522. Book 4 abruptly ends with this line. There is a considerable lacuna
between book 4 and book 5 as we now have them. The gap leaves unsung
many important events. As we have noted (see above, book 3, line 88,
note), Laelius returned to Spain with a message from Syphax, indicating
that the king would welcome a visit from Scipio. The Roman general re-
sponded and with a small escort crossed the Mediterranean to meet the
king. He was nearly captured en route by Hasdrubal's fleet and chance
brought both the Carthaginian and the Roman leaders simultaneously to
the court of Syphax. Both sought the king's support. Persuaded by Scipio's
charm, Syphax promised to cooperate with the Romans, abandoning his
former ally (Livy 28.17.18). Scipio went back to Spain and in the spring of
205 B.C., having cleared the Iberian peninsula of the enemy and with the
prospect of a powerful ally in Africa, he returned to Rome. He was elected
consul that same year and—against strong opposition—persuaded the Sen-
ate to approve his plan to invade Africa. In the spring of 204 B.C., having
in the meantime wrested the city of Locri in Bruttium from the Cartha-
ginians, he sailed from Lilybaeum with an expeditionary force estimated at
thirty-five thousand and landed near Utica. (Scullard, *Scipio Africanus*,
pp. 108-15, provides a good account of the events of the year preceding
the invasion.)

Before embarking, the Roman leader had received some disconcerting
news from Syphax. The king reported that he had married Sophonisba,
daughter of Scipio's adversary Hasdrubal, and had reverted to the Cartha-
ginian alliance. Scipio was more fortunate in his other African ally, Massin-
issa, son of Gala, king of the Massylii, who inhabited the region between
the domain of Syphax and the city of Carthage. Massinissa too had been an
early ally of the Carthaginians and had fought with them against Scipio in
Spain. But, like Syphax, he had changed sides, coming over to Scipio at the
end of the Spanish campaign (Livy 28.35). Unlike Syphax, the prince, who
had become king through the deaths of his father and uncle, remained loyal
to Rome. A year after Scipio's landing in Africa the Roman army, aided by
Massinissa's cavalry, defeated the Carthaginians and Syphax at the battle
of the Great Plains, near Utica. Syphax fled, with Massinissa in hot pursuit.

Book 5 opens with the entrance of the latter into Cirta, previously held by Syphax.

Scholars have long sought for an explanation of the lacuna and debated its significance. Martellotti (*Scipione*, p. 13) saw it as indicative of a shift in inspirational currents; for him the first four books would be of a visionary color, under the star of Macrobius; beginning with book 5 we move into history under the aegis of Livy. It is certainly true that the opening lines of book 5 give a sense of brisk emersion into action after the meditative and reminiscent tone of book 4. The reader does recognize a shift of gears and a fresh start—even though it must be conceded that there is plenty of Livy in the first four books and a good deal of "visionary" material yet to come in the last five, including a full-fledged dream in book 9. Martellotti's theory is, however, more an interpretation than an explanation of the lacuna. The gap may be attributable, of course, simply to missing pages. It is also possible to believe that the material that called for exposition in the interval spanned by the lacuna may have offered special problems to the poet. For, in fact, between the mission of Laelius and the Battle of the Great Plains with the sequent irruption of Massinissa into Cirta, much of the activity of Petrarch's hero had been political rather than military, and politics is not appetizing meat for the Muse. Furthermore, not all of Scipio's actions in that period were of such nature as to arouse admiration. Some had seen his visit to Syphax (which is given ample treatment in the *De viris illustribus*) as an act of rashness, and his misplaced tolerance of his subordinate Pleminius, who had dealt harshly with the Locrians, had compromised the general; Fabius even moved for his recall (see Scullard, *Scipio Africanus*, pp. 112-15). Bernardo comments that the "substance [of Livy's account covering the period of the lacuna] must have proved difficult for the poet to raise to a poetic plane"—an opinion anticipated by Corradini (see Bernardo, pp. 142 ff., and Corradini's lengthy note, pp. 434-37).

In connection with the lacuna, an interesting theory was proposed by Festa, first in the *Giornale dantesco* (27 [1924]:97-101), and later in the preface to his edition of the *Africa* (pp. lxv-lxviii). Festa argues that the elaborate descriptive passage in book 3 (lines 109-328 in our version) was intended by Petrarch to portray not the palace of Syphax but the Palace of Truth to which Lady Truth alludes in the opening pages of the *Secretum*. In the poet's plan, Festa maintains, Scipio, at some later point in the narrative, would have visited some such extraterrestrial and suggestive palace; Petrarch's editor therefore concludes that the passage referred to might be seen as "in part" filling up the lacuna at the end of this book. For a discussion of Festa's thesis see Bernardo, pp. 130 ff.

BOOK 5

The story of Massinissa and Sophonisba had a great attraction for Petrarch. It is told again, at some length, in the "Triumph of Love" 2.3-87.

1. The great-souled conqueror: Massinissa. See Livy 30.7-9.

2. Cirta: although defined by Livy as Syphax's capital, Massinissa thinks of it as his city. It lay within the domain of his people.

16. The queen is Sophonisba; she had turned Syphax against Scipio (see above, book 4, line 522, note, and below, lines 469-98). For the story of Massinissa and Sophonisba Petrarch follows Livy (30.12-15) very closely. According to de Sanctis (*Storia dei Romani*, 3.2.517, note), who says her native name was Saphanba'al, Livy's account is "already romanticized"; he suspects Ennius may be the source of the "poetic invention."

35 ff. Sophonisba's tresses are borrowed from Laura; see *Rhymes* 90. Nor are they her only borrowings; as Martellotti puts it (p. 639, note), "the reader will see for himself the accumulation of Laura's perfections in Sophonisba." Corradini (pp. 437-38) supplies further specific references.

55. See above, book 3, line 221, note.

80. An allusion to *Aeneid* 1.227 ff., where Venus asks Jupiter to help Aeneas.

82. See *Met.* 15.761 ff., where Venus appeals for the salvation of the life "that alone remains to me from Dardanian Iulus."

90 ff. Petrarch refers to this passage in *Fam.* 18.7.

170 ff. A reference to Massinissa's earlier alliance with Carthage. See above, book 4, line 522, note.

205. Manes: the spirits of the dead.

210. Euripus: the strait between Boeotia and Euboea.

212 ff. The language and imagery seem to echo *Rhymes* 189.

266. The distant leader is Scipio.

307. We adopt Martellotti's suggestion (p. 651, note) of *mens* for Festa's *gens* (line 231 of the Latin).

309. In "The Triumph of Love" 2.56 Massinissa states that he is of the same age as Scipio; Sophonisba was perhaps ten years younger.

312-13. Petrarch remarks elsewhere on the equalizing virtue of love, notably in *Ep. Met.* 2.9.

325. The Etruscans were said to have invented trumpets. Petrarch's "tuscus clangor" here echoes Virgil's "Tyrrhenus . . . clangor" (*Aeneid* 8.526).

330. The planet Venus is called Vesper (Hesperus) at dusk and Lucifer at dawn.

348-58. A possible interpretation of the dream would have the higher mountain stand for Scipio, the lower one for Massinissa, and the torrents for their eloquent speeches. Such is Corradini's interpretation, cited by Martellotti (p. 653, note), who prefers to see the torrents as signifying Sophonisba's tears.

425 ff. On Scipio's visit to Syphax see above, book 4, line 522, note.

486. Penates: the household gods.

509. Scipio has here in mind the "hopes" springing from his first negotiations with Massinissa. See above, book 4, line 522, note.

516-18. Again, a reference to their first meeting.

519. This self-satisfied affirmation of temperance and the praise of self-control in the face of temptation is from Livy 30.14.5 and 6. Martellotti (p. 661, note) believes that Petrarch also had in mind Seneca, *Ad Luc.* 51.6.

564-65. See above, book 4, line 522, note, for Sophonisba's marriage. On Hasdrubal, son of Gisgo, see above, book 1, line 168 and note.

604. Massinissa's anguish is recorded by Livy (30.14.1-4), as indeed are all the details of the lovers' tragedy.

626. The reference is to Apollo's love for Daphne.

676. The Blessed Isles, *Insulae Fortunatae*, were located far in the western sea; they are sometimes identified with the Canaries.

730. The phrase "starry heights" suggests that Scipio is destined to dwell in the highest physical heaven, that of the fixed stars.

855. Charon.

858. Proserpina.

861. Elissa: Dido. The short catalogue of tragic heroines derives from *Aeneid* 445-51. In the "Triumph of Love" 1.139-44 there is a similar grouping.

862. Medusa.

863. Laodamia, daughter of Acastus. She followed to Hades her husband Protesilaus, slain by Hector (Ovid, *Epistulae ex Ponto* 3.1.110).

865. Procris: daughter of Erechtheus, king of Athens, killed by her husband Cephalus in the forest when he mistook her for a wild beast (*Met.* 7.694 ff.). The bane of Troy: Helen.

866. Phaedra, who killed herself for love of her step-son Hippolytus (*Met.* 15.500 ff.).

867. Ariadne: daughter of King Minos; she was abandoned by Theseus but rescued by Dionysus, who put her crown as a constellation in the heavens (*Met.* 8.172 ff.).

870. As Petrarch says of his Laura in *Rhymes* 350.9-10. Corradini (pp. 442-43) cites other resonances of the *Rhymes* in Massinissa's lament.

877 ff. Massinissa seems to believe in the Pythagorean idea of reincarnation.

883. Orpheus.

896. Martellotti (p. 677) notes that Petrarch's line (684 of the original) combines two half-lines from Horace, *Odes* 1.1.2 and 1.3.8.

977 ff. These lines recall the curse of Dido on the Romans *(Aeneid* 4. 612-29). Sophonisba's prayer will be fulfilled. Scipio, disgusted with the ingratitude of his fellow citizens, went into voluntary exile in Liternum, Campania (see above, book 2, line 702, note). He gave orders that his body should not be buried in Rome. He accompanied his brother Lucius Scipio in the latter's campaign against Antiochus. Lucius was accused by Cato of taking bribes. Scipio's son Gnaeus was taken prisoner by Antiochus and did not acquit himself well under interrogation. Petrarch gives a detailed account of these matters in his *De viris illustribus.*

992. It is said that Scipio caused to be engraved on his tomb the bitter statement: "Ingrata patria, ne ossa quidem mea habes" (Livy 38.53; Val. Max. 5.3.2b).

993 ff. The spouse is Massinissa. For the fate of his family see Sallust, *Jugurtha* 5.5; 12.5, and 26.3. The bloody churl is Marius (for his origins see Sallust, *Jugurtha* 63.3), springing from the very stock of Massinissa's allies, the Romans, and destined to overthrow Jugurtha and the descendants of Massinissa.

BOOK 6

1-2. In the beginning Zeus divided the world into three domains: his own realm would comprise the sky and the land; the sea would be ruled by Poseidon; and the underworld by Pluto.

4. Corradini (p. 445) is reminded of Petrarch's vision of Laura's arrival in Heaven *(Rhymes* 346).

14. Minos: one of the judges of the underworld; his appearance here recalls his aspect in the *Divine Comedy (Inferno* 5.4-6), where he also has the role of assigning sinners to their appropriate circles.

16. the second cell: see Virgil, *Aeneid* 6.426 ff.

19. Rhadamanthus: another judge of the lower world; see *Aeneid* 6.566-69.

23. Aeacus: third judge of the lower world; mythical king of Aegina and grandfather of Achilles and Ajax.

50-51. See *Aeneid* 6.443.

53. See *Aeneid* 6.653-55.

55-63. A similar passage is found in the "Triumph of Love" 4.137 ff. The unhappy lovers in the following lines also appear in the "Triumph of Love."

65. Iphis: a youth of Cyprus; his love for Anaxarete was not reciprocated and he hanged himself in despair. See *Met.* 14.699.

66. Byblis: guilty of incestuous love for her twin brother. She was

turned into a fountain (*Met.* 9.580). Hyginus, *Fabulae* 2.43, says that she hanged herself.

68. Myrrha, cursed by Venus, fell in love with her father; she was turned into a myrtle tree (*Met.* 10. 298).

70. For the story of Orpheus and Eurydice see *Met.* 10.11-63.

77. Oenone, a nymph of Phrygia whom Paris first loved, then abandoned. See Ovid, *Heroides* 5.

78-79. The reference is to Helen of Troy.

80. Lavinia was betrothed to Turnus but became the wife of Aeneas. Her story is told in *Aeneid* 7-12.

82. two others: these are the young lovers Pyramus and Thisbe. Pyramus, believing Thisbe dead, killed himself; she, finding his body, also committed suicide. From their blood grew the mulberry (*Met.* 4.55-166).

94. Massinissa died in 148 B.C.

107 ff. Scipio's concern for Massinissa is recorded in Livy (30.15.9-11).

121. Procne: the swallow; see *Met.* 6.668.

137 Syrtes: sandbanks, Syrtis Major and Syrtis Minor (now called Sidra and Cabes) on the coast of North Africa.

174 ff. Hamilcar is called "a second Mars" by Livy (21.10.4); the four sons of this lion were Hannibal, Hasdrubal, Mago, and Gisgo (Corradini, p. 446). At the time of Scipio's speech only Hannibal survived.

206. See Livy 30.15 for the gifts to Massinissa.

285. Livy (30.16) tells of the return of Laelius to Rome with the prisoner Syphax. The latter's soliloquy is Petrarch's contribution.

308. Trinacria: Sicily.

375. Tunis: mentioned by Livy (30.16).

400. treachery: because their purpose was not truly to seek peace but to gain time until Hannibal should return (Livy 30.16). Petrarch's account of the negotiations closely follows Livy (loc. cit.).

494. Thetis: a sea nymph, daughter of Nereus and Doris and mother of Achilles. See Ovid, *Met.* 11.221 and 13.162.

495. Nereus: a sea god, father of fifty daughters, the Nereids (*Met.* 2. 268).

506. Bruttium: ancient name for the region now known as Calabria. Petrarch's account follows Livy 30.20.

554. Claudius ordered the head of Hasdrubal, Hannibal's brother (defeated and killed at the battle of the Metaurus, 207 B.C.), to be cast in front of the outposts of Hannibal's army. Hannibal then withdrew to Bruttium (Livy 27.51).

577. Hanno: the leader of a Carthaginian faction opposed to Hannibal and his policies.

590. Croton: now Crotone, in Calabria. Founded by the Achaeans, it was an important city in antiquity, famous for its sacred grove, its temple

of Juno Lacinia, and a massive column of pure gold, indicative of its wealth. In the sixth century it was the seat of the school of Pythagoras. See Livy 24.3; *Aeneid* 3.552.

605. It was said that Zeuxis, after surveying many maidens, chose five and represented the best features of each in one statue. See Livy 24.3 and Pliny 35.10.36.

620. The massacre is mentioned by Livy (30.20), as are Hannibal's self-reproaches (below, lines 669 ff.).

659. His daughter: Minerva; see above, book 3, lines 257-59, note.

669. Bomilcar: one of Hannibal's generals; according to Livy (22.51), however, it was Maharbal, commander of the cavalry, who urged Hannibal to move at once on Rome.

709. In 211 B.C., hoping to divert the Romans from the siege of Capua, Hannibal moved north from Campania to attack the capital city itself. Three miles from the walls, as he prepared to do battle with the Roman army, a great storm broke and made fighting impossible. The same phenomenon was repeated the following day. The Carthaginians saw an omen in this celestial intervention and Hannibal withdrew (see Livy 26.11).

731. The Latin reads: "et quarto linquebat litora lustro" (line 556), but it was just barely into the fourth lustrum. Hannibal had been in Italy from 218 to 203 B.C., a little more than fifteen years.

732. These lines are a direct quotation from Livy 30.20.7.

758. See *Aeneid* 3.414 and 420.

759. The legendary monsters, Scylla and Charybdis, symbolized the dangers of the passage of the Strait of Messina. See *Aeneid* 3.557 ff; Ovid, *Met.* 14.68-77.

770-71. There may be a reference here to the ill-fated Athenian expedition against Sicily, led by Alcibiades. See Justin 45.

775. Marcellus: see above, book 1, line 502, note, and book 3, line 671, note.

783. Cynthia: see above, book 2, line 431, note.

828. Regulus: see above, book 3, line 672, note.

832. Bágrada: see above, book 1, line 256, note.

834. In the course of the First Punic War a great serpent appeared in the Bágrada; it filled the stream and crushed in its toils the Roman soldiers attempting to cross, thus impeding the advance of Regulus. The Romans finally killed the monster; its blood polluted the river and the surrounding area was poisoned by the stench. The skin, measuring 120 feet, was sent to Rome. See Livy, "Periocha" 18; Val. Max. 1.18; Pliny 8.14

844. Xanthippus: a Spartan ally of the Carthaginians in the First Punic War; it was he who defeated Regulus and took him prisoner. See above, book 3, line 672, note.

853. Their leader: Regulus.

858. It was said that Xanthippus, having served the Carthaginians loyally, was betrayed by them and drowned on his homeward voyage. No such account is found in Livy and all historians doubt its veracity. It is found in Val. Max. 9.6, ext. 1, and Silius Italicus, *Punica* 6.682 (a work unknown to Petrarch). See de Sanctis, *Storia*, 3.1.3.151, note.

871. An allusion to the battle of the Aegates; see above, book 3, lines 590-92, note.

905. Anchises, father of Aeneas, died on the voyage and was buried on the Sicilian coast (*Aeneid* 3.707 ff.).

928 ff. Petrarch's account follows Livy 30.21-29 very closely.

953. For this debate see Livy 30.23.

959. Metellus: This is Q. Caecilius Metellus (see above, book 2, lines 181-86, note). He was a faithful partisan of Scipio. Livius and Laevinus were of the other faction. See Scullard, *Scipio Africanus*, pp. 169-70.

987. Aquilo: the north wind. On the storm and its sequel see Livy 30.25.

1082. Festa's text indicates a lacuna after this line (832 of the original).

1085. both chieftains: Hannibal and his brother Mago.

1090. Mago had been wounded in battle before embarking to return from Liguria to Carthage (Livy 30.18).

1095 ff. The Ligurian and Tuscan coastline observed by Mago is also given full and warm treatment in Petrarch's *Itinerarium Syriacum*, composed in 1358. For Mago's voyage and death see Livy 30.19.

1103. Siestrum: Sestri Levante.

1109. Meroë: see above, book 3, line 464, note.

1115. The island is Palmazza; the port is Portovenere.

1117, Eryx: Lerici. In a letter to "Lelius," written April 29, 1346, Petrarch refers to this passage.

1121. the Corvinian cape: Capo Corvo.

1128. Macra: now called the Magra.

1129. Luni: an ancient city that stood on the left bank of the Magra.

1136. Igilium: now known as the Isola del Giglio.

1139-40. Piombino and Monte Argentaro.

1141-42. Port' Ercole, on the shore of the Argentaro peninsula. The village of Talamone, now a part of Orbetello (Grosseto province) stands nearby.

1143. Umbro: now called the Ombrone.

1151-99. This is the passage circulated without Petrarch's consent and much to his displeasure (see introduction).

1191. According to Livy (13.19.5) Mago died off the coast of Sardinia.

BOOK 7

11. Hanno: see above, book 6, 577, note.

40. Leptis: Leptis Minor, an ancient city in Libya. For Hannibal's landing see Livy 30.25.11-12.

54. The uneasiness in Rome is recorded by Livy (30.28).

67. A similar observation occurs in *Fam.* 14.5.

80. For the gloomy predictions of Fabius see Livy 30.28. The Delayer was opposed to Scipio's policies; he had, in the words of Scullard (*Scipio Africanus*, p. 168), "attacked and fought Scipio's African project tooth and nail. Besides the military and strategic issues at stake . . . the men were divided by an essentially different approach to Rome's future. Fabius represented a more old-fashioned agrarian outlook; he wished to finish the war with all speed, to heal the wounds which it had inflicted on the Italian countryside, and possibly to develop northern Italy. . . . The other view, represented by Scipio . . . , was that a purely Italian policy was outdated and that Rome must become a Mediterranean power."

115-82. Hannibal's march, the reception of the Carthaginian scouts (to which Petrarch refers again in *Fam.* 12.2), and the meeting of the leaders all follow Livy 30.29. Naraggara (variously called Nargara, Nedagara) was about one hundred miles southwest of Carthage; the modern town Sidi Youssef stands on the site. For Zama see the discussion following the notes to book 7.

195. See above, book 1, line 502, note, and line 506, note.

213. Typhoeus: a Titan, third son of Gaea (Earth).

214. the sons of Earth: the Titans.

218. Pallas: Minerva; see above, book 6, lines 659-61 and note.

242 ff. An allusion to the battle of the Ticinus; see above, book 4, line 236, note.

247. For the storm see above, book 6, line 709, note.

265. An allusion to the Metellus episode; see above, book 4, lines 267 ff. and note.

270. the king: Syphax.

278 ff. In Livy too (30.30-31) both generals make speeches; Hannibal's is closely reproduced by Petrarch, Scipio's considerably enlarged.

303-04. Another allusion to the Ticinus; see above, line 242, note.

335. Trebia: now called the Trebbia, a river flowing into the Po near Piacenza; the scene of Hannibal's victory over the Romans, 218 B.C. (Livy 21.54-56).

383. Petrarch, speaking through Augustine, returns to this thought in *Secretum* 3. The line (292 of the original) appears again in *Ep. Met.* 2.14. 273.

395. Cyrus, founder of the Persian Empire, was defeated and killed by the Messagetae, a Scythian tribe ruled by the queen Tomyris. Cyrus provided a stock example of pride brought down; see Dante, *Purgatorio* 12.55.

400. Pyrrhus, king of Epirus. After early victories over the Romans he was defeated by them at Benevento, 275 B.C. The year before he had been victorious over the Carthaginians in Sicily (hence the allusion in line 411) and had earlier made himself co-ruler of Macedonia. But he too came to a tragic end; fleeing from his unsuccessful siege of Sparta (272 B.C.), he fell beneath a shower of stones hurled by a mob in the town of Argos.

419. Regulus: see above, book 3, line 672, note.

442. Probably an allusion to the terms made after the battle of the Caudine Forks (321 B.C.), in which the Samnites defeated and humiliated a Roman army (Livy 9.5 ff.).

466. Aeolia's triple realm: Sicily ("Trinacria").

475. See *Aeneid* 1.286.

509. An allusion to the battle of the Aegates; see above, book 3, lines 590-92, note.

519. Saguntum: a Spanish city allied to Rome. Its capture and sack by Hannibal (218 B.C.) was the occasion of the Second Punic War.

648-62. This scene of military preparation is reminiscent of *Aeneid* 7. 632-40.

662. Festa's text indicates a lacuna after this line (499 of the original).

675. The first matron is Rome. Carthage is the second matron (line 682).

698. For Juno's connection with Carthage see *Aeneid* 1.15 ff.

714. Favonius: another name for the west wind.

726. The reference is to Hamilcar, "the second Mars"; see above, book 6, line 174, note. He was ambushed and slain in 229 B.C. near Castrum Album, now Alicante (Livy 21.41.3).

754. Boreas: the north wind. Riphean crags: see above, book 2, line 262, note.

769. The boy is Scipio.

863 ff. A reference to Christianity, as in line 881 below.

914 ff. The allusion to "mortal bodies" is a little unexpected. Perhaps Petrarch is thinking here of his own misplaced devotion to Laura, a "cosa mortale," as he defines her in *Rhymes* 365.

948 ff. A prediction of the Incarnation.

962. Saturn completes its revolution every twenty-nine and one-half (earth) years. Christianity was brought to Rome by St. Peter in 42 A.D.

963 ff. Jupiter sees himself as the infant Jesus, an example of syncretism no less bold (if perhaps less tasteful) than Dante's ". . . o sommo Giove/ che fosti in terra per noi crocefisso" (*Purgatorio* 6.118-19).

987. For the preliminaries of Zama, disposition of troops and so on, and the battle itself, see Livy 30.32-36.

1006. Cyllenius: Mercury, born, according to legend, on Mount Cyllene in Arcadia.

1034. In Livy too (30.32) both generals address their troops.

1058. the consul: Terentius Varro, who joined battle with Hannibal at Cannae against the advice of his colleague Paulus (Livy 22.44).

1059-60. Before the battle of the Ticinus there were adverse omens; see Livy 21.46. The commander on this occasion was Publius Scipio, our Scipio's father. Flaminius, defeated and slain at Trasimenus, was also notoriously "ill-starred" (Livy 21.62-63).

1062. Sempronius: the Roman leader defeated at the Trebia; see above, line 335, note.

1063 ff. At both the Ticinus and Cannae dust storms blinded the Romans (Livy 21.46; 22.40); Livy speaks (22.24) of a mist at Trasimenus and of the cold that numbed the Roman army at the Trebia; Hannibal had prepared his troops against it by ordering them to anoint themselves with oil "to make their joints supple" (Livy 21.55.1).

1115. Polyphemus: the one-eyed Cyclops blinded by Ulysses. In *Bucolicum carmen* 1.115 and in the interpretative letter (*Fam.* 10.4) Petrarch refers to Hannibal as "Polyphemus."

1130. Bruttians: Calabrians.

1138. The king is Massinissa, hated by the Numidians still loyal to Syphax. Numidia was the homeland of the Massaesyli and the Massylii.

1175. More than a peck of gold rings, plucked from slain Roman knights, were brought to Carthage after Cannae (Livy 23.12).

1223. The elephant stampede is mentioned by Livy (30.33.13-16).

1287. The combatants reproach each other for past outrages: the Romans had exacted too harsh a tribute from the Carthaginians after the First Punic War; the Carthaginians had behaved savagely when they took Saguntum.

1333. For the tidal wave that brought an island to the surface and the prophecy of Roman domination, see Justin 30.4. Ancient Therasia, an island in the Aegean, is now called Santorin.

1452-53. Livy (30.34) describes the different fighting styles of the Romans and the Carthaginians.

1484 ff. Laelius and Massinissa, who had been pursuing the Carthaginian cavalry, turned and took the enemy in the rear (Livy 30.35).

1498. Hadrumetum: a town now called Sousse, in North Africa, southeast of Carthage; it was Hannibal's base (Livy 30.29 and 35).

Historians today, although they might not call on celestial authority for support, would agree with Petrarch's assessment of the importance of the battle of Zama. Scipio's victory assured that western and not eastern traditions and institutions would prevail in Europe and eventually throughout the western world. Nor would scholars fault the poet's description of the combat, for which Livy is still the most respected source. It may be noted that Scipio's army numbered about thirty-five thousand and Hannibal's

perhaps as many as fifty-five thousand. But if the Roman general was out-
numbered, he had two advantages over his opponent. He had cavalry more
numerous and more skilled than Hannibal's; and he had, aside from Massin-
issa's contribution, a homogeneous force, whereas, as Petrarch indicates,
Hannibal commanded a very mixed army. This permitted Scipio to employ
his tactics of envelopment; he could count on his well-disciplined and
unified center to hold its own against the unreliable allies of Hannibal
while his cavalry broke the Carthaginian wings and eventually attacked the
enemy from the rear. His device for dealing with the elephants was also
successful and seems to have been novel. It is curious that an engagement
of such importance has still not been securely fixed either in time or in
place. The exact date is unknown; the battle took place in either the late
summer or early fall of 202 B.C. The site is still under dispute; the question
is complicated by the fact that there were at least two Zamas. Scullard
seems inclined to accept a site twenty-seven kilometers east of Sidi Youssef
(Naraggara). See his comments in *Scipio Africanus*, pp. 271-74, and also
F. G. Moore's appendix to vol. 8 of his *Livy, with an English Translation
in Fourteen Volumes*, "The Zama Problem," pp. 543-54. For a description
of the battle, see B. H. Liddell Hart, *A Greater than Napoleon*, pp. 164-90.

BOOK 8

1-3. Petrarch speaks of the "folk of the Antipodes" in *Secretum* 3 and
Rhymes 50.1-3.
   18 ff. For Scipio's assault on the Carthaginian camp see Livy 30.36.1.
   63-64. These lines are reminiscent of Virgil's *Georgicon* 4.184-85.
   92. Hannibal's eye became infected in the damp marshes of the Arno.
Lack of sleep and proper medication resulted in its loss (Livy 22.2 ff.).
See above, book 2, line 43, note.
   113. For the disposition of Hannibal's troops, including elephants, see
Livy 30.33.
   120. Italians: the Bruttians of book 7, line 1130 above.
   123. Gaetulian: from Gaetulia, a region of northwest Africa.
   143. For Hannibal's ranking of great generals see Livy 35.14.5-11.
Petrarch refers to it again in his *Invectives against a Certain Doctor*, 3.
   149. Porus: an Indian prince defeated by Alexander at the battle of the
Hydaspes, 326 B.C. Darius III, king of the Persians, was defeated by
Alexander at Issus (333 B.C.) and Arbela (331 B.C.).
   160. Scipio's outline of Hannibal's virtues and defects follows Livy
(21.4) quite closely. On his temperance, Justin (32.4) notes that the
Carthaginian never drank more than a pint of wine at a time.
   184. For Hannibal's faults see Livy 21.4 ff. Petrarch mentions them
also in *Sen.* 10.2.
   186. The disparagement of Alexander, beginning in this passage, lends

support to the notion of Enrico Carrara (*Da Rolando a Morgante*) that the *Africa* may have been in inspiration, at least in part, a kind of "Antigualtherus"—that is to say, written with the intention of opposing the exaltation of Alexander in the medieval poem of Walter of Châtillon (the *Alexandreis*, composed in 1178-82 in the Virgilian style and widely read up to Petrarch's day) the glorification of Scipio. Carrara finds many parallels between the two poems that seem to justify his opinion. Scipio here makes it clear that as a general Alexander was inferior to Hannibal— and very far below him in the conventional human virtues. And of course on both military and moral grounds the reader will perceive that Scipio is himself superior to Hannibal. Petrarch, whether or not he had Walter in mind, could find ample authority for his criticisms of Alexander in Livy 9. 17 and 18.

187. See Quintus Curtius 5.7.

190. See Quintus Curtius 8.1 and Justin 12.6.3.

192. See Quintus Curtius 3.5.

194. See Quintus Curtius 6.6 and 10.5; Justin 12.3.8.

210. This thought, echoed in line 266 below, is almost literally from Quintus Curtius 10.5.

216. Festa's text indicates a lacuna after this line (154 of the original).

238. The four great battles are the Ticinus, the Trebia, Lake Trasimenus, and Cannae.

241 ff. For this Alexander and his fate see Livy 8.24. Aulus Gellius (*Noctes Atticae* 17.21.33) relates that Alexander of Epirus as he sailed for Italy remarked that he was going to the men's quarters while his nephew was bound for the women's quarters. See also Livy 9.19.10 ff. and Justin 12.2.

320. A play on *sol/solus*. See Cicero, *De natura deorum* 2.27.

346. See Livy 30.36.

396 ff. Livy (30.27) quotes Hannibal's speech advising his countrymen to make peace with the Romans.

437. This is Antiochus III; see above, book 2, line 162, note, and line 176, note.

442 ff. For Hannibal's flight to Antiochus see Livy 33.48.

448-50. Vulcan (in Italian Vulcano), named for the god whose forge was said to lie under the volcanic island. See *Aeneid* 8.416-22.

460 ff. Petrarch refers to this episode also in *Fam.* 9.5. The headland, variously styled Peloris, Pelorian, Peloros, stands on the northeast coast of Sicily; it is now known as Capo di Faro or Capo di Messina. The murder of the Pilot Pelorus, suspected of treachery, is recounted by Strabo (1.1.17), but Strabo's Pelorus is the Greek pilot of the Persian fleet, killed by his suspicious commander after the battle of Salamis. The association of the tale of Pelorus with Hannibal (historically without basis) is found

in Valerius Maximus and Pomponius Mela (*Chorographia*); the latter
authority places the incident, as Petrarch does, on the occasion of Hannibal's
voyage to the East. See Pauly, *sub voce* Pelorus.

483. There are two Methons, one in the region of Messenia in the Pelo-
ponessus, the other in Macedonia, where Philip lost an eye in battle. As
Corradini notes (p. 461), Petrarch confused them.

492. Knossos: an ancient city on the northern coast of Crete.

514. The brothers are our Scipio and Scipio Asiaticus; see above, book 2,
line 162, note.

515 ff. For Scipio's actions here see Livy 30.36.3 ff.

580. These are two promontories on the Bay of Carthage.

595. On the battle with Vermina see Livy 30.26.7-9.

622 ff. This is a puzzling passage. Petrarch's Latin (lines 437-79) is
somewhat ambiguous. Develay translates (5.52): "Qu'il aurait mieux valu
pour lui tomber sur un monceau de cadavres, si les destins l'eussent permis,
que de partager la prison de son malheureux père à Albe et son sépulcre à
Tibur." Barolo's version (p. 250) reads: "Misero lui! Quanto miglior
destino/tra i soldati esser caduto e al padre,/consentendolo i Numi, ne
l'Albano/carcere andar compagno e riposare/insieme ne la tomba Tiburtina."
Develay suggests that Vermina was later to share his father's fate; Barolo
implies that an even sadder destiny is in store for the prince. But in fact
there is no historical basis for either suggestion. Far from being "infelix,"
Vermina not only survived the battle but later recovered his kingdom. Livy
(31.19.5-6) records his treaty with the Romans, who kept him in power
as a check on Massinissa, their volatile ally (Scullard, *Scipio Africanus*,
p. 159).

628. See Livy 30.36.

657. The news of the defeat of Vermina and of the victory over Hanni-
bal reached the Roman Senate, sitting in the Temple of Bellona, on the
same day (Livy 30.40).

661 ff. As in Livy 30.38.

679. Latona's offspring: Apollo and Diana.

682. The sister of Mars is Bellona. Leda's sons: Castor and Pollux.

690. For the ill-starred voyage of Claudius see Livy 30.38-39. Scullard
(*Scipio Africanus*, p. 171) thinks Livy's account is somewhat unfair to
Claudius.

710. Laurentian: Latin; the adjective comes from the ancient town of
Laurentum, between Ostia and Lavinium.

717. The brothers: the winds. The description of the storm has echoes
of *Aeneid* 1.80-124.

731. The Tyrrhenian hills form part of the shore line of Tuscany.

754. Populonia: an ancient Etruscan city, near Livorno.

795. Livy (30.40) speaks of the ambitions of Lentulus, "a Cornelius but
no friend of Scipio" (Scullard, *Scipio Africanus*, p. 172).

818. See Livy 9.18.

865. Byrsa: see above, book 1, line 258, note. For Scipio's statement see Livy 30.44.3.

874. This is Scipio Africanus the Younger; see above, book 1, line 3, note.

876. See Livy 30.36.9 ff.

930 ff. Scipio's peace terms are recorded in Livy 30.37.1-6.

975. Hasdrubal Haedus: no kin to Hannibal but a member of the faction led by Hanno, bitterly opposed to Hannibal's family and policies. See Livy 30.42.11-18 for the reception given Hasdrubal and his speech. Petrarch has considerably enlarged on the Carthaginian's plea.

986. Bellona: see above, line 682, note. Her temple near the Circus Maximus was a place of assembly where the Senate met with missions not allowed to enter the city.

1005. The youth is Hannibal.

1017. Hanno: see above, book 6, line 577, note.

1024. For Hannibal's famous oath see Livy 21.4.

1038. See Livy 21.3.

1056-62. Livy (23.12-13) quotes Hanno's speech on this occasion.

1105. As in line 1005 above, the youth is Hannibal.

1187 ff. The question and riposte are taken almost verbatim from Livy 30.42.20-21.

1216. The reference is to Ganymede; see above, book 3, line 173, note.

1221. Appian gate: marking the terminus of the Appian Way.

1225. Evander: the Arcadian founder of a settlement at the foot of the Palatine. See *Aeneid* 8.

1229. See Livy 1.7.

1232. Carmenta: Arcadian prophetess, mother of Evander and one of the Latin Muses (*Aeneid* 8.333 ff.). Petrarch speaks of her with admiration in *Variae* 22.

1241. For the story of Cacus and the cattle stolen from Hercules see *Aeneid* 8.193 ff.

1246. The famous tale of Horatius holding the bridge is found in Livy 2.5.

1248. The frowning maid is Cloelia, the Roman girl of legend who, given as a hostage to Porsenna, swam the Tiber to return to Rome (Livy 2.13).

1257. It was said that the Carthaginians, digging ground to found their city, unearthed the head of an ox. This was seen as an indication of fertile soil but also as a symbol of permanent enslavement. So the Carthaginians chose another site (Justin 18.5).

1274. The bird memorializes the geese, whose honking alerted the Romans to the night attack of the Gauls (Livy 5.47).

1285. Suburra: a quarter of Rome, northeast of the Forum.

1290-91. The hill is the Viminal.

1308-13. The story of Brutus; see above, book 3, lines 867 ff.

1317. If the temple to all the gods is the Pantheon, Petrarch is guilty of an anachronism, for the Pantheon was not built until 27 B.C. But his guided tour is as much for the benefit of his readers as for the visiting Carthaginians.

1321. The tomb of Romulus: or the Meta Romuli. "A name sometimes given in the Middle Ages to a pyramidal monument that stood between the mausoleum of Hadrian [the Castel Sant'Angelo] and the Vatican" (S. B. Plattner, rev. by T. Ashby, *A Topographical Dictionary of Ancient Rome*, p. 340).

1323 ff. While Romulus was conducting a review of his troops on the Campus Martius, near the marsh of Capra, a sudden storm arose and the hero was veiled in a dense cloud. When the cloud cleared Romulus had vanished. In spite of the assertion of a senator that the father of Rome had been borne aloft by a blast, there was some uneasiness about his fate and even a rumor that certain senators had done away with him. But one Proculus Julius stated that he had had a vision in which Romulus came down from Heaven before him and assured him that Rome would conquer the world (Livy 1.16).

1331. The hill is the Janiculum.

1336. Italus: "An ancient king of the Pelasgians, Siculians or Oenotrians from whom Italy was believed to have derived its name" (Smith, *Biography*, 2:634). See *Aeneid* 1.530-33.

1338. Picus: legendary Italian prophet and demigod. See *Aeneid* 7.48.

1342. Clusium: modern Chiusi; Etruscan capital of the Tarquins. Lars Porsenna was the Tarquin champion.

1344. C. Mucius Scaevola burned off his right hand to punish it for failing to kill Porsenna (Livy 2.12).

1346. The bridge of Fabricius and Cestius spanned an island in the Tiber now called the Isola Tiberina. It was at one time known as the Lycaonian island. The origin of this appellation is obscure; Besnier (*L'Île tibérine dans l'antiquité* , p. 867 concludes that "dans l'antiquité quelque monument de l'île, une statue sans doute, devait rappeler le roi d'Arcadie Lycaon ou la contrée de Lycaonie."

1348 ff. The island was formed, legend says, by the debris of the plunder of the Tarquins' palace cast into the Tiber (Livy 2.5).

1352-54. See above, book 3, line 662 and note.

1400. For the release of the prisoners see Livy 30.43.

1430. Livy does not mention the sacrifice of a sow. It is not clear why the animal was chosen; perhaps a memory of *Aeneid* 1.530-33.

1437. See Livy 30.44.

1449-60. Following Livy 30.43.13. Petrarch speaks of Scipio's distinctions again in *Fam.* 22.14.

1505. See *Matthew* 18:8-9.

1533. Livy quotes some historians (unnamed) as saying that the fleet numbered more than five hundred ships.

BOOK 9

13. For Ennius, see above, book 2, line 575, note. He was a personal friend of the Scipios; his statue was a part of the family tombs. For his being a "witness and companion" of Scipio during the campaign in Africa Claudian is our only authority. Martellotti (p. 690, note) believes that the Ennius episode here has its "remote origin" in Claudian, citing *De consulatu Stiliconis*, 3, *praef.*

27. The Castalian spring was on the slope of Helicon, the mountain of the Muses.

59. That is, there will be no example of virtue more lofty than Scipio.

60. Our eloquence: *"nostra peritia"*: it is quite possible that "nostra" may here be translated "my."

68. The king is Alexander; see Cicero, *Pro Archia* 10.24. The story appears also in *Rhymes* 187.

89. The Maeonian bard is Homer.

95-101. Martellotti (p. 694, note) remarks that here Scipio proposes for Ennius the two subjects of Petrarch's coronation speech: the relationship between truth and poetry and the significance of the laurel crown. Before Martellotti, Corradini (p. 469) had noted that the substance of Ennius's discourse is similar to that of the coronation speech. For a translation of Petrarch's oration see E. H. Wilkins, *Studies in the Life and Works of Petrarch*, pp. 300-13.

110. Pierian: *i.e.*, of the Muses, in legend daughters of Pierus, king of Thessaly, also associated with Mount Pierus.

117-19. Another echo of Claudian, *De consulatu Stiliconis* 3.5-6 (Martellotti, p. 695, note).

123 ff. Petrarch here gives his prescription for the use of allegory and his definition of poetry; he touches on the subject again in *Sen.* 4.5. Martellotti (p. 695, note) notes how closely his thought follows Lactantius, *De divinis institutionibus* 1.2.24-25.

151. For the "never-dying green" and the immunity to thunderbolts (lines 158-59) see Isidore of Seville, *Etymologiae* 17.7.2 (Martellotti, p. 697, note).

156. Pierides: the Muses; the Cyrrhaean cavern: *i.e.*, on Parnassus.

161-62. One may see in these lines a faint adumbration of the *Triumphs*.

175. In the *De remediis* 2.57, Petrarch speaks of the uses of pleasant discourse in shortening a wearisome journey.

217. Ennius's dream of Homer at the beginning of the *Annales* is mentioned by Cicero (*De re publica* 6.10).

251 ff. Corradini (p. 471) finds an echo of *Aeneid* 2.285 ff. in these lines.

260-72. The wonder that the blind Homer could make others see is expressed in Cicero, *Tusc.* 5.39.114. Petrarch mentions the scope of Homer's vision also in *Ep. Met.* 2.10.244-49.

274-78. An echo, probably, of *Aeneid* 6.136.

288. In the *De remediis* 2.97, Petrarch mentions the case of the philosopher Democritus, said to have removed his eyes because they kept him from the ways of truth. The source is Aulus Gellius, *Noctes Atticae* 10.17. 1-4.

294. A lacuna follows this line.

296. a valley closed: Vaucluse, where Petrarch, the "youth" of line 295, was living when he began the *Africa*. See introduction.

323. An allusion to Petrarch's coronation, April 6, 1341.

332 ff. Augustine chides Petrarch for his devotion to the laurel in *Secretum* 3.

343. The last Roman coronation before Petrarch's took place in 238 A.D.

345. After his coronation, Petrarch went to St. Peter's and left his wreath on the altar. See *Ep. Met.* 2.1 for details.

352. An allusion to the *De viris illustribus*, begun in 1338.

365. Reference is to the *Rerum memorandarum libri*, begun in 1344.

384. Speaking of his residence in Vaucluse, Petrarch in his *Letter to Posterity* states: "almost all my little works were either completed or begun or conceived there" (translated by Morris Bishop, *Letters from Petrarch*, p. 9). See also *Fam.* 8.3.

413. Cynthia: the moon; her brother is Apollo, the sun.

423. See above, book 2, lines 572-75.

470. For Scipio's triumph see Livy 30.45. Petrarch has added somewhat to its glories. Livy states that Syphax died before the triumph took place; he adds however that Polybius, "an authority not to be scorned," says that the African king was a part of the triumph. Nor does Livy mention any brother of Hannibal and in fact none survived at this time. Festa (p. 274, note to line 357 of the Latin) suspects an erroneous emendation of a faulty text. Nor is Sopater present in Livy's account.

524. Terentius Culleo: a Roman senator, captured by the Carthaginians and freed after Zama. He remained deeply grateful to Scipio for his liberation. See Livy 30.45.5.

536. Tibur: Tivoli; Soracte (now Soratte), a mountain (altitude 691 meters) some twenty-five miles north of Rome.

537. Praeneste: Palestrina.

545. On Scipio's restraint see Livy 30.45; Justin 3.7.

550. See above, book 2, lines 155-57.

570. See above, lines 303 ff.

592. Robert: see above, book 1, line 26, note, and introduction.

Works Cited

Abbreviations used are given in parentheses.

Alighieri, Dante. *Divina Commedia [The Divine Comedy]: Inferno; Purgatorio; Paradiso.*

——. *Convivio.*

——. *De monarchia.*

——. *Epistole.*

Augustine. *De civitate Dei [The City of God].*

Barolo, Agostino. *L'Africa di Francesco Petrarca in versi italiani.* Torino: Chiantore, 1933.

Bernardo, Aldo. *Petrarch, Scipio and the "Africa": The Birth of Humanism's Dream.* Baltimore: Johns Hopkins Press, 1962 (Bernardo).

——, trans. *Francesco Petrarca: Rerum familiarium libri I-VIII.* Albany: State University of New York Press, 1975.

Besnier, Maurice. *L'Île tibérine dans l'antiquité.* Paris: A. Fontemoing, 1902.

Bishop, Morris. *Letters from Petrarch.* Bloomington: Indiana University Press, 1966.

——. *Petrarch and His World.* Bloomington: Indiana University Press, 1963.

Boethius. *De consolatione philosophiae* (Boethius).

Caesar. *De bello civili.*

Carrara, Enrico. *Da Rolando a Morgante.* Milan, 1932.

Cato the Elder. *De re rustica.*

Charles-Picard, Gilbert. *Hannibal.* Paris: Hachette, 1967.

Cicero. *Cato Major de senectute.*

——. *De natura deorum.*

——. *De officiis.*

——. *De re publica.*

——. *Epistulae ad familiares.*

——. *Pro Archia.*

——. *Pro Sulla.*

——. *Tusculanae disputationes [Tusculan Disputations] (Tusc.).*

Claudian. *De consulatu Stiliconis.*

Corradini, Francesco. *Africa Francisci Petrarchae nunc primum emendata*. In *Padova a Francesco Petrarca nel quinto centenario della sua morte*. Padua: premiata tipographia del Seminario, 1874 (Corradini).

Curtius. *De rebus gestis Alexandri Magni [The Life of Alexander the Great]* (Quintus Curtius).

Develay, Victor. *L'Afrique, poème épique, traduit pour la première fois par Victor Develay*. Paris: Librairie des Bibliophiles, 1882 (Develay).

Ennius. *Annales*.

Festa, Nicola. *Francesco Petrarca: L'Africa. Edizione critica*. Florence: Sansoni, 1926 (Festa).

——. *Saggio sull'Africa del Petrarca*. Palermo and Rome: Remo Sandron, 1926.

Florus, Lucius Annarus. *De gestis Romanorum epitome [Epitome of Roman History]* (Florus).

Gaudo, G. B. *L'Africa . . . versione con note*. Oneglia: G. Ghilini, 1814.

Gellius, Aulus. *Noctes Atticae*.

Giornale dantesco.

Homer. *Iliad*.

——. *Odyssey*.

Horace. *Carmen saeculare*.

——. *Odes*.

Hyginus. *Fabulae [Fables]*.

Isidore of Seville. *Etymologiae*.

Josephus. *Antiquities of the Jews* (Josephus).

Justin. *Epitome in Trogi Pompeii historias [Epitome of Trogus]* (Justin).

Juvenal. *Satirae [Satires]*.

Lactantius. *De divinis institutionibus [The Divine Institutes]*.

Liddell Hart, B. H. *A Greater than Napoleon*. Boston: Little, Brown and Company, 1928.

Livy. *Ab urbe condita [History of Rome]* (Livy).

Lucan. *Pharsalia* (Lucan).

Macrobius. *In somnium Scipionis [Commentary on Cicero's "Somnium Scipionis"]*.

Marretti, M. Fabio. *L'Africa del Petrarca in ottava rima*. Venice: D. Farri, 1570.

Martellotti, Guido. "Africa." In *Francesco Petrarca: Rime,*

Trionfi e Poesie Latine. Milan and Naples: Riccardo Ricciardi, 1951 (Martellotti).

——. *Francesco Petrarca: La vita di Scipione l'Africano.* Milan and Naples: Riccardo Ricciardi, 1954 (*Scipione*).

Martianus Capella. *De nuptiis Mercurii et Philologiae.*

Mela, Pomponius. *Chorographia.*

Moore, Frank Gardner. *Livy, with an English Translation in Fourteen Volumes.* Cambridge, Mass.: Harvard University Press, and London: William Heinemann, 1949.

Mussato, Albertino. *Ecerinis.*

Nolhac, Pierre de. *Pétrarque et l'humanisme.* Rev. ed. Paris: H. Champion, 1907.

Orosius, Paulus. *Historiarum adversus paganos: libri VII* (Orosius).

Ovid. *Epistolae ex Ponto.*

——. *Fasti.*

——. *Heroides.*

——. *Metamorphoses (Met.).*

——. *Tristia.*

Padoan, Giorgio, ed. *Petrarca, Venezio e il Veneto.* Florence: Olschki, 1976.

Palesa, Agostino. *L'Africa recata in versi italiani.* Padua: Fratelli Salmin, 1878.

Pauly's Real Encyclopädie der classischen Altertumswissenschaft. Rev. ed. Stuttgart: J. B. Metzler, 1894-1963 (Pauly).

Petrarca, Francesco. *Posteritati [Letter to Posterity].*

——. *Africa.*

——. *Bucolicum carmen.*

——. *Canzoniere [Rhymes].*

——. *Coronation Speech.*

——. *De otio religiosorum.*

——. *De remediis.*

——. *De viris illustribus.*

——. *De vita solitaria.*

——. *Epistolae: Familiares (Fam.); Seniles (Sen.); Variae.*

——. *Epistolae metricae (Ep. Met.).*

——. *Invectivae contra medicum quendam [Invectives against a Certain Doctor].*

——. *Itinerarium Syriacum.*

——. *Rerum memorandarum libri.*

——. *Secretum.*

——. *Trionfi [Triumphs].*

Pingaud, L. F. *Petrarchae Africa quam recensuit, praefatione, notis et appendicibus illustravit L. Pingaud, scholae Normalis alumnus.* Paris: E. Thorin, 1872.

Platner, Samuel Bald. *A Topographical Dictionary of Ancient Rome.* Completed and revised by Thomas Ashby. Oxford: Oxford University Press, and London: H. Milford, 1929.

Pliny the Elder. *Historia naturalis [Natural History]* (Pliny).

Polybius. *History.*

Robinson, James Harvey, and Henry Winchester Rolfe. *Petrarch: The First Modern Scholar and Man of Letters.* New York: G. Putnam's Sons, 1898.

Rossi, Vittorio, and Umberto Bosco. *Francesco Petrarca: Le familiari.* Florence: Sansoni, 1933-42.

Sallust. *Catilina.*

——. *Jugurtha.*

Sanctis, Gaetano de. *Storia dei Romani.* Florence: La Nuova Italia, 1968-69 (*Storia*).

Scullard, H. H. *Scipio Africanus: Soldier and Politician.* Ithaca: Cornell University Press, 1970.

Seneca. *Ad Lucilium epistolarum moralium libri XX (Ad Luc.).*

Seung, T. K. *Cultural Thematics: The Formation of the Faustian Ethos.* New Haven: Yale University Press, 1976.

Silius Italicus. *Punica.*

Smith, William. *Dictionary of Greek and Roman Biography and Mythology.* Boston: Charles C. Little and James Brown, and London: Taylor, Walton and Maberly and John Murray, 1849 (*Biography*).

——. *Dictionary of Greek and Roman Geography.* Boston: Little, Brown and Co., 1857 (*Geography*).

Statius. *Achilleid.*

——. *Thebaid.*

Strabo. *Geography* (Strabo).

Suetonius. *Vitae Caesarum [Lives of the Caesars]* (Suetonius).

Valerius Maximus. *Factorum et dictorum: libri IX* (Val. Max.).

Virgil. *Aeneid.*

——. *Georgicon.*

Walter of Chatillon. *Alexandreis.*

Westin, Henrik. *Afrika, episk dikt af Petrarca: öfversättning från det latinska originalet.* Göteborg: Göteborgs Handelstidning Aktiebolags Tryckeri, 1889.

Wilkins, Ernest Hatch. *Life of Petrarch*. Chicago: University of Chicago Press, 1961.

——. *Studies in the Life and Works of Petrarch*. Cambridge, Mass.: Mediaeval Academy of America, 1955.

Index

The index lists names of places and persons (including legendary characters) as they appear in the text and notes. We have not listed every incidence of every name: of the abundant appearances of *Rome, Italy, Carthage*, and the like, a majority are not truly pertinent; we have listed only those that seem to us to be so. In the case of Scipio and a few others, we have enlarged our warrant to permit reference to significant passages that include pages where the name may not actually appear.

Save for books of the Bible, authors are listed but not titles of books. In a few cases, however (e.g., Petrarch and Cicero), where the references are numerous and to more than one work, we have listed the individual titles under the author's name.